PRAISE FOR
GOSNELL

"*Gosnell* reads like a literary *Criminal Minds*. This deftly written, gripping, and graphic account of the arrest and grand jury investigation into Kermit Gosnell's nightmarish house of horrors reveals the truth about the monster who murdered with no compunction and kept ghastly trophies of his victims. *Gosnell* thoroughly reports the facts the mainstream press largely ignored: that, for years, complaints about unsafe conditions and even fatal malpractice at Gosnell's clinic were met with *zero* action, so concerned were the powers that be with protecting unfettered access to abortion. *Gosnell* indicts a system that, in the name of women's 'reproductive health,' failed to do anything to protect the women and born-alive infants who were slaughtered at 3801 Lancaster Avenue."

—**MARIA MCFADDEN MAFFUCCI**, editor of *Human Life Review*

"Warning: once you start reading this, you will not be able to put it down. It will grip you from the first page and not let you go. No matter what prejudgments you may have when you begin, they will be challenged."

—**CONNIE MARSHNER**, pro-life strategist and CEO of Connie Marshner & Associates

"Hollywood could not conjure up a villain more barbaric and cold-blooded than true-life serial killer Kermit Gosnell. Investigative journalists Ann McElhinney and Phelim McAleer take you face to face with Philadelphia's baby butcher in this gripping exposé. But the story is especially chilling because **he did not act alone**. The true horror lies in Gosnell's ghoulish gallery of enablers—feckless government bureaucrats, abortion radicals, and an AWOL media. McElhinney and McAleer are unflinching torchbearers of truth. This book is a public service."

—**MICHELLE MALKIN**, founder of Twitchy and author of *Invasion* and *Culture of Corruption*

"Ann and Phelim courageously tell the heart-wrenching, shocking story previously ignored, one that every American needs to read. With each page, abortionist Kermit Gosnell takes his place in American history as a monster whose victims were the most innocent and helpless among us."

—**KATIE PAVLICH**, reporter, commentator, and author of *Fast and Furious: Barack Obama's Bloodiest Scandal and Its Shameless Cover-Up*

"In this historic book, Ann McElhinney and Phelim McAleer meticulously record the harrowing true-crime story of Kermit Gosnell's barbaric abortion and infanticide business. Every American needs to read Gosnell, because the atrocities he committed, with the knowledge and support of public authorities, demand that we answer what we really believe about human dignity and the law's equal protection for the most vulnerable."

—**DAVID DALEIDEN**, the undercover reporter behind the Center for Medical Progress videos that exposed Planned Parenthood's baby parts business

GOSNELL

GOSNELL

**THE UNTOLD
STORY OF
AMERICA'S
MOST PROLIFIC
SERIAL KILLER**

ANN McELHINNEY AND PHELIM McALEER

REGNERY
PUBLISHING
A Division of Salem Media Group

Regnery® is a registered trademark of Salem Communications Holding Corporation

Cataloging-in-Publication data on file with the Library of Congress

This paperback edition published in 2018, ISBN: 978-1-62157-858-1

Published in the United States by
Regnery Publishing
A Division of Salem Media Group
300 New Jersey Ave NW
Washington, DC 20001
www.Regnery.com

Manufactured in the United States of America

10 9 8 7 6 5 4 3 2 1

Books are available in quantity for promotional or premium use. For information on discounts and terms, please visit our website: www.Regnery.com

In memory of our mothers
Monica and Rita
Absent, unseen, forever near

CONTENTS

"People often ask: Where was God in the Holocaust? It is the wrong question. The real question is: Where was man?"
—RABBI JONATHAN SACKS[1]

"I will give no sort of medicine to any pregnant woman, with a view to destroy the child."
—THE ORIGINAL HIPPOCRATIC OATH[2]

"Planned Parenthood is rooted in the courage and tenacity of American women and men willing to fight for women's health, rights, and equality. Margaret Sanger, the founder of Planned Parenthood, is one of the movement's great heroes."
—PLANNED PARENTHOOD WEBSITE[3]

"The most merciful thing that a large family does to one of its infant members is to kill it."
—MARGARET SANGER, *Woman and the New Race*, 1920[4]

FOREWORD

ALAN ROBERTSON

The first time I met Ann McElhinney and Phelim McAleer was on a cruise ship. We were the guests on a panel discussion about media and entertainment and its effect on our culture. It was on that panel that I learned they were journalists and it was also how I learned how passionate they were about digging for truth and exposing it for the world to see. That day gave me a glimmer of hope that there were still committed journalists out there who understood why our founders protected the rights of a free press to watch the powerful, the secretive, and looked to expose hidden monsters. That was also the day I learned about Dr. Kermit Gosnell.

Like most Americans, I remembered something vaguely about the Gosnell trial "somewhere up north." I could certainly give you a lot of details about O. J. Simpson, George Zimmerman and Trayvon Martin, or Ferguson, Missouri, but nothing concrete about Dr. Kermit Gosnell. When Ann and Phelim told me about this case I asked,

"Why haven't I heard more about this?" They invited me to watch their movie about this case, which is amazing by the way, and then I began to understand why the American press didn't want to do an exposé about this story. This book gives much more depth and detail about one of the most shocking stories that I have ever read about or even heard of.

When I watched the Gosnell movie, I think shock was the overwhelming emotion that I felt, and then sadness for so much killing. When I read the book, anger became the overwhelming emotion. A lot of the anger was aimed at Dr. Gosnell himself, as well as some of his staff for what they did to babies and also young women, but I was surprised at how much anger I had for the system that claims to care about women's health.

When you read about Gosnell in this book, you find out how the abortion industry really doesn't give a hoot about women's health and even less about the lives of millions of unborn girls, who NEVER had the chance to become women! The Gosnell case was said to not be about abortion, but the facts that came out of the trial show that this industry cares nothing about women or children.

Page after page of this book shows how many people whose job it was to protect women and children instead failed them miserably. It started with a greedy Dr. Gosnell and his untrained and severely flawed staff. Dr. Gosnell's wife, Pearl, became his willing accomplice instead of his ultimate accountability. The Pennsylvania Department of Health and other higher government officials, including a Republican governor, failed to protect and do their jobs. They ignored truth, looked the other way, and did not enforce the law. The local and national media did nothing to shine light on this story and even when shamed to cover the trial did the minimum in terms of reporting. Talk about a basket full of deplorables that appear to be irredeemable!

Why all this failure? Why all this looking the other way while women were being mistreated, maligned, and abused? Why were the bodies of babies mutilated and displayed for decades in this barbaric clinic serenely named the Women's Medical Society? Because the abortion industry is a powerful and greedy force in this country and the peer pressure coming from the pro-choice movement does everything possible to ignore the abuses of women and children. My first thought after reading this book was, "How many more places are there out there like this house of horrors?"

I thank God for Ann and Phelim and their courage for pursuing this story and telling the world about Dr. Kermit Gosnell. The country of Ireland has given America a lot of treasure in many great men and women over the last few hundred years, but none better than these two jewels. I pray that our culture can come to grips with the loss and pain that abortion causes. I also applaud the truth seekers who are exposing the greed and malpractice that are going on every single day in our country in the abortion mills. I hope this book and the movie can shine some much-needed light on a dark, dark place.

Alan Robertson,
of A&E's *Duck Dynasty*

PREFACE

ANN McELHINNEY

I never trusted or liked pro-life activists. Even at college I thought them too earnest and too religious. I thought the shocking images they showed were manipulative. I distinctly remember my argument: a heart transplant is gross to look at, too. I don't want to look at pictures of that, and heart transplants are brilliant. So back off, pro-lifers with your scary pictures. I also didn't trust the provenance of the pictures; I was sure they had been photo shopped.

If the anti-abortion position was so strong, it should be able to argue without resorting to emotionally manipulating its audience with fraudulent horror pictures.

Once you have this mentality, it's very easy to completely dismiss pro-life activists. And the universities of the world are teeming with young people just like that young person I once was.

Fast forward to April 2013 and Kermit Gosnell's trial in Philadelphia, when everything changed.

Nothing in the intervening years had shaken my feelings on the subject.

But the images shown in the courtroom were not from activists, they were from police detectives and medical examiners and workers at the 3801 Lancaster Ave clinic. The expert testimony describing "good" abortions was from OB/GYNs who had been performing abortions for thirty years. The witnesses swore an oath to tell the truth and to present the evidence, and they did, under pain of penalty for perjury.

What they said and the pictures they showed changed me. I am not the same person I was.

Abortion arguments from pro-abortion advocates tend to avoid any actual talk of how an abortion is done and what exactly it is that is being aborted. I know a lot about both now.

I now know that what is aborted is a person, with little hands and nails and a face that from the earliest times has expression. The humanity in all the pictures is unmistakable, the pictures of the babies that were shown as evidence in the Gosnell trial—first, second, and third trimester babies, in all their innocence and perfection.

I also know that in a proper, legal abortion babies are poisoned in their mother's womb by injecting a needle filled with potassium chloride into the baby's heart. Then the baby is suctioned out in pieces. If the baby is bigger, forceps are used to pull it out in pieces—an arm, a leg, the head often torn from the torso. If the head is too big to pull out, the abortionist makes a hole in the base of the skull and the brain is sucked out to collapse the skull so the head can come easily. That's how it's done when it's done well.

Reading the testimony and sifting through the evidence in the case in the research for this book and for writing the script of the movie has been brutal. I have wept at my computer. I have said the Our Father sitting at my desk. I am no holy roller—I hadn't prayed in years—but at times when I was confronted with the worst of this story I didn't know what else to do.

I have had a profound sense of the presence of evil in the actions of Gosnell and his staff and their complete lack of conscience. Most disturbing of all is the banality of the evil; in the clinic they joked and laughed amidst the carnage.

I am absolutely certain that the dead babies spoken of in court were unique people whom the world will now never know. I hope this book and the movie go some way to mark the fact that they lived and in their short lives made a difference. Time will tell. This story can change hearts and minds; it has mine.

I can't reconcile the certainty of the babies' humanity with the fact that killing babies in the womb at these same ages is perfectly legal in many parts of the U.S. Kirsten Powers put it eloquently: *"Regardless of such quibbles, about whether Gosnell was killing the infants one second after they left the womb instead of partially inside or completely inside the womb—as in a routine late-term abortion—is merely a matter of geography. That one is murder and the other is a legal procedure is morally irreconcilable."*[1]

The jurors had to listen to the stories of the lives and deaths of Baby Boy A Abrams (29.4 weeks), whose photograph is on the Internet; Baby Boy B (twenty-eight weeks), whose frozen remains were found in the clinic—the medical examiner's photograph of him with his neck slit is online—Baby C, who breathed for twenty minutes before Lynda Williams "snipped" his life; Baby D, who was delivered in a toilet and tried to swim to safety before Adrienne Moton slit his windpipe; Baby E, who cried before Dr. Gosnell cut his neck; and Baby F, who moved his leg up to his chest before he was killed. They saw pictures of the forty-seven dead babies discovered at the clinic the night of the raid, their remains stuffed into old milk cartons and kitty litter containers.

These babies sent Gosnell to prison. But more than that, they are the most eloquent evidence we have ever had of the reality of abortion. The media have tried to ignore their stories.

We will not.

ONE

FROM DRUG BUST TO HOUSE OF HORRORS

*"Jim Wood is remarkable. He just gets it.
He's very, very bright, and he was like, no, this isn't
right.... They couldn't have done this case without
him. He was obsessed; he was Mrs. Mongar's
champion. He was the only one."*

—FORMER PHILADELPHIA ASSISTANT DISTRICT ATTORNEY
CHRISTINE WECHSLER [1]

*"In the good cop–bad cop routine,
Jim Wood was the good cop."*

—DR. KERMIT GOSNELL [2]

It wasn't a homicide case—until it was. Originally the authorities weren't investigating murder, or even illegal late-term abortions. They were just trying to bust a prescription drug mill. But they wound up discovering something far worse.

The work of putting Dr. Kermit Gosnell behind bars required the effort and resources of many dedicated people in law enforcement and the district attorney's office, but one man deserves the lion's share of the credit.

Detective Jim Wood was working as an undercover narcotics investigator for the Philadelphia DA's office back in 2009. Wood's friends call him Woody, and he has many, many friends. He's a soft-spoken family man, the product of a close-knit Catholic family of eleven children. Woody's round, smiling, boyish face makes him appear unthreatening and a pushover. He's neither.[3] His tenacity and professionalism have earned him much admiration among his colleagues and peers. Christine Wechsler, one of the Gosnell prosecutors, described him as "remarkable."[4] Assistant District Attorney Joanne Pescatore told us, "Jim Wood is the reason this case exists."[5]

If what happens in our lives makes us into the people we become, then Woody was made from tragedy. His father, James Morgan Wood Sr., was a Philadelphia police officer who developed multiple sclerosis when he was thirty-eight years old. He quickly went blind and was unable to work. So his wife Sally had to go to work and take charge. She became a meter maid for Lower Merrion Police Department in the suburbs of Philadelphia. But at that time the job involved a little more than just issuing parking tickets. Part of the job was to be a "Police Matron," searching and guarding female prisoners as they passed through the police station. She would do that and then go home and look after her eleven children.

"She put us all through private schools," Jim Wood says. "That's what she had to do. So me with five kids, I look at them and that's nothing."

Jim, the second eldest, was only sixteen when his father went from being a healthy provider for a big happy family to being so unwell he never worked again. His mother's strength and resilience through it all has left a lasting impression on him. But his father's illness was just the beginning.

Three of Wood's siblings died under tragic circumstances.

Woody's eldest sister, Sally, was the smartest in the family. She was a lawyer at a top Philadelphia firm with a bright future ahead of her. Then she suddenly took ill and died of cancer in 1999. She was only thirty-five years old.

Three years later, Woody's youngest brother Tom was killed in a car accident on his way home from a baseball game. He was just twenty-one.

And Jim's baby brother Richard had lived for just two hours after his birth, but in that brief period his mother had him baptized—Richard Michael Wood.

Despite all this tragedy, Jim Wood's faith was not shaken: "I never questioned God...God knew what he was doing."

Woody thinks of his infant brother almost every day. Richard is like his guardian angel. When Woody's first child was born prematurely, weighing in at just four pounds, four ounces, he named the boy Richard in tribute to the brother he never got to know.

Woody and his wife Angela were young and unmarried when Richard was born. She was nineteen, he was twenty-one, and they were both scared. But Woody remembers the music playing in the delivery room. It was Kenny Loggins singing "Danny's Song." Recalling that night, Wood smiles and begins singing sweetly.

And we've only just begun.

Think I'm gonna have a son.

He and Angela now have five grown children: Richard, Jimmy, Angela, Andrea, and Jennifer. Jimmy was born prematurely like Richard and has struggled with serious health problems all his life. Jim and Angela brought him home from the hospital on a heart monitor. He had sleep apnea, and his parents constantly worried he would die in his sleep. He started having seizures at the age of two, and they continued for four years. Woody recalls coming home from a shift at midnight to find his son in a full seizure. He saved his life by giving him mouth-to-mouth resuscitation.

When Jimmy got to high school and started playing football, he soon started complaining of back pain. His doctor initially dismissed it as nothing serious, but Woody and Angela were nervous. They sought a second opinion and had a biopsy taken. Jimmy was diagnosed with Ewing's Sarcoma. He went through painful radiation and chemotherapy treatments, and he's been cancer-free for nearly a decade. But the boy's thick head of hair never fully came back. For Woody, it's yet another reminder of his family's penchant for tragedy.

He isn't at all bitter. If anything, life's misfortunes have made Woody stronger in his faith. "I learned a lot from the Gospels and found a lot of answers in the Gospels. There is a spirit inside all of us. We have to nourish that spirit to get through this life; we will see our loved ones again."

Woody could have retired by now, but he continues to work in law enforcement. He has a lot of fight in him, coupled with a strong sense of morality and a bedrock commitment to doing the right thing. When he talks about his career, he brings up the parable of the talents. "I think God sets us up in ways where we can handle certain things," he says. "We are born alone and we die alone. What we do in between must be to help people."

When it comes to police work, Woody believes common sense is a cardinal virtue. And Woody has common sense in spades. Not everyone does. The veteran detective observes that too many young guys join the force without street smarts. That gets people hurt. Getting a hunch about a case and cultivating a gut instinct are vital for good police work. It was that instinct that helped uncover Kermit Gosnell's sordid house of horrors and put him away for the rest of his life.

In 2009, Woody was a detective with the Philadelphia district attorney's office, assigned to a joint federal and local task force set up to fight the city's growing illegal prescription-drug trade. The powerful painkiller oxycodone had become the street drug of choice, and oxy mixed with codeine cough syrup was the new heroin. Pills sold for upwards of eighty dollars per tablet. For a dealer with access to prescriptions (normally through a criminal and an unethical doctor), this was a highly lucrative business. Wood's undercover assignment in the spring of that year was to turn drug peddlers into informants, find out where they were getting their illicit prescriptions, and cut off those prescriptions at their source.

Woody's modus operandi was simple and effective. He'd tail known dealers, wait until they committed a traffic violation, and pull them over. Then he would break the news: he knew their names, he knew their associates, he knew their comings and goings. And he knew their car was full of drugs.

"So here's what's going to happen: I'm going to take you down to the station and you're going to go to prison for a really, *really* long time...or you can cooperate."

As he gave suspects their choice, Woody never stopped smiling.

Everyone wanted to cooperate.

By turning dealers into confidential informants, or CIs, Woody was able to unravel the network of prescription drug dealers and suppliers in Philadelphia. And in the process Wood just happened to land the strangest and most important case of his career.

One night, Woody, another undercover detective we'll call Mike, and two uniformed patrol officers were running surveillance on a suspected dealer's house. The plan was to go with the tried-and-true traffic stop routine.

"The guy comes out. We follow him a couple of blocks. I'm in touch with the uniform. They pull him over," Woody recalls. "So I go up to the car, and right away I just introduced myself. I said, 'Hey,

Jeff'—we can make him Jeff Smith. I don't want to divulge his real name because he's still out there. I said, 'I'm Detective Wood from Philadelphia district attorney's office. I know a lot about you. I know you're selling OxyContin. I know where you're getting it from. I know who is supplying you with the prescriptions. I even know you're about to get married in two weeks."

"You have a couple of choices here," Woody told the suspect. "You can either go to jail or you can cooperate with me."

Naturally, Jeff decided to cooperate. He let the officers search his car and his house, and he agreed to wear a wire. Woody's team seized a lot of drugs that night.

With Jeff on board as a CI, Wood and the task force began pursuing a host of leads. One of the first names Jeff provided was that of Robert Carey. Carey ran a multimillion-dollar drug racket in northeast Philly and Bucks County to the northeast of the city. Jeff's information and Woody's investigation led to Carey's being charged with felony identity theft for forging prescriptions for at least 142,428 tablets of OxyContin and Percocet between January 2008 and February 2010. Carey was also suspected in the likely contract killing of a New Jersey couple and another unsolved murder—the beating death of a man over a drug debt. The victims of the possible contract killing were Danielle Imbo and Richard Petrone, last seen on February 19, 2005, leaving a bar on South Street in Petrone's black 2001 Dodge Dakota pickup truck. Neither the truck nor the couple have ever been found, and the case remains open.

Carey hanged himself with his own shoelaces in his cell on April 14, 2010, before he could be convicted on the ID theft charges. He must have figured his luck had run out. His days making millions of dollars selling Oxy and beating people to death were over.

Turning Jeff into an informant was paying dividends. The smiling Jim Wood was getting results.

Next Jeff introduced Woody and Undercover Mike to a woman named "Fiona" (we've changed her name, too). It was through Fiona that Woody heard Kermit Gosnell's name for the first time. But initially all the detectives knew was that Fiona was buying prescriptions from a doctor and moving a lot of pills. They began an undercover sting, buying Oxy from Fiona.

The U.S. Drug Enforcement Administration provides the money for undercover "buy-walks"—deals in which police purchase drugs and let the dealer walk away. Woody's contact at the DEA was Steve Dougherty, an old friend. He and Woody had grown up in the same Philly neighborhood and known each other for years. Dougherty worked closely with Woody and Undercover Mike, and he stayed on the Gosnell case until the end.

"It's hard for civilians to understand that, when you do these types of investigations, you've got to put up the money and pills are very expensive," Woody explains. "An Oxy 80 milligram tablet street buy is worth $80." But drug dealers offer bulk discounts, since their cost is considerably lower than eighty dollars a pill. (The basic principles of capitalism work in the criminal world, too.) An undercover officer would typically buy eighty pills for thirty-two hundred dollars, or forty dollars apiece.

All of Woody's drug buys were recorded, and the tapes make compelling listening—none more so than the recording of Woody's conversation with "Fiona" the afternoon of May 12, 2009.

> Wood: Yo, Fiona?
> Fiona: Yeah. I'm listening.
> Wood: Everything cool?
> Fiona: No. Not now. Tomorrow I'll get another 120. I'll call you then. You be on standby. Or in the morning, text you or something.
> Wood: Well, can you talk because I wanted to talk about the other thing that we were going to do?
> Fiona: When do you want to do it?

Wood: That's what I'm saying. My question to you is how
do I know when I go in there I'll definitely get it. I don't
want to waste my $135 or $145 going in there if, you
know what I mean? Is it definite or...?

Fiona: Right.

Wood: I don't want to go there and get bullshit Vicodin. I'm
there for Oxys...Who are you taking me to so I know?

Fiona: You're talking 'bout what doctor?

Wood: Yeah.

Fiona: I'm talking about Gosnell.

Wood: Who?

Fiona: Dr. Gosnell.

Wood: Dr. Darnell?

Fiona: God. G-O-S-N-E-L-L. Gosnell.

Wood: When do you think we can do that?

Fiona: When do you want to go?

That was the first time Woody heard Gosnell's name. When he
took the name and began to investigate the doctor, he found reason
to suspect that Gosnell was one of the city's biggest suppliers of illegal
prescriptions. It would eventually emerge that Gosnell was, in fact,
one of the biggest suppliers in the entire state of Pennsylvania.

But Woody had no idea that he had also just stumbled upon
America's most prolific serial killer.

Woody calls Gosnell's prescription drug operation a "typical pill
mill smurfing scheme."

"Smurf" is the term cops use to describe the junkies who buy up
dozens of prescriptions (scripts) from doctors. Smurfs are phony
patients. Fiona was a smurf.

Woody tried to get Undercover Mike an appointment with Gosnell. Fiona had told them Gosnell would meet anybody. But the day

they visited the Women's Medical Society clinic on Lancaster Avenue, the door was locked.

Woody says he often thinks back on that day. If only they'd known what was really going on behind that locked door.

The Gosnell investigation hit a snag when Fiona was charged in a separate case in Delaware and had to go to prison. This is one of the downsides of working with criminal informants. They're criminals. Without Fiona's cooperation, the task force faced the real possibility that they would have to drop the investigation into Gosnell—which, though they didn't know it at the time, would have allowed the doctor to continue his killing.

But Fiona was so friendly with Undercover Mike that she invited him to her "going away to prison" party. She introduced him to her girlfriend, a dealer called Susan (not her real name). Mike could work with Susan while Fiona was locked up.

Woody and Mike made three or four buys from Susan before something changed. Suddenly, Susan had gotten nervous. Woody believed she had figured out that Undercover Mike was a cop. One afternoon, Woody and Mike watched Susan enter a pharmacy. Woody got out of the car and followed her in. He decided that even if she didn't sell to Mike that night, they were going to bring her in for questioning.

Woody pretended to be a customer and lingered around the shelves looking at merchandise. He was unshaven and wearing a baseball cap.

Susan walked up to the pharmacist's counter and ordered a prescription. She had to wait for it to be filled. Woody was practiced at going unnoticed, but he had to keep Susan in his line of sight, and as he watched her from a nearby aisle one of the pharmacists noticed him and asked, "Who're you?"

"Oh, I'm waiting for a friend," Woody replied. "He's supposed to pick up a prescription."

But as more minutes passed, the pharmacist grew suspicious: "Who is it exactly that you are waiting for?"

The pharmacist likely thought Woody was a junkie or a shoplifter. He certainly looked the part.

Woody was playing it cool. He didn't want the attention, and he really didn't want to blow his cover. Woody remembers thinking, *If he only knew I was a cop.* The last thing he needed was for Susan to get scared and bolt.

Finally, Susan got her pills and walked out.

She took a few steps outside the building and all hell broke loose. Suddenly, she was surrounded by FBI agents. Unbeknownst to Wood, the DEA had given the FBI information about Susan, and they had been watching her, too.

Jason Huff was the lead FBI agent on the case. He has worked for the FBI for more than ten years. At the time of the raid he was working on the Bureau's Healthcare Fraud Squad, where he investigated cases of prescription drug dealing.

Huff, Wood, and DEA agent Dougherty became "the three amigos" on the case that day. The three of them would work the Gosnell case until the end, and they remain friends to this day. But at the moment of Susan's arrest, none of them suspected any other criminal activity going on at 3801 Lancaster.

The federal agents stepped aside and let Woody deliver his pitch to Susan. He offered her the same choice he'd given Jeff, except he had far more evidence lined up against her.

"Look, Susan, here's the deal," Woody said. "You know what's going on. You know Mike is a cop, so you're in deep doo-doo. You have the opportunity to help yourself out."

Well, *boom.* She said, "Yeah."

Susan agreed to become a CI and get prescriptions from Gosnell's clinic. The three amigos video recorded all of her buys. First she saw Randy Hutchins, one of Gosnell's assistants, and explained her various fabricated ailments to him. Then Hutchins showed her in to see

Gosnell himself. He wrote her five prescriptions—for sixty 80 mg tablets of OxyContin; ninety tablets of Xanax; eight ounces of Phenergen with codeine; sixty tablets of Bactrim DS, an antibiotic; and sixty 10 mg tablets of Lexapro, an antidepressant.

Meanwhile, the team identified Latosha Lewis as a potential informant and witness. Lewis, who goes by Tosha, worked the front desk at Gosnell's clinic and was seen handing over prescriptions to fake patients—including an undercover cop.

Once the three amigos had sufficient evidence on Lewis, they brought her in for questioning. She told them everything they wanted to know about Gosnell's pill-smurfing business. Bizarrely, Tosha seemed to be enjoying explaining Gosnell's criminal enterprise—at one stage she used a white board in the interview room to map out exactly how the operation worked.

Tosha explained that Gosnell had three types of patients: seekers (drug dealers and users); procedures (women seeking abortions); and sick.

Gosnell's scheme allowed drug dealers to collect multiple prescriptions on the same day for numerous fake patients. For example, Gosnell had been selling prescriptions to Fiona under twenty-six different patient names. On a typical night, Gosnell would sell two hundred scripts.

He would write prescriptions for OxyContin, Percocet, Xanax, and codeine syrup for anyone who wanted them.

For the prescription drug side of Gosnell's practice, "patients" weren't given appointments. They had to write their name on a list and wait for hours until the doctor would see them. The initial consult with the doctor cost one hundred and fifty dollars. Gosnell would do a cursory examination and write a prescription—and often more than one—for whatever they told him they wanted.

But then the patients—really drug dealers—weren't required to return for a follow-up for six to nine months, and often not at all. They could simply call for new scripts every three to four weeks; a staffer would take orders over the phone. Gosnell would usually arrive at the Lancaster Avenue clinic around 7:00 p.m. each day, when he would fill out prescriptions from the forms his staff left for him based on the "orders" they had received that day.

The following day, the dealers would go to the clinic to pick up their prescriptions. They had to pay twenty dollars for the script to whoever was working the front desk. And Gosnell would pay a tip of ten to twenty dollars to that day's front desk employee for her work with the prescriptions.

In one conversation between Tosha and Gosnell that was recorded by the three amigos, February 6, 2010, the doctor justified selling the prescriptions to drug dealers as a way of improving the local economy: "And so part of me is also being understanding that economically, in a recession, and when people don't have jobs, these prescriptions may be a lifeline to survival to some people." Apparently Gosnell considered himself a Good Samaritan, helping dope peddlers make ends meet through tough economic times. It was a pathetic lie—made worse by the fact that Gosnell was a doctor and an addiction expert. He knew very well the horrific consequences of Oxy addiction, he just didn't care. He loved the power he got from supplying addicts, and he loved the money.

Later, when Gosnell was confronted about his illegal prescription business, he claimed that he was prescribing the drugs for people's "emotional well-being." A serial killer's rationalizations can't always be consistent, it seems.

In the initial interview with Tosha, the subject of the conversation soon turned from smurfs and Oxy buys to the disgusting conditions in Gosnell's clinic.

Tosha told the three amigos that unlicensed workers were treating patients. Decomposing medical waste made employees ill, she said. One of the cats Gosnell kept in the building had died from a flea infestation. The equipment was old and in most cases did not work.

And then she told them about an Asian woman named Karnamaya Mongar who had died in the clinic the previous November. According to Tosha, her death "just wasn't right."

Sometimes abortions go wrong, and sometimes women die. But something about the story struck Woody. Whatever else could be said about Tosha Lewis, she had the sort of common sense smarts that Woody respected. If she thought something wasn't right, chances are she was not mistaken.

Woody called his lieutenant and asked him to look for the police report of Mongar's death.

There was none.

"I couldn't believe it," Woody recalls, "because anytime there's a hospital case call, anywhere, from someone with a small injury to a very bad injury—not just a shooting or stabbing—police officers would ride with the medical unit. I guess they did away with that policy, because I'm thinking, 'How could this woman die, and there's no police report?'"

Woody contacted the medical examiner's office. "Do you have a woman who died?" He gave her name. "She was of Asian descent. It was in November…"

The medical examiner replied, "3801 Lancaster Avenue?"

So Woody and DEA agent Steve Dougherty went downtown to meet Gary Collins, the doctor who had performed Mongar's autopsy. He had the toxicology report on her, too. It showed that she had had a high concentration of Demerol in her system. Mongar's death had been ruled accidental. But Woody didn't buy that for a moment—not after he had heard Tosha describe how patients were being treated by unqualified staff.

Ordinarily, the Philadelphia police department's homicide unit would investigate a suspicious death like Mongar's. Woody was a narcotics detective. But because her death was part of a larger drug case, he was allowed to stay on it. Still, he knew it was a sensitive matter; cops and prosecutors tend to be territorial. So he consulted with assistant district attorney Ed Cameron. Woody outlined the case and explained that he would be asking for a warrant related to a possible homicide. Cameron gave him the go-ahead.

Sure enough, one of the narcotics deputy district attorneys got wind of Woody's investigation and went ballistic. Even though prosecutors in the district attorney's office all "play for the same team," they jealously guard their own turf. And the narcotics DA didn't want his prescription drug investigation to veer off into a homicide case. But Woody was undeterred. He wanted to get to the bottom of what had happened to Mongar, and a search warrant for Gosnell's office was the way to do it.

Wood obtained four warrants altogether, all connected with Mongar's death. In the meantime, FBI agent Huff was assembling the evidence against Gosnell, including all the buys the three amigos had done with Tosha and Fiona. He was also writing a federal search warrant for Gosnell's office. And Dougherty had a separate warrant for the DEA's investigation.

Dougherty, who often acted as liaison between the task force and other agencies, contacted the state Department of Health and the Pennsylvania Department of State, which oversees professional licensing.

The raid on Dr. Gosnell's Women's Medical Society abortion clinic at 3801 Lancaster Avenue was set for the evening of February 18, 2010.

The task force met for a pre-raid briefing at FBI headquarters on 600 Arch Street, Philadelphia. Huff, Woody, and Dougherty all had teams from their agencies. Sherry Gillespie was on hand from the Department of State. The Department of Health sent two registered nurses, Darlene Augustine and Elinor Barsony. In all, more than twenty people would participate in the raid.

Everyone was psyched.

Except for Darlene Augustine, one of the nurses from the Pennsylania Department of Health. Woody recalls how she sat across from him at the FBI conference table "just stone dead."

"We were all sitting around, talking, having a good time, waiting for everything to get set," Woody told us. "This one nurse, Darlene Augustine. I didn't know at the time there was a reason Darlene looked like that."

Augustine was a health quality administrator. She had worked for the state health department since 1989 and supervised the inspectors who responded to complaints at health care facilities. So she knew about Mongar's death, and she knew who Gosnell was. She told the grand jury that she had, in fact, received a fax from Gosnell on November 24, 2009—the day before Thanksgiving—notifying the state that Karnamaya Mongar had died following an abortion at his Lancaster Avenue clinic.

Gosnell listed the wrong date for Mongar's death on the form, a typically careless mistake, not surprising given the way he ran his filthy Lancaster Avenue clinic.

What happened when his fax arrived in the pristine offices of the Department of Health in Harrisburg, however, defied any professional standard of conduct—and even any rational explanation. Augustine passed the fax along to her boss, Cynthia Boyne, who directed the Pennsylvania Health Department's Division of Home Health, which is "inexplicably," as the grand jury report puts it, the division in charge of "overseeing the quality of care in abortion clinics." (What exactly does abortion in a freestanding ambulatory surgical center like Gosnell's clinic have to do with "Home Health" care, the grand jury wondered.) Boyne in turn discussed the situation with her superior, Janice Staloski, head of the entire Bureau of Community Licensure and Certification. These two women were responsible for regulating the care in all abortion facilities in the state.

They decided to do nothing.

They did not follow up with the medical examiner's office, or the Hospital of the University of Pennsylvania where Mongar was taken by ambulance and later died. They did not call the responding paramedics or the Philadelphia police department. And before the February 18 raid by the three amigos' taskforce, no one from the Department of Health bothered to visit 3801 Lancaster Avenue to speak with Gosnell or anyone else about Mongar's death. The grand jury in Gosnell's case would later learn that Department of Health attorneys had actually ordered Darlene Augustine to say nothing about Mongar's death to law enforcement during the raid. In fact Augustine had told Elinor Barsony, the other nurse, not to mention that they even knew about Mongar's death. These government employees were accompanying law enforcement officers into a potentially hazardous situation but were deliberately withholding relevant information they possessed about the target of the raid. No wonder Darlene Augustine was looking sick.

Apparently a narcotics detective cared far more about the death of a refugee from Bhutan than one of the state's own "health quality administrators"—or anyone else in the Department of Health. The grand jury would lambaste health department bureaucrats for their inaction, concluding that their passivity cost at least two women their lives.

FBI agents had been watching Gosnell's truck at his other clinic in Delaware all afternoon. They followed the doctor back to Philadelphia and informed the team that Gosnell was en route. He pulled up to the clinic around 8:30 p.m. The search warrant team wanted to meet him before he went inside rather than risk walking in on an abortion in progress.

"He pulls up," Woody remembers. "I approached him with my supervisor and Steve Dougherty. He's on the phone with his wife, and he's sort of telling her real quick—I didn't realize he was on the phone at the time. He's telling her the police are here."

Gosnell told us he initially thought the police were investigating a shooting at a nearby bar. But he was quickly notified that he and his clinic were the target of the investigation. Jim Wood was the bearer of bad news, but it seemed to have little effect on Gosnell's demeanor.

"I said, '*Doc, get off the phone*,' I want to explain. I tell him we have a warrant for his office. And he was cooperative."

"He was typical Gosnell, like, this…how do you describe this…like a calm Hannibal Lecter-type mentality, like, what's all this about?"

Gosnell was not flustered. He asked if he could bring his dinner with him.

When the investigators saw the inside of the abortion clinic, they couldn't understand how anyone could work in the place, much less eat dinner there. Even though Tosha Lewis had told them about the clinic's appalling conditions, nothing could prepare them for the stench. As soon as the agents and officers entered the building, they were assaulted with the rank odor of cat feces, formaldehyde, and human urine.

"There was a cat running around the clinic," FBI Special Agent Huff testified at trial, "and I actually saw urine on the stairs going up to the second floor. There were places where you could see blood on the floor. There [were] piles of trash all over the place. The smell was very bad."[6]

Team members would describe the scene to the grand jury using such words as "filthy," "deplorable," "disgusting," "very unsanitary, very outdated," "horrendous," and "by far, the worst" conditions these experienced professionals had ever encountered.

Everything was covered in cat hair—the chairs, blankets, and all the surfaces. Investigators saw semi-conscious women moaning in the waiting room. The clinic's two surgical procedure rooms were filthy and unsanitary. DEA agent Dougherty would later compare them to "a bad gas station restroom." Instruments were not sterile. Equipment was outdated and rusty. Women recovering from their abortions sat on dirty recliners covered with bloodstained blankets that employees said they "tried" to have cleaned weekly. Unlicensed employees had sedated all of the women, long before Gosnell arrived. Staff members couldn't say for certain which medications they had given or what dosages they had administered. Many of the medications that the agents and detectives found in inventory were well past their expiration dates.[7]

The pre-op and post-op areas shared the same space, which health department inspector Elinor Barsony called "unusual." But Gosnell made no effort to protect his patients' privacy or dignity. "There was no separation anywhere. All the females were sitting in chairs in rows. There was no curtains, no drapes, nothing for privacy, confidentiality, or anything," said Barsony. Two dusty old portable electric heaters warmed the room. An oxygen concentrator, covered in dust, looked like it didn't work.[8]

Woody remembers expressing his shock and disgust to Darlene Augustine, the nurse who—though he didn't know it at the time—was implicated in the Department of Health's dereliction of duty in Karnamaya Mongar's death—but she would not accept the evidence in front of her eyes. She was the DOH official who had received the fax about Mongar's death, which her superiors had decided to ignore, and, as we have seen, that very night she was under orders from Health Department lawyers not to reveal anything about the Mongar case to the task force—orders she had passed along to her fellow nurse Elinor Barsony.

"Well, you're just saying that because you're a cop," Augustine told Woody.

"I'm saying it because I'm a human being," he replied.

Everything about the raid was bizarre. Gosnell walked into the clinic carrying one bag containing his dinner and another full of clams.

"What are the clams for?" Woody asked.

"To feed my turtles," Gosnell answered, pointing to the (illegal) sea turtles in a dirty tank that dominated his waiting room.

As Woody tells it, Gosnell put away the bag of clams, then "he comes out with two of them, and he walks over to the fish tank and smashes them together and then just drops the whole, everything, the shells and the clam, right in the turtle tank."

"With patients around, with workers around, with FBI agents in there," Woody recalls with amazement.

The officers and agents wanted to separate all of the staff for questioning. Woody explains that the investigators wanted to know all that was going on in the clinic. "Not just the drug stuff, but other stuff, like Mrs. Mongar's death, the people administering medicine without being trained. All that type," the detective says. "There were a whole bunch of questions."

Gosnell employed numerous assistants on his staff. Sherry West, Lynda Williams, Madeline Joe, Ashley Baldwin, Liz Hampton, and Eileen O'Neill were all working the night of the raid.

Liz Hampton, a housemate of Gosnell's wife Pearl in foster care as a child, a tenant in his mother's house as an adult, and one of the doctor's longest-tenured employees, was in the recovery room, crying hysterically and saying she was going to have a heart attack. Police finally had to escort her out. Lynda Williams, whose only qualifications to administer dangerous drugs were an eighth-grade education and a phlebotomy certificate authorizing her to draw blood, appeared fidgety, nervous, and confused. She couldn't tell the Pennsylvania Department of Health nurses the names of the medications the patients had been given. Instead, Health Department nurse Elinor Barsony recalled, "she went to the cabinet and pulled out the bottle and said, 'This is what I gave.'...Her hand was almost shaking when she was telling you this stuff."

Barsony was on the raid to look for violations of the Pennsylvania Abortion Act. Her description of the facility, from her testimony at the trial, sounds like a scene from a horror film.

"It was dimmed. There was [sic] females sitting in lounge chairs, like, there was one lounge chair. Then there was four [more]," she said. "Then you had to go down two steps and there were three more females sitting in a chair. Chairs down there were just regular hard-back chairs. The ones in the other [recovery] area...were kind of like a La-Z-Boy chair."

Five women sat in the post-op area in those chairs, covered with dark blankets. "The first one was kind of somnolent. She was sleeping," Barsony recalled. "The second and third one were quite [un]comfortable, saying that they had cramps and...[that] they were bleeding. The fourth and fifth ones were kind of awake with it. They were the more talkative, more verbal."[9]

One patient had brought her children, and they were running wild as investigators tried to sort out the situation. Of the eight patients at the Women's Medical Society clinic that night, none of them had been given the twenty-four-hours-in-advance counseling that Pennsylvania state law requires before every abortion. An abortion is a big decision, and the rule is supposed to give a patient time to change her mind. But in Gosnell's clinic, investigators found piles of pre-signed twenty-four-hour counseling forms. He didn't want his patients to change their minds. Once a woman turned up, he took her money, and she often had the procedure done that same day—illegally.

The post-op women were not hooked up to any kind of monitoring devices. "There was one automated blood-pressure cuff that was not used," Barsony said. "I don't know when it was used last. It was dusty and dirty."

When nurse Barsony tried to talk with the first patient, she said, "I had to actually tap her on the knee to wake her up. The other two were in so much pain, they weren't sleeping.... [They] were having abdominal cramping and holding their stomachs and trying not to be loud, but they were having pain and in discomfort."

"The other two were drowsy but arousable," Barsony said. "And they were talkative. They were upset." Because of the conditions? No—it was the police presence. They were angry that law enforcement was interfering with their abortions.

Barsony found the procedure rooms in an even worse state than the recovery room. "They had the trays for the procedure already opened; so they were sitting there exposed...they're supposed to be covered," she explained. All medical instruments are supposed to be sealed until the doctor is ready for them. That's when the sterilization seal is broken. Gosnell followed none of those basic medical protocols. In fact, all of the metal instruments Gosnell used were unsanitary and unsafe.

Barsony also saw that the suction machine used during some of the abortions was in a terrible state of repair. Attached to the suction machine are tubes, which are connected to jars that fill with fetal parts as the baby is suctioned out of the mother's womb. These tubes were corroded and had lost their pliability. The suction gauge was unreadable. That meant the doctor couldn't measure how much suction he was using. Then Barsony realized the clinic only had one of the machines, which was used for both vaginal *and oral* suction.

Barsony decided that the two patients in the most distress—the ones crying and bleeding heavily—needed to be hospitalized. Paramedics arrived quickly, only to discover that the emergency exit door from the recovery room was chained shut and blocked by broken and discarded furniture and equipment, including a wheelchair with a missing wheel. Nobody could find the key for the padlock.[10]

It eventually transpired that the emergency door had also been padlocked when paramedics showed up in November for Karnamaya Mongar. The grand jury concluded that the lock had delayed Mongar's treatment and may have contributed to her death. In the three months between Mongar's death and the taskforce raid on his clinic, Gosnell had never gotten around to getting the door fixed.

Because the paramedics couldn't use the emergency exits, they had to take the women out the front door. The problem was the corridors were narrow and curved awkwardly. Worse, they were cluttered with file boxes, jugs of water, and plants. So the EMTs couldn't even get a stretcher into the building. They had no choice but to walk the patients out.

Health Department nurse Darlene Augustine went into the basement with two police officers. The stairs were rickety and dangerous, and it took them awhile to find a light switch. The basement was filled with bags of fetal remains that reached the ceiling. Behind the bags they could see medical files and more old and broken equipment. Plants lined one of the walls, behind a pane of glass. The floor was covered in more cat feces. They also found unsecured medical supplies—syringes, expired medicines, and some biologicals that should have been in a temperature-controlled environment. The Philadelphia police, FBI, and DA's office photographed everything.

The clinic felt like a maze. Gosnell actually owned three buildings, which he had connected haphazardly. The clinic was a warren, with stairs going everywhere, strangely shaped rooms, and corridors leading to more corridors. It was easy to get lost. CSU police officer John Taggart testified during the trial to the complexity of the building: "It's kind of like taking out an auditorium and building rooms in there yourself but not squaring them off because it is a rectangle and a triangular building."

Wood, Huff, and Dougherty had planned to interview Gosnell while the other agents would pair up and interview his assistants. Soon after they arrived, however, Huff's supervisor from the FBI approached the two Health Department nurses to let them know that one of the patients had a problem and needed assistance. What the patient really wanted was for her abortion to proceed. Health Department nurse Elinor Barsony phoned her supervisor Cynthia Boyne, who in turn called hers, Janice Staloski in Harrisburg. We have already met these officials—the directors of the Pennsylvania Department of Health's Division of Home Health and its Bureau of Community Licensure and Certification, responsible for overseeing abortion clinics, who had decided to do absolutely nothing about Gosnell's clinic in response to the fax notifying the Health Department of Karnamaya Mongar's death. And as we shall see in the next chapter, Staloski had visited Gosnell's clinic as early as 1992, in her then position of state health inspector, and found "no deficiencies" despite multiple violations of the law and threats to patient safety. Still, even in the light of her appalling track record to this point, Staloski made a virtually incredible decision on the night of the raid. She said the Health Department had no jurisdiction to stop Gosnell from doing the abortion—he should *be allowed to perform the procedure.* Huff's FBI supervisor concurred.

Wood and Huff objected strenuously. They were trying to interview Gosnell and couldn't believe that Barsony, Augustine, and the FBI supervisor had seen the state of the place and allowed Gosnell to continue to treat patients. Months later, Huff and Woody were still talking about how Gosnell was allowed to do an abortion in the middle of a raid.

"We couldn't believe it," Woody told us. "He could have hurt that woman, too. I don't know why that decision was made." Wood and Huff aren't medical experts, but they showed more concern for that woman's health and wellbeing that winter night than the so-called professionals from the Department of Health.

It was extraordinary, to say the least. A Department of Health official in Harrisburg allowed an abortion at a filthy, flea-infested, excrement-covered clinic with expired medicine, broken machinery, and unsanitary instruments—staffed by unlicensed, untrained employees. The Pennsylvania Health Department let a known drug dealer and suspect in a possible homicide carry out the procedure. Health inspectors routinely shut down restaurants for less, but somehow in this case they decided their hands were tied. It's difficult to find the right word to describe the Department of Health's functionaries and their judgment that night, but despicable, unconscionable, criminal, inexcusable, and morally bankrupt all come to mind.

The patient, who was later identified by her initials S. W. or Patient Number Six, explained to investigators that she had sought the abortion because "I don't want no more children." It was the fourth time she had terminated a pregnancy.

When Gosnell had finished S. W.'s procedure, he walked into his office, where Woody, Dougherty, and Huff were waiting to pick up where their interview had left off. Jim Wood described to us what happened there: "He comes back with torn surgical gloves, his hands covered in blood and proceeds to eat teriyaki salmon with chopsticks in front of us."

FBI agent Huff told the story on the witness stand during the abortionist's murder trial. "When Gosnell came back, we continued the interview. He also got food and he actually—he actually was still wearing his bloody latex gloves that had some holes in them and he actually ate his dinner with the gloves on."

The assistant district attorney interjected, "He didn't take the gloves off?"

"No," Huff answered.

"Were the gloves whole or were they ripped too?" the prosecutor asked.

"Yeah, they had some rips in them," Huff replied. "They had blood on them."

Smelling the food, a cat walked into the office. Gosnell, using one of his chopsticks as a pointer, said to the detectives, "See that cat? He's killed two hundred mice in this clinic." Gosnell accidently dropped the chopstick onto the dirty floor. Without a moment's hesitation, he picked it up and continued eating.

"Jason Huff can't eat salmon teriyaki to this day," Woody told us.

According to Gosnell's staff, he ate food even during abortions. "Dr. Gosnell would always eat during a procedure, a sandwich or a bowl of cereal, the door to the operating room would remain open during the procedure and one of his two ailing cats could and did wander in and out."[11]

His own explanation of why he wore gloves to eat his dinner on the night of the raid is bizarre, as we found out when we interviewed him in prison. In contradiction to the sworn testimony of three law enforcement officers—that he ate in bloody surgical gloves—Gosnell insisted, "I washed and scrubbed post-operatively." He admitted he was wearing gloves, but he told us that he had them on for a reason that had nothing to do with performing abortions: "While being questioned I used non-sterile gloves as I was cleaning a special terrarium as an entry for that year's Flower Show of the Year in the PA Horticultural Society."

Woody questioned Gosnell about Mongar's death while Huff and Dougherty focused on the prescription drug allegations. Woody asked who had medicated Mongar. Gosnell said he had asked Lynda Williams (the phlebotomist with the eighth-grade education) to give her some medication, and he had administered more himself. Gosnell claimed he had been present whenever Mongar was given medication.

But down the hall, Williams was telling investigators a different story. She admitted to medicating Mongar on her own. Gosnell wasn't even in the building at the time; she had called him and he had said, "Med her up."

Williams also told detectives that Gosnell regularly manipulated ultrasounds to falsify fetal ages—to make the fetuses look younger than they really were. She said that Gosnell didn't charge for this service, and that she believed he did it because patients would cry and beg him to. In reality, Gosnell was trying to cover up the illegal late-term abortions he was doing: Pennsylvania law prohibits abortions after twenty-three weeks and six days.

Gosnell seemed to enjoy talking to Woody and the federal agents. He was very cooperative, and he seemed to have an answer for everything. He was polite and composed, and nothing fazed him. This was classic Gosnell. Even during his murder trial, he was smiling and sociable. He displayed the same relaxed demeanor to us when we met him at Huntingdon Prison. But the night of the raid, he was underestimating how much law enforcement knew. The three amigos all noticed the doctor's expression change when Woody started asking pointed questions about manipulating the ultrasounds.

"His face changed color. Turned like an ashy color. His lips started to quiver, and he dropped his head, and it looked like he was trying to compose himself because he wasn't expecting that," Wood told us. "I think that's when he figured out that we were getting information from the other workers and now he's in big doo-doo."

It was the one and only time Gosnell showed weakness.

Gosnell admits his demeanor changed the night of the raid, but he disputes the reason. "It happens to be quite true that I was 'rattled' during this phase of the six-hour interrogation [according to both the official records and Jim Wood, the interview, which was continually interrupted, actually lasted for less than an hour], but not for the reason assumed by the officers." Gosnell says he was realizing that he had been "mistakenly" rounding down the ages of the babies he was preparing to abort. "My confusion was not of guilt as supposed—it was more like—how could I have gotten myself into an apparent bind."

In any case, on the night of the raid, Gosnell composed himself and tried to deflect attention from his wrongdoing. "I had a friend in Kansas," he said, "who was shot and killed in his church."

His friend was George Tiller, the infamous late-term abortionist in Wichita who was murdered by an anti-abortion militant named Scott Roeder on May 31, 2009. Roeder shot Tiller through the eye at point blank range. Roeder was convicted in 2010 and received a life sentence without possibility of parole for fifty years. He is fifty-seven.

Abortion providers know and refer patients to each other. Karnamaya Mongar, for example, had come to Gosnell from a clinic in Washington, D.C. Gosnell received regular referrals from clinics in Virginia, Maryland, New York, Connecticut, and New Jersey. Sometimes women would come from as far away as Florida, Georgia, and Puerto Rico.

Abortionists even have an annual convention in Las Vegas where they gather for seminars and training and a bit of fun. That's where Gosnell met Tiller and they became good friends.

Wood wasn't interested in Gosnell's friendship with Tiller. What about the ultrasounds? Why manipulate them?

But Gosnell's mention of Tiller wasn't irrelevant; he was bringing up their relationship to give a reason that he would never have done illegal late-term abortions in Pennsylvania—because he could refer those cases to his friend who did *legal* late-term abortions in Kansas, where the law was different.

Gosnell told the detectives that abortions are legal in Pennsylvania up to twenty-four and a half weeks. (The limit is actually twenty-three weeks and six days.) The doctor went on to explain that if a woman sought his services past (his mistaken idea of) the legal limit, he would refer her out of state, usually to Kansas or Colorado.

But that wasn't quite true. Jim Wood told Gosnell that his colleagues had discovered a lot of aborted fetuses in the basement. Hypothetically, Woody asked, how many of those fetuses might turn out to be older than the legal limit when they're examined by the coroner?

"Not a whole lot," Gosnell replied. "Maybe 10 to 20 percent." He assured Wood and his colleagues that he tried not to perform abortions past the legal limit.

The doctor had casually admitted to a serious crime—several, in fact—in front of a police officer and two federal agents.

It was a long night for everyone. Investigators collected what evidence they could and took hundreds of pictures. Wood searched for anything he could find that might shed light on Karnamaya Mongar's death.

In one room, Wood came upon a metal cupboard. He opened it and found a shelf full of jars—five of them—containing little baby feet.

He looked at DEA agent Dougherty and wondered aloud, "Is this *normal?*"

"I've never been to an abortion clinic before. I didn't know if that was normal. It didn't look normal, but crazy things happen in this world," Woody told us.

He closed the cupboard and left the feet where they were. The contents of the jars did not constitute material evidence for his search warrant, he didn't understand why they were in the cupboard, so he didn't have probable cause to take the feet. He kept looking.

Woody looked in refrigerators and freezers, which were placed throughout the building, including in some of the bathrooms. He kept finding containers filled with fetal remains. Not just glass jars but empty water and milk jugs, cat food containers, and Minute Maid juice bottles with the necks cut off.

Investigators found the remains of forty-seven babies in all.[12]

Dr. Sam Gulino, Philadelphia's chief medical examiner, would later detail for the court what they found:

There [were] a great variety of the types of containers. Some of them were, in one case a distilled water jug where

the top had been cut off of it. Others were drink containers, like I think one was a cherry limeade container that
had been used. There were others that I recognized. It was
a container that you would have either cat or dog food in
because I had actually used that brand of cat food with my
cat, so I knew what the container was by its very distinctive
shape. And in most of the cases, the tops had been cut off
so that the opening was larger; and then they contained in
them usually some amount of bloody liquid that was frozen, fetal tissue. And then, as I said, some of them also
contained other objects such as gloves or gauze or, in some
cases, some of the cervical dilators.[13]

The search took hours to finish. By the time it was over, the detectives and agents were physically and emotionally exhausted. They
also weren't sure what they had found. How much of what they had
seen and heard was legal and how much wasn't? "We knew there
were fetuses in the freezer during the search," Woody recalls. "But
we still didn't know the extent of all the other information. We didn't
know as far as the legitimacy of all the stuff that these workers were
saying about Gosnell."

The next morning, Wood, Huff, Dougherty, and their teams
reconvened after just a few hours' sleep to meet with First Assistant
DA Joe McGettigan. McGettigan is a highly respected prosecutor
who first made a name for himself in the 1997 murder prosecution
of multimillionaire John E. du Pont and later in the conviction of
former Penn State football coach and serial child molester Jerry Sandusky. Now in private practice, McGettigan has also had a successful
career as a screenwriter in Hollywood, off and on between cases.

McGettigan wanted to know how the detectives planned to proceed, because the investigation was clearly expanding beyond the
scope of a single suspicious death.

The problem for investigators was that Gosnell still had full access to his Lancaster Avenue clinic. He hadn't yet been arrested or charged with any crime. And other than the evidence the agents had collected for the drug case, they hadn't taken anything else—none of the files and none of the babies' remains. "We knew we needed to get back to the clinic with either a search warrant or consent to search to get the fetuses out, to get more evidence of other crimes that may have been committed," Wood explains.

The decision was made that Wood and a lieutenant should pay a visit to Gosnell at his other clinic in Delaware and obtain consent for another search of the Philadelphia clinic, this time to remove the fetuses and take more pictures of the clinic's filthy condition, the cats, and the bloodstained floors.

The police officers went to the Atlantic Women's Medical Services at 2809 Baynard Boulevard in Wilmington, Delaware. A staff member told them Gosnell was in the middle of an abortion and would join them as soon as he was finished. As they waited, however, Gosnell's lawyer called the office and asked to speak to John McConnell, the lieutenant who was there with Jim Wood. The lawyer wanted to know if they planned to arrest his client that evening. McConnell answered no, and the attorney said, "That's fine," and hung up.

Gosnell emerged from the clinic at 8.30 p.m. He wanted the detectives to know he had done nothing wrong and was willing to cooperate. He signed their consent form and asked them to wait for him to finish up so he could follow them back to Philadelphia. They left for Lancaster Avenue twenty minutes later.

Homicide detectives joined them at the Women's Medical Society clinic not long after they arrived there. There was some tension that night. Homicide cops are busy; Philly is a dangerous town. They always have plenty of other cases to cover, and they weren't even sure this one qualified as a homicide. The detectives didn't want to interview Gosnell at the clinic; they wanted to take him downtown to police headquarters at 8th and Race.

"No, I don't want to go to 8th and Race," Gosnell told them. "I want to go home to my wife. I've had a long day."

He wasn't under arrest, so the detectives let him leave. It was a missed opportunity. The next day, Gosnell refused to answer any questions and referred the police to his attorney. It was not the only time when a disconnect between homicide and the team that had been investigating Gosnell would adversely affect the investigation.

But that night, before the homicide detectives arrived, Gosnell was still in a cooperative mood as McConnell and Wood went about their search. The doctor walked up to a freezer in one of the rooms they were searching, pointed at a container, and said, "Oh, by the way, that's Mrs. Mongar's fetus." Wood remembers the creepy exchange vividly. Karnamaya Mongar had died months earlier, yet her baby remained in the freezer. Gosnell behaved as though this was not at all strange.

"I'll never forget it," Wood told us. "You open up the freezer door—and you know how you have one side [of a refrigerator] is the freezer. Well, Mrs. Mongar's baby was there...in a clear bag. It was the only one in a clear bag, wrapped in a paper towel." A medical examiner later determined that Mongar's baby, a girl, was nineteen weeks old.

No files were removed during the second search on February 19, which lasted until the next morning. Once again, the police and federal agents lacked the necessary warrants. FBI agent Huff had taken pictures of some of the files the night of February 18. Latosha Lewis had shown him a shelf where second-trimester abortion files were kept. But when Huff finally returned with another warrant, on April 2, those files were gone.

On February 19, police removed the forty-seven fetuses and delivered them to the medical examiner's office. But they left the jars containing baby feet. Detectives still weren't certain whether there was anything illegal about the feet being stored as they were. Only later were the feet also seized and taken to the medical examiner.

Gosnell had told Kareema Cross—another underqualified clinic employee who drew blood, did ultrasounds, and even injected labor-inducing drugs—that he kept the feet for "DNA purposes." But that was just another lie. A small tissue sample is all that is required to obtain DNA, even assuming that there was any legitimate reason to do DNA testing on any of the fetuses Gosnell had aborted. According to Adrienne Moton, in her three years of working at the clinic, nobody ever asked for a DNA test.[14]

It's something of a mystery why Gosnell kept the feet, how long he kept them, and why he eventually chose to dispose of some but not others. Kareema Cross supplied detectives with photographs that she had taken in the clinic in 2008. We have seen the pictures; one shows at least twenty jars with baby feet. And Ashley Baldwin, a teenaged employee of Gosnell's whose mother eventually pled guilty to corruption of a minor for bringing her daughter to work with her at Gosnell's house of horrors, would also testify that she saw at least twenty jars of feet at one point.[15] But when the police conducted their search, they only found five.[16] Apparently Gosnell severed babies' feet for his own amusement and secretly disposed of them when it suited him, in a course of conduct shocking for a doctor—though not for a serial killer.

Over the next several weeks after the initial February 18 raid and the follow-up the next night, investigators made numerous return visits to 3801 Lancaster Avenue. On February 22 a police officer removed Gosnell's medical license from a wall. One detective told us there was blood on the frame. The contrast between the clean space it left and the rest of the wall showed just how disgustingly dirty the place was; it seemed that no cleaning had been done since the license was hung more than thirty years before.

Woody's videotape of a later search makes for disturbing viewing. The filth, the garbage piles, the bags of fetal remains scattered about—it's nauseating. Some of the workers pointed to the stains on the walls. Those were where patients would urinate because the toilets didn't work. Later, at trial, it was revealed that the toilets were often backed up with fetal remains.[17] Bathrooms had vomit on the floor—from the drug addicts Gosnell happily supplied, it was revealed in later interviews.

In one part of Wood's video, he walks through the office of Eileen O'Neill, the unlicensed medical school graduate who would be tried alongside Gosnell for theft by deception, conspiracy to commit theft, racketeering, conspiracy related to corruption, perjury, and false swearing. She was lucky they didn't charge her with practicing medicine without a license. O'Neill maintained that she worked upstairs and had no idea what was going on.

In O'Neill's office was a plaque in the shape of a dog bone. It read: "We got rid of the kids because the dogs were allergic." Woody took a picture of it, and it's still a screensaver on one of his home computers—a regular reminder of the most important case of his career.

Pennsylvania Department of Health nurses Darlene Augustine and Elinor Barsony inexplicably waited until four days after the February 18 raid to return to the Lancaster Avenue clinic. On that occasion they were accompanied by Susan Mitchell, a health inspector who had visited Gosnell's clinic twice before over a twenty-year span. They described to the grand jury a facility that was clean, uncluttered, and smelling strongly of disinfectant. There were no cats in sight. The delay by the Department of Health had given Gosnell plenty of time to clean up.[18]

Still, on that visit the DOH did make some gruesome discoveries. According to their report, which we have seen, they found that "Five containers from second trimester abortions for the month of 12/09 were located on a shelf in a cabinet above the sink between the 2 procedure rooms."

The same day, February 22, the Pennsylvania Board of Medicine temporarily suspended Gosnell's medical license. Sherilyn Gillespie served the petition for Immediate Temporary Suspension on Dr. Gosnell. Juan Ruiz, the prosecuting attorney for the Department of State, insisted that she have someone with her "due [to] the dangerous area and practice of the doctor." Gosnell voluntarily surrendered his "wall certificate, registration certificate and wallet card." Steve Dougherty from the DEA accompanied Gillespie and asked Gosnell to voluntarily surrender his DEA license; Gosnell refused, saying he wanted a hearing.

Four days had passed after the initial raid and its grisly revelations, and Gosnell had been free to destroy evidence, practice his horrific brand of medicine, and butcher babies and women. The Harrisburg bureaucrats didn't deem it necessary to interrupt their weekend. Department of Health officials didn't even initiate the paperwork to shut down the clinic until March 12, almost a month later.[19]

On April 2 FBI Agent Huff obtained a warrant to search Gosnell's home at 646 North 32nd Street. Once again, Woody documented the search on video. The team wore hazmat suits. Given the state of the clinic, they weren't taking any chances. Once inside, they were all grateful for the protection.

What the amigos found was like something out of an episode of *Hoarders*. Everywhere they turned there were clothes and rubbish, bits of food, plastic bags, teddy bears, and other stuffed animals. The garden was overgrown, with empty cardboard boxes strewn about, lots of empty flowerpots, and pieces of old furniture in the yard. Inside the house, most of the curtains were pulled closed and every room was dirty, filled with trash and books and files and stacks of old mail.

Most of the bathrooms were stuffed with rubbish and filth, the dust clearly visible where it had accumulated over the years.

Like many hoarders, Gosnell and his wife, Pearl, were big shoppers. Philadelphia police officer John Taggart described to us the brand new, often unopened merchandise they found. "He had DVDs and movies that he never opened. Stacks of them all around the bedroom. There was a 60-inch TV. Nobody even saw it because it had clothes on it until we moved them," Taggart explained. "And Pearl had a lot of Coach bags. I don't know if they were real. They were on top of the bed. A lot of them were still in boxes like she [hadn't] even opened them."[20]

In what appeared to be Pearl's office, detectives saw a large collection of DVDs. Some of the titles seem ironic now, like *Hide and Seek*, *I Tried*, and *Labor Pains*. All the rooms were painted in vivid reds, navy blues, and purples. Almost every room had a fridge, including the bedrooms and bathrooms. No fetal remains were found in the home, however. And there was one room, a bathroom, which stood out as the only clean space in the house. It's a mystery to the police why that one room was clean.

Gosnell was home at the time of the search. He was smiling and relaxed, as usual. Noticing one of the officers was Hispanic, Gosnell offered to cook him Spanish eggs. The offer was declined.

At one point Philadelphia Assistant District Attorney Christine Wechsler had to leave the house to make a phone call. From outside, she heard music coming from the house. Outraged that someone would put music on during a search, she ran back inside, only to discover Gosnell playing Chopin on his piano whilst surrounded by police officers in hazmat suits. In a surreal case this was one of the most surreal moments.

On the third floor, officers found Gosnell's fifteen-year-old daughter in bed. Jenna Gosnell's room was painted pink and purple, with a bookcase crammed with stuffed animals and soft toys. Bizarrely, she had a shelf full of dolls that resembled real babies. There were lots of unopened toys, too. It looked liked any other teenage girl's room, with a few notable exceptions. Her door had a lock on the outside. In her closet were two mink coats that had recently been dry cleaned. And in a trunk beside her bed were a .380-caliber Mauser semi-automatic pistol and $241,147.00 in cash. Gosnell had told Wood he owned two guns, but detectives only recovered the one in Jenna's room.

Assistant DA Christine Wechsler and one of the officers decided to search the basement, though Gosnell strenuously advised them not to. As Wechsler and the officer descended the stairs, they could hear a strange noise, but they couldn't work out what it was. The basement was very dimly lit, and once their eyes adjusted to the light, they could see that their hazmat suits were turning black from the bottom up. They raced back upstairs, covered in fleas. The noise they had heard was the fleas jumping on their hazmat suits.

At the top of the stairs, Gosnell smiled and said, "See I'm not such a bad guy, I told you not to go down there."[21]

Meanwhile, the investigation had taken a more sinister turn. On March 24, a dive team searched the waters off the dock of Gosnell's beach house in Brigantine, New Jersey. Gosnell had been seen going into the house very late at night with medical waste bags. He didn't turn on the lights, and soon afterward he was seen leaving the house with two other men. All three went out on the dock by the house. Gosnell appeared to be emptying something from the bags into the water. Investigators also heard that he was seen removing material from bags and putting it into crab traps as bait. But the dive team did not find any evidence—investigators believe fetal remains would likely have been completely eaten by the crabs that crawl in those waters.

Jim Wood has seen a lot in his many years in law enforcement, but the searches of Gosnell's clinic and home had a profound effect on him.

During the search of the Women's Medical Society clinic, officers opened a safe and found an envelope with money still in it. It was Karnamaya Mongar's payment for her abortion.

"It was $330," Woody told us. "There was some put on a VISA account." On the envelope was written: "Karna Mongar, 830.00, 500.00 visa, 330 cash Wednesday 11/18."

"We never opened that envelope. That envelope is still in our evidence today, not opened. We have pictures of that. It was just eerie to see. A woman paid for her own death."

"It's like…Frank Rizzo, former mayor of Philadelphia said to police officers, [being a Philly cop], it's a free ticket to see the greatest show on earth. It really is."

"I don't know if it's free though."

TWO

"MURDER IN PLAIN SIGHT"

*"When once a certain class of people has been placed
by the temporal and spiritual authorities outside the
ranks of those whose life has value, then nothing comes
more naturally to men than murder."*

—SIMONE WEIL [1]

*"Murder is unique in that it abolishes the party it
injures, so that society has to take the place of the
victim and on his behalf demand atonement or grant
forgiveness; it is the one crime in which society has a
direct interest."*

—W. H. AUDEN [2]

"Murder in plain sight."

—GRAND JURY REPORT IN THE GOSNELL CASE [3]

The grand jury system is a mystery to most Americans. Grand juries decide if particular cases deserve criminal proceedings. They have a very broad investigative reach. A grand jury hearing is not a trial. But as at trial, witnesses may be compelled to appear, but not to testify—the Fifth Amendment guarantees the right to avoid self-incrimination. Grand jury rules vary from state to state, but in Pennsylvania witnesses can bring a lawyer to the proceedings. Unlike at trial, although lawyers are present in the grand jury room, they can only consult with their clients—they cannot make objections. The prosecutors can ask leading questions and can ask for hearsay and other evidence that would not normally be admissible during a trial—which can make for surprisingly candid testimony.

The County Investigating Grand Jury XXIII, as it was officially known, met for almost a year in the Gosnell case. Wading through all of the facts, deciding what crimes might have been committed, listening to unprepped witnesses telling their stories—it was a strange, uncertain process. The final report, published on January 14, 2011, is a complete page-turner, a chronicle of how America's biggest serial killer got away with murder for more than thirty years. In its gruesome 261 pages, the grand jury named and shamed—and in some cases recommended charging—the doctor, his wife, and most of his staff, along with officials in numerous state government agencies, all the way up to the governor.[4]

Judge Renée Cardwell-Hughes oversaw the grand jury proceedings in the Gosnell case.

Cardwell-Hughes is a tall, elegant African American woman who spent fifteen years on the bench, hearing homicide cases for most of that time. Originally from Lynchburg, Virginia, she graduated from Georgetown University Law School in 1985 and took a job in Philadelphia at Mesirov, Gelman, Jaffe, Cramer & Jamieson, one of the oldest and most respected white-shoe law firms in the city. She has presided over some of Philly's biggest grand jury investigations. In 2008, she supervised the grand jury impaneled to investigate extensive and unprecedented allegations of sexual abuse within the Catholic Archdiocese of Philadelphia. That grand jury handed down multiple indictments against clergy and church employees who had helped cover up decades of child abuse by moving pedophile priests to different parishes where no one had the slightest idea who they were or what they had done.

Judge Cardwell-Hughes is divorced and raised her son Alec largely on her own. She speaks of his achievements often. Alec is a West Point graduate, and a second lieutenant in the U.S. Army. But when he was still a little boy, his mother, whose day job involved putting some of Pennsylvania's most vicious criminals in jail, received a chilling anonymous letter that described, in detail, how she and Alec spent their days—where they went, who they met. The author even knew the two sports Alec played and where he played them and what the judge did in her spare time. The experience was frightening, but Judge Cardwell-Hughes didn't resign and run away. She stayed in her job, but she and her son lived with round-the-clock police protection for two years before it was judged that the threat no longer existed.

But that's all behind her now. Today, Cardwell-Hughes is CEO of the Southeastern Pennsylvania chapter of the Red Cross, based in Philadelphia. She invited us to the Red Cross office on Chestnut Street, where we met in a very corporate conference room.

Cardwell-Hughes first explained to us how the grand jury system works. Grand jury proceedings are secret, so a panel is often convened when witnesses are afraid to come forward.

Grand jury cases tend to be complex, Cardwell-Hughes said. "They can't be investigated quickly. So it's not like we saw you selling drugs on the corner and the police arrest you, or the bank was broken into and there is a videotape and somebody fits the profile. No. This is [a process] where you know something is not right and you want to do an investigation. And as the investigation is going, you need a grand jury," she said. Once the grand jury has heard all of the evidence, the panel recommends whether to proceed with an indictment, as well as what the charges should be. The judge agrees and signs off.

The judge didn't detail the behind-the-scenes negotiations and politicking that come with any controversial grand jury investigation. In reality there is bound to be a lot of back-and-forth about what direction the investigation should go in. And the Gosnell case was certainly controversial, with the grand jury investigating abortion, racial issues, and dereliction of duty by government officials.

When the news first broke that Cardwell-Hughes was presiding over the Gosnell grand jury, she told us, members of the black community inundated her with questions. They couldn't understand how the allegations against Gosnell were even possible.

> I have all these people...in their sixties and above—what I would call blue-blood African American Philadelphians. Philadelphia is an old community and there is a cadre of 'firsts.' You know, first doctor, first judge—you name it, first, right? They were a very small, close-knit community. And they were all completely stunned.
>
> They all said to me, "Renée, it can't be true. He was such a good man; he was really smart, dedicated to his practice and the community." And all I could say to them was, at some point greed took over and he is not the man that you know.

"When you talk with people," Cardwell-Hughes told us, "you get the stories of him being one of the first African Americans to graduate from University of Penn. Medical School; how smart he was; how committed to the community he was. You get this picture of him that is a complete contradiction [of what happened] at the clinic on Lancaster Avenue. Just a complete contradiction."[5]

That picture of Gosnell makes some sense of an odd filing Gosnell would submit to the appeals court after his conviction. He claimed to have been called up for service in Vietnam, assigned to "Military Detoxification for Addicted Combatants," but released from service with an honorable discharge when Philadelphia locals were so concerned about losing his expertise that they sent three thousand letters to the military on his behalf.[6]

Assistant district attorney Christine Wechsler was one of the original prosecutors on the Gosnell case. She is naturally curious and smart—a short, blond, fast-talking dynamo with a knack for thinking up unthinkable questions and unafraid to hear the answers. She's also the mother of four young children; she would run back and forth from her office to her son's kindergarten to the medical examiner's office.

Christine Wechsler described the Gosnell grand jury to us as a gradual process, with evidence building on evidence. "It was like light bulbs going off. When you're in the grand jury, and I did a lot of grand jury work, you're asking questions that you don't know the answers to. That's what I tell the grand jurors. You have a nice audience. They get to know you every week. And you really are pulling people in. You don't know what they're going to say. There's no script. It's not like you're putting on a presentation like on trial where you know what you are putting on show."

The grand jury can ask anything and everything. With the Gosnell case, the panel had to determine whether there was enough evidence to suggest that Karnamaya Mongar's death wasn't just accidental. They had to decipher Gosnell's medical files, which showed how he fabricated ultrasound readings to skirt the state's late-term abortion law. They had to ask detailed questions about how the fetal remains the police had removed from Gosnell's freezer came to be there. How did Gosnell remove the babies from their mothers? Why did he cut off their feet and store them? The grand jury also had to probe what the Pennsylvania Department of Health and the

Department of State did or—more importantly—did not do about Gosnell's house of horrors.

"It was all over the place," Wechsler said. "It was crazy."

Wechsler recalled for us what it was like for her working homicide cases. "I was very young in homicide," she says—a thirty-year-old mother of four surrounded by mostly older men. Wechsler had been on maternity leave with her third child during the latter half of 2009, and she returned to work a month before the drug task force executed the search of Gosnell's offices in February 2010. "There hadn't been a baby born in homicide in ten years. The attitude is that we don't have babies here."

Ann Ponterio, chief of the Philadelphia DA's homicide unit, tapped Wechsler and her colleague Joanne Pescatore to lead the prosecution. "[Ponterio] pulled me into the office one day and said, 'I'm clearing all of your cases and you're going to work on something just for me.'"

The homicide unit chief paired her with Joanne Pescatore because, as Wechsler memorably explained, Pescatore is "anal" and Wechsler most definitely is *not*. Pescatore keeps her files immaculate and her cases well organized. The brilliant but flighty Wechsler needed someone like that to keep her focused. "It was funny," she says. "We have very different approaches to things in the way we work through stuff. But we work really well together."

The two women were also at different stages of their lives during the investigation and trial. Pescatore was in the middle of a divorce. Wechsler had young children to care for.

The two women supported each other during the case, and they often needed each other. By the time it was over, they were good friends. "She was like my mom," Wechsler told us. "She'd packed me peanut butter and jelly sandwiches [for] every grand jury [hearing]— on white bread! I never let my kids eat white bread. It's so good. Her daughter babysat for me one summer. We are very, very close."

The whole team working the Gosnell case bonded, brought together by a common dedication to justice and a shared sense of outrage at Gosnell for what he had done and at those who had allowed him to get away with it for so long.

They all had their own ways of doing things, and they had to learn to get along. Wechsler tells the story of the first day the investigators got together to start sifting through patient files and pictures of the dead babies. "We were sitting there with all these detectives, we were all sitting around. Woody was there, getting out their papers, and I'm about to start asking all these terrible questions about the pictures that I know are coming, and he was like, 'Can you order us a pizza?'"

Wechsler couldn't believe it.

"I'm like, 'You're not going to want to eat that pizza!' And he says, 'What? We're not going to have pizza?'"

That was a veteran detective. It didn't matter if the conference table was covered with crime scene photos—a cop has got to eat.

"That's [what] we would do," Wechsler said. "We ate and drank. We talked twenty-four hours a day."

The case took a heavy emotional toll. "My days were crazy," she told us. "I couldn't sleep once we started piecing everything together. I used to watch *I Love Lucy* reruns at night. Thank God for the Cartoon Network. And we all drank a lot. I would call my husband [and say], 'You need to bring home wine, there's no way I'm going to sleep.'"

She would try to take her mind off the gruesome details by reading trashy novels. "I started reading 99-cent novellas. My husband would [ask], 'Are you still awake?' Yeah, I'm on my second 99-cent novella."

As the case progressed and more and more evidence emerged, Wechsler really needed those novels. The details of Gosnell's crimes were a heavy burden, and getting heavier.

Because of the secrecy of the grand jury, Wechsler and Pescatore weren't allowed to share what they were doing even with their fellow prosecutors. Both women got a lot of grief from colleagues whose workloads increased while they only had one case to handle. They weren't very popular in the office for the year the case played out.

Pescatore and Wechsler are both educated, independent women with many children between. But as they delved into Gosnell's crimes, they realized how little they knew about abortion—either the medical procedure or the law surrounding it. In fact, neither of them knew the first thing about abortion law before they were assigned the case. When they read the state statute together for the first time they were flabbergasted at how late a woman in Pennsylvania could obtain an abortion. A paralegal had retrieved the statute, and both women's eyes fell on the gestational age limit—abortion is legal up to twenty-three weeks and six days in Pennsylvania—at the same time. They looked at each other in disbelief. The idea that a woman could wait so long and still terminate a pregnancy legally seemed incredible to them.

"This is controversial, but twenty-four weeks—give me a break," says Wechsler, who describes herself as pro-choice. "You're six months pregnant...you're big. Babies are kicking around in there."

In fact, the twenty-four-week Pennsylvania gestational age limit, so late it shocked Pescatore and Wechsler, is more restrictive than the law in some states. According to the pro-abortion Guttmacher Institute, only "43 states prohibit abortions, generally except when necessary to the woman's life or health, after a specific point in pregnancy." In other words, seven states have no limit at all on how late abortions can be done—right up to the moment of birth. That's why Dr. Gosnell tried to tell investigators on the night of the initial raid on his clinic that he had sent late cases out of state to Colorado or Kansas. Colorado has no gestational limit.[7] And Gosnell's friend Dr. Tiller—until he was murdered by anti-abortion militant Scott Roeder in 2009—was able to exploit the health-of-the-mother exception in Kansas's law to abort late-term fetuses "even into the ninth month of pregnancy," long past the point at which they could have lived outside the womb.[8]

In a case filled with ghastly details, establishing the cause of death for the forty-seven babies recovered from Gosnell's freezer was a part of the investigation that left a permanent mark on Wechsler's psyche. She was pregnant with her fourth child during the early part of the investigation, but that didn't exempt her from thoroughly sifting through the evidence—which included examining all of those tiny babies' bodies inside and out.

The Philadelphia medical examiner's office on University Avenue is a ten-minute drive from Lancaster Avenue. It's an uninviting place at the best of times. Pescatore and Wechsler worked with Sam Gulino, Philadelphia's chief medical examiner. Gulino was relatively new to that position when the Gosnell case began to unfold, and he wasn't keen to be enmeshed in controversy. The prosecutors had questions for the ME that he couldn't seem to answer at first. Part of the challenge for the prosecutors was the secrecy of the proceedings. Just as Wechsler and Pescatore couldn't discuss the case with their colleagues in the DA's office, they couldn't tell the ME exactly what they were investigating, either. All Wechsler could do was ask him to answer questions based on the evidence before him. She couldn't tell him why she was asking those gruesome questions.

Wechsler had to establish whether the babies had died inside or outside the womb. Their location at time of death could spell the difference between the death penalty for Gosnell or total exoneration. In the strange world of abortion law, a few inches were vitally important.

But how could they tell from those forty-seven bodies just where they died? In a late-term abortion method called intact dilation and extraction (by abortionists) and partial-birth abortion (in the federal and state laws banning the practice) the fetus is delivered in a breach presentation and its brains are sucked out *in utero* after everything but the head of the baby is outside the woman's body. This has the effect of crushing the skull, making it easy for the largest part of a large fetus to be removed safely—safely for the woman, that is.

If the forty-seven babies found in the clinic had no brains, then they would probably have been killed when at least the head was still in the birth canal. Even though the torso and legs would have been outside the woman, it would not have been a legal murder. Gosnell could possibly have been charged with violating the 2003 federal Partial-Birth Abortion Ban Act, but he could not have been indicted for the murders of live babies outside the womb.

Wechsler recalls phoning Dr. Gulino and asking whether any of the fetuses he was examining had their skulls crushed. "They're too big. How would they have gotten out? He didn't know." She became exasperated with the medical examiner. He didn't seem to know very much about fetal or infant anatomy. "I remember fighting with him," she said. "Well, didn't you read up on abortion? How do you do an abortion? If you don't know how to do an abortion, how did you know what you're doing?"

Gulino explained how he was measuring heads to determine fetal age, but he hadn't thought about how the fetuses had ended up outside the women's bodies in their intact state.

Wechsler really needed to know.

"I wanted to make the argument that they were delivered, that...[Gosnell] fed the women these drugs, he pushed these babies out, they came out, they were crying, they were fine." And then?

Gulino invited Wechsler and Pescatore down to the morgue to look at the bodies for themselves. Crime scene investigator John Taggart of the Philadelphia police department went with them.

The ME, who didn't know as much about abortion as the team who had been studying it for months, brought out the fetuses and asked what they wanted to see. "It's got a cut in the back of its neck," Wechsler said. She wondered if in fact the brain had been sucked out through this hole. "But its head seems perfect to me. Is it?"

"I don't know," Gulino replied.

So he invited her—a thirty-year-old attorney and a mother with a baby of her own at home—to cut it open.

"He was like, just cut it in fours, and we can see," Wechsler recalled Gulino telling her. "Again, they're little, and they're not hard. It's not hard. It's malleable still. It's soft. These heads have been pre-served to a certain degree."

And that is how Christine Wechsler, the diminutive former cheer-leader, Catholic schoolgirl, and mother of four came to be in a morgue preparing to cut open the skulls of forty-seven babies.

She didn't hesitate. She lifted the scalpel and started cutting.

"We had an assembly line of these babies that we knew nothing about. But you needed to know. We needed to know. Was [the head] crushed? Was it perfect? Was it round?"

"And we discovered they were perfect. They were intact," she said. That proved the brains hadn't been suctioned out of the babies' skulls in utero. Their mothers had delivered the babies alive.

Investigators initially struggled to explain the cuts on the back of the aborted fetuses' necks. If the hole wasn't to suck the brains out in utero, then why would the stab wounds be there?

Wechsler had seen plenty of dead bodies during her time in the DA's homicide unit. She'd seen a lot of dead children, too. But her visit to the ME's office to examine Gosnell's victims left a deep impression, and the memory remains vivid even today.

"So I saw them, literally—they were immaculate little specimens. You held them in your hands." Looking back, Wechsler told us she felt privileged, in a way, to see those fetuses. "You would never get to hold an infant at that age."

"Some of them were pristine," she recalled. "I saw them rehydrated with not an ounce of blood on them. They were perfect little things. You almost couldn't believe they were real."

"That was one of those *I-Love-Lucy*-lots-of-wine nights," she said.

In the course of interviews with some of the women who assisted Gosnell, the grisly truth about the neck cuts emerged. Prosecutors heard how he would use scissors to finish the babies off after they were born. "I had girls who were saying that that's how he accomplished the demise," Wechsler told us. "A lot of them had these marks in the back of the neck. We couldn't tell that they were perfect scissor marks"—not all of the cuts on the necks were precise or clean. According to Wechsler, some of the incisions looked torn. "That was gruesome. That was when it was like, *this* is disturbing." In Gulino's opinion, the marks could have come from scissors.

Wechsler told us that story on the deck of her beautiful home in Ardmore, Pennsylvania. The two-story house sits on a ten-thousand-square-foot lot overlooking the Merion Golf Club. The sun was shining; around the yard were children's toys and a swing set, all the domestic accessories that make up a normal family life. The contrast with the attorney's descriptions of the horrific deaths and mutilation of small babies could not have been more stark.

———

The team of prosecutors and investigators met regularly to sift through evidence. It was a huge learning exercise. So much of the information was scientific or medical. They all learned how to read ultrasounds.

"We would go through files," Wechsler explained, "and we had five ultrasounds, and we date them based on the BPD reading"—BPD stands for "biparietal diameter," a measurement of the distance between two sides of a fetus's head used to assess gestational age. "Joanne and I knew them by heart. I'd be like, 'I have thirty-seven weeks.' [Joanne Pescatore would say] 'I have twenty-nine.'"

They had to educate themselves, often staying up late reading medical textbooks and surfing the web for information. "I'm going to be on the federal watch list because of all these abortion websites that I'm on trying to figure out all this junk," Wechsler joked.

One question confronting the prosecutors was what to do about the feet that Gosnell had severed and stored. There were long legal arguments about the relevance of the feet, but the crucial question was whether severing them was even a crime.

"My family had a very bad New Year's Eve that year," Wechsler recalled. "We drove to the Poconos, and I was on the phone the whole time. We were re-reading *Planned Parenthood v. Casey*, re-reading the progeny of cases, because we were still fighting over the feet" —specifically how to get the feet into evidence and find some way of charging Gosnell for cutting them off and preserving them.

Wechsler said she had screaming matches with her bosses, Ron Eisenberg and Joe McGettigan. They didn't want to use the severed feet. But the young assistant district attorney was adamant. "I was like, 'What do you want me to do? I need to make it relevant. If you don't give me a charge, the feet are not relevant…so you have to give me a charge.'"

Round and round they went until McGettigan finally gave Wechsler the crime she was looking for: abuse of corpse.

"We were asking, '*Is it a corpse? Were these alive? Do you have to be alive to be a corpse? You're a fetus.*' I'm like, '*Then what the hell is it?*' It was insane," Wechsler said.

All through the investigation the team had to confront existential questions—not exactly something in a prosecutor's job description. Ultimately, Gosnell was charged with five counts of abuse of corpse. According to the law, "It is a crime for a person to treat a corpse in a way that he knows would outrage ordinary family sensibilities."[9]

And so that was how, on March 18, 2013, Desiree Hawkins, a twenty-year-old woman from West Virginia, received a strange voicemail. A police officer had called and asked her to call back.

When she did, she was asked if she had had an abortion in Philadelphia in 2009.

The police officer from Philadelphia told her that Gosnell, her abortion doctor, had been arrested. She explained to Desiree that he'd been allegedly delivering babies alive and then killing them. The officer said she was calling because during the investigation police officers had discovered Gosnell had kept trophies. He had severed babies' feet and kept them in labeled jars.

One of the jars had a label with the name Desiree Hawkins.

Desiree was stunned. She had had an abortion at Gosnell's clinic when she was sixteen and in high school. Her mother told her if she had the baby she'd have to leave the house because there just wasn't enough money.

The first clinic she went to, Hagerstown Reproductive Services, refused to do an abortion because at nineteen weeks she was too far along. They did, however, write Gosnell's name on a piece of paper. At Hagerstown she was confronted by pro-life protestors who she said scared her. But she was questioning her decision. "I kept asking myself is this the right thing to do. Should I be doing this? Should I hate myself for doing this?"

In December 2009 Desiree had the abortion at 3801 Lancaster Avenue. She woke repeatedly during the procedure at Gosnell's clinic and felt something being pulled or tugged from her. "I remember I kept coming to because I kept feeling pinching. It wasn't cutting because there were no marks there later. But I kept feeling pinching and pulling. Which is the reason why I felt I kept waking up. Every time I wake up, I feel it."

The last time she came to, she was still in the procedure room. She was very groggy but she remembers seeing Gosnell. "I just remember him picking up something and walking out [of] the room. To this day, I don't know if that what he picked up was my baby or not. I don't know. I think I've convinced myself that's what it is. But I don't know."[10]

In an interview with Kirsten Powers for *USA Today,* Hawkins revealed that she was not in fact nineteen weeks pregnant when she had her abortion. In the subsequent fallout from the Gosnell case she had retrieved her file. She was actually twenty-three weeks pregnant, not nineteen, when she went to Gosnell. "I was so overwhelmed and hurt," said Hawkins. "If I had known I was 23 weeks, I would have [chosen] adoption," she said.[11]

Interviewed for the documentary *3801 Lancaster: American Tragedy,* Desiree Hawkins said the discovery that Gosnell had kept her baby's foot as a trophy had exacerbated her trauma. "It gets worse because the one picture of the specimens they showed online...the very last one where part of the label is showing, that's mine. You don't even know how to respond when you find that a human or somebody else has kept the foot of your baby. You don't know how to answer that. You just want to cry. You just want to get sick. You don't want to believe it. And I still don't."[12]

That picture of Desiree Hawkins's baby's foot is online to this day. A permanent reminder.

―――

The grand jury report describes the corpses in long, technical, and frankly repetitive detail.

One twenty-one-week fetus of unknown gender was found in a plastic bleach bottle wrapped in a red biohazard bag. Both feet had been severed.

The feet of a twenty-two-week fetus were found in separate jars labeled with the same name and date, December 5, 2009. The left foot of another nineteen-week fetus was found in another jar. Investigators didn't find the right foot.

The grand jury heard evidence of how Gosnell would sever the spinal cords of live babies and place their bodies in "cut-off milk jugs, water containers, and juice cartons." One of the babies Gosnell was charged with murdering—the twenty-eight-week-old called "Baby Boy B"—was found in a bag inside a plastic water container, along with the placenta and several gauze pads.

The medical examiner provided a professional perspective to the grand jury. "Certainly things like drink containers, milk containers, water containers—this is not something we do in medical practice," Gulino testified. "What I do does not deal with living patients, and I would not put something in a plastic drink container. It just…it feels wrong I guess is what I'm saying. It feels wrong."

During the trial, assistant DA Ed Cameron told the jurors about a relative of his who had delivered a stillborn baby. The family held a funeral because, "Stillborns are treated like human beings. They are due the respect that any dead person should be given, either proper disposal through cremation at a medical facility, burial, whatever one wants to do—not put in a jar on a shelf," he said.

The prosecutors squarely confronted the grisly results of abortion. And they discovered that nobody really wanted to talk about it. In fact, they learned first hand how blinkered the medical profession could be when it came to abortion. Among the unpleasant surprises they encountered early on in the investigation was the nearly universal unwillingness of doctors to help them. Hardly anyone wanted to talk. A few were sympathetic but balked at testifying. Many more weren't so kind. Medical professionals didn't want to contribute to any official proceeding that might shine a negative light on abortion. The prosecutors were encountering the same reluctance to speak up and do the morally and ethically right thing that had allowed Gosnell to continue killing for years.

"I was calling doctors every day," Wechsler recalls. "People were hanging up the phone on me. People were cursing at me." She even made an inquiry with her own OB/GYN. "I had just had a baby at this practice. I was like, would you guys help me? They were like, no, go to so and so."

Why the silence? "Because everybody knew about Gosnell," Wechsler told us. "He was in the community. And the Planned Parenthood people and the [pro-choice] community would tell you that everybody knew about him, and they all warned one another internally about him. So when...he got arrested, and we were investigating, no one wanted to unearth it. It was very taboo." It seems the medical establishment cared more about the principle of unfettered access to abortion than the safety of real-life women.

The prosecution team learned that abortion was a very widespread procedure in Pennsylvania. Women could get abortions at places most people wouldn't suspect are abortion clinics. It isn't widely advertised, but the Hospital of the University of Pennsylvania performs abortions. No one knew Abington Hospital in the northern Philly suburbs performed abortions, either, until the hospital planned to merge with the Catholic-run Holy Redeemer Health System. It turned out that Abington was one of the biggest abortion providers in Montgomery County. Predictably, the merger ended the abortion services. As Wechsler put it, "The nuns went nuts."

At one point, Wechsler spoke off the record with an abortionist from Abington. The doctor explained how the drug dosages Gosnell and his untrained, unlicensed assistants gave Karnamaya Mongar would never have been administered at her facility. But she wasn't willing to testify to that effect.

Wechsler recalled how the abortionist was apologetic but firm. She didn't want the world to know how she made her living. "I know I could never help you," she told Wechsler. "I'm a mom, I'm a soccer mom. I'm like you, you're a lawyer. My kid's friends' parents don't even know what I do."

The lack of cooperation from the medical community created huge problems for the prosecutors. They could read ultrasounds day and night, but they needed professionals to help them understand what the ultrasounds meant. They could listen to Gosnell's assistants tell them how much of what drugs they had administered, but they needed experts to tell them the effects and proper dosages—and to give evidence in court. At this stage the assistant DAs and detectives knew more than most about abortion, but their opinions and findings were not good evidence—for that they needed qualified, experienced experts. If they couldn't find them, Gosnell was literally going to get away with murder.

The team adopted what Wechsler called "a grassroots approach." In reality it was straightforward desperation. They called anyone— friends, relatives, *anyone* they knew—who might be able to help.

The pressure was intense. A new DA, Seth Williams, had been sworn into office in 2010. Wechsler and Pescatore were called into meetings with their supervisors every day. And their colleagues still had no idea what they were working on. "You have to remember, it was a big secret, it was a grand jury. It was a dirty topic, and there was a lot of pressure on this new DA."

Finally Wechsler persuaded her children's pediatrician to help. She recalls walking on the street talking with the doctor, who was also a family friend and married to a former assistant district attorney. He helped decipher the medical records and explained what many of the drugs did. In time, Pescatore and Wechsler were able to find doctors who were willing to appear before the grand jury and at trial. But it wasn't easy.

Crime scene investigator John Taggart remembered one of the doctors they persuaded to help them. "She was a doctor that did abortions at Abington Hospital. Very attractive young lady. We brought her in on a Saturday. She's never been into court and we asked her a whole bunch of questions."

At one point, the prosecutors looked at Taggart and asked him if he had any questions for the doctor. He did. He wanted to know what happened if a baby was born alive during an abortion.

"She goes, 'The way I do it, it can't happen.'"

Taggart followed up. "What happens if everything doesn't line up one day?"

"She goes, 'It can't happen.'"

"I said, 'All right, it can't happen. One day, it does happen. What do you do?' She started crying. She said she never even thought about it."

For Taggart, learning the reality of abortion for the first time was shocking. "Even if it's done right, it's barbaric," he told us. "I'm no holy roller, but if you see the way they actually have to do it, it's barbaric." The learning experience was one shared by Wechsler, Pescatore, Wood, and the rest of the team.[13]

THREE

DERELICTION OF DUTY

"The Department's mission is to promote healthy lifestyles, prevent injury and disease, and to assure the safe delivery of quality healthcare for all Commonwealth citizens."

—PENNSYLVANIA DEPARTMENT OF HEALTH MISSION STATEMENT

Judge Cardwell-Hughes describes the grand jury that sat through some two years of evidence as exceptional. "Really dedicated, bright, and just an extraordinary cross-section of people," she told us. "There were people with high school degrees, people with graduate degrees. They asked really good questions. They were really thoughtful, committed. Absolutely committed. Good people."[1]

Good people performing what was, by any reckoning, a ghastly job.

The grand jurors heard from Gosnell's former patients and workers at the clinic, including Ashley Baldwin, the girl whose mother eventually pled guilty to corruption of a minor for bringing her daughter to work at the Lancaster Avenue clinic when she was just fifteen.

They had to sit through testimony from Gosnell's janitor, Jimmy Johnson, who described toilets blocked with fetal remains.

They listened as a woman from the National Abortion Federation who had inspected the Women's Medical Society described it as the worst facility she had ever seen. She turned down Gosnell's application for accreditation, walked out the door—and did absolutely nothing else. She didn't bother to report Gosnell to the Department of Health or the Department of State.

As the grand jury put it in its final report, "Of course, she rejected Gosnell's application. She just never told anyone in authority about all the horrible, dangerous things she had seen." In any case, as the grand jury had learned, it's unlikely that officials from either department would have acted even if she had.

The grand jury's final report mysteriously did not name the evaluator from the National Abortion Federation even though she had failed to report probable criminal activity at Gosnell's clinic. It was a strange decision for a report that named names and shamed those who failed to protect Gosnell's patients. A source close to the investigation says the name of the investigator was withheld at the insistence of Judge Cardwell-Hughes, who did not want the report to criticize the abortion establishment.[2]

The investigation also discovered that Gosnell was guilty of medical insurance fraud. He was not an approved provider for Keystone East Health Insurance patients, yet he treated their patients and charged the insurance company. According to the grand jury's report, "Gosnell simply asked Dr. Agnes Simmons, a fellow West Philadelphia doctor who was a Keystone provider, to pretend that she worked at the Women's Medical Society so that the clinic could bill Keystone under her name."

We asked the Pennsylvania Department of State what, if anything, it had done in response to the grand jury's discovery of insurance fraud. Had there been any investigation of Dr. Simmons's practice? A public information officer told us to make a formal Right to Know application, so we did. The DOS has an entire department devoted to responding to Right to Know Law requests. First we heard that our request would take many weeks to process. Then they denied our request, citing numerous statutes. We had a right to appeal, but as their denial letter helpfully explained, "Please be advised that the Office of Open Records has addressed appeals of the department denial of RTKL requests in this nature and has upheld the Department's denial in *all cases*" [emphasis added].

We did learn, however, that Dr. Agnes Simmons has no history of disciplinary action against her.

The *Philadelphia Daily News* offered some background on the Simmons-Gosnell fraud allegations in a March 28, 2011, story:

> Simmons hasn't been charged. Ruth Stoolman, a spokeswoman for Keystone's parent agency, Independence Blue Cross, said, "We cannot comment on ongoing investigations or litigation."
>
> Simmons vehemently denied the allegations and insisted she isn't under investigation before booting a *Daily News* reporter out of her West Philadelphia medical office earlier this month.
>
> "Y'all make me sick! I just threw up a little in my mouth," the 68-year-old bespectacled physician said at her office on Chestnut Street near 62nd.
>
> She then hired an attorney.
>
> "She will not be charged. No way, no how," said Chuck Peruto Jr. "Not only are we going to sue this a--h--- who implicated her, but after we sue him, I'm going to beat him up. I'm going to sue him and then beat the blabbermouth up. That's how strongly I feel she didn't defraud anyone."[3]

Simmons's bravado—and her lawyer's threats of physical violence—seemed to reflect a culture in Pennsylvania and Philadelphia, where unethical and possibly illegal behavior is tolerated even among professionals such as lawyers and doctors.

Simmons's attorney Chuck Peruto also described Simmons as a longtime friend of Gosnell's who was "horrified" by the charges against him. "What she read, that was not the Gosnell she knew," Peruto told the *Daily News*. "The Gosnell she knew had tremendous bedside manner, really cared about his patients and was very dedicated back in the day. She just kept saying, 'My, my, my!' She's surprised by it all."[4]

Kareema Cross, the clinic employee who gave the police her photos of Gosnell's collection of baby feet, told investigators that on one occasion Deborah Collins from Keystone Health Plan East came to the clinic because Gosnell's patients had complained that even though they had insurance, Gosnell still charged them one hundred and fifteen to one hundred and fifty dollars for their first visit. Collins told Gosnell that if he wanted to bill under KMHP he would have to refund that fee. He did not refund the money.

Instead Gosnell told staff that if people wanted to follow the insurance rules he would prescribe Motrin instead of OxyContin and codeine syrup (the cocktail of choice for drug addicts in PA).

The complaints stopped immediately—and Gosnell continued to get payments from KMHP.[5]

Assistant DAs Wechsler and Pescatore made many visits to the shuttered Lancaster Avenue clinic over the course of the investigation. Pescatore remembers the unnerving feeling she had every time she was there. "I felt like people were touching me inside that building," she said.[6]

It was so disturbing to Wechsler that she couldn't even bear to keep the clothes she wore anytime she visited 3801 Lancaster. She would immediately return home and throw her clothing into the garbage. She wanted nothing to remind her of that horrible place.

Even hardened FBI agent Jason Huff had a similar reaction after the first raid. He told friends the first thing he did when he got home was to take off and wash every stitch of clothing that he had worn that night.[7]

It was important to the prosecutors that the grand jury have an opportunity to see—and smell—Gosnell's house of horrors for themselves.

But first Judge Cardwell-Hughes had to inspect the clinic and decide if the jury should see the place. The police made Cardwell-Hughes wear a hazmat suit. "I have never seen anything so incredibly dirty in my life," the judge told us. "There were cat feces everywhere. I'm certain there were rodent feces, too. There were animal feces in the building. There were wild plants growing all over the place. There was dirt. This is not dirt because we had closed the building. This is dirt that had been there for a long time. It was filthy."

"You cannot process how dirty it was," the judge said. "There's a turtle tank in the window. And Gosnell spent more time asking me about those turtles than he did asking me about anything else. The turtles. It was crazy. It was absolutely crazy."

Wechsler told us Gosnell's turtles caused her no shortage of grief. To this day she gets irritated at the memory of the fuss over those animals. She recalls her husband asking her late one night what she was working on. "I'm like, 'A motion to protect, to preserve, the turtles.' What a contrast. We're throwing babies out in the trash, but, oh, we care about these turtles…. It was ridiculous," she said. There Wechsler was, in the midst of building a complicated case against this mass murderer, expending time and energy to make sure nothing bad happened to Gosnell's pets. The turtles ended up at a preserve in New Jersey.

Seeing the conditions at the clinic convinced the judge that assistant DAs Pescatore and Wechsler were right. The grand jury had to see the place.

It fell to Philadelphia PD crime scene investigator John Taggart to bring the grand jury members through the clinic. Because of the unsanitary conditions, the prosecutors discussed requesting hazmat suits for everyone. But with sixty people visiting the site—including the grand jury panelists, attorneys, and police—full hazmat gear for everyone would have been a logistical nightmare. Luckily for the prosecutors, everyone opted to wear masks and booties instead. Taggart and the other police officers took the grand jury in ten at a time. The rules for such visits are strict. The police can explain what each room is, but there can be no additional questions. The jurors walked through the obscene filth in silence. They were horrified.

The building was so maze-like—so complicated—that when Taggart finally got all the jurors back on the bus, he realized the jurors had missed the entire third floor. But they had seen enough.

Taggart made an interesting observation about the clinic when we met with him. Even after it was shut down, there were plenty of drugs and drug paraphernalia still left in the building. "That's one of the things that's really crazy," he told us. "All those junkies out there, nobody ever f---ed with that place. Nobody. It's weird. They're spooked out by it. Folks steal copper from a place that is fully occupied. That place has a lot of stuff still in there. Nobody has broken in there or tried to break in there."[8]

And it was true. When we visited the clinic, there were no obvious signs that anyone had tried to break into the building. As we stood outside on the sidewalk taking it all in, a passerby stopped and said, "There's evil in that place."

The overarching question in the case—the one everyone asks—is how could Gosnell's crimes have gone on for so long? Surely somebody must have complained? Surely state health inspectors would have had some clue about Gosnell's irregular and illegal practices? Surely the disgusting conditions at the Women's Medical Society should have drawn scrutiny long before Karnamaya Mongar's suspicious death attracted Jim Wood's attention?

The grand jury report devotes eighty-one detailed pages to answering these questions. In the end, the report is a scathing rebuke of the scores of bureaucratic automatons and pathetic paper pushers who failed to do their jobs. The grand jury used phrases such as "abdication of responsibility," "purposeful neglect," "chose to look the other way," "feeble excuses," "'it's-not-my-job-description' mindset" to excoriate local and state agencies.

The fact is, Gosnell's clinic should have been closed *decades* before his license was suspended in 2010. The evidence of malpractice and criminal activity was plentiful. His clinic wasn't even qualified to provide abortion services. Under Pennsylvania's Abortion Control Act, any facility providing abortions must have on staff or at the very least as a consultant a doctor who has completed a residency in obstetrics and gynecology. "In fact," the grand jury report notes, "40 years ago, [Gosnell] started but failed to complete a residency in obstetrics and gynecology." As we shall see, while there was apparently an OB/GYN on staff at Gosnell's clinic when Pennsylvania first licensed it in 1979, even the appallingly lax inspection schedule followed by the Department of Health established the fact that Gosnell was working alone by 1989—but the Health Department did nothing.

So the incompetents in Harrisburg, Pennsylvania's state capital, knew or should have known that, even by their own lax rules, Gosnell should not have been carrying out abortions—but they didn't care.

The Pennsylvania Department of Health certified the clinic at 3801 Lancaster Avenue to provide abortions on December 20, 1979. According to their records from the time, Dr. Joni Magee, an obstetrician-gynecologist, was the medical director and Gosnell was a staff physician. A registered nurse worked two days a week, four hours a day. The certification may have been accurate at the time. (Except for the notation that the clinic allowed easy access for stretchers. Given the complex and confusing layout of the building it was unlikely to have been true then, and it was certainly not true thirty years later, when paramedics lost forty-seven precious minutes trying to get the dying Karnamaya Mongar out of the building.) But on December 20, 1980, the clinic's operating license expired. This set no alarm bells ringing in Harrisburg among any of the regulators tasked with ensuring patient safety during abortions.

The Department of Health supposedly returned for a site visit in 1986, but state officials were unable to provide the grand jury with documentation establishing that the inspection actually took place.

On August 16 and 17, 1989, almost ten years after the state first certified the clinic for operation and nine years after its license to operate had expired, two inspectors finally appeared at 3801 Lancaster for a site review—Elizabeth Stein and Susan Mitchell. Stein and Mitchell noted at the time that Gosnell was the only physician at the clinic; there was no OB/GYN employed or on contract as a consultant, as the law required. They also noted other serious violations, including the fact that no registered nurses were on staff. And yet Stein and Mitchell ended up recommending that Gosnell's operating license be *extended* for another year. Mitchell's name would be connected to the clinic again years later. She was asked to join law enforcement on the night of the February 2010 raid.

In March of 1992, state health inspectors Janice Staloski and Sara Telencio paid a visit to the clinic. Staloski would eventually be promoted to Bureau Director for Community Program Licensure and Certification, becoming the Harrisburg official responsible for overseeing all Pennsylvania abortion facilities. In that capacity, she decided that Gosnell should be allowed to proceed with the abortion the night of the original February 2010 raid. At the time of the 1992 inspection, Gosnell was still the only doctor at the facility, but a Dr. Martin Weisberg was listed as a consultant. Again, there were no nurses. Crucially, in light of the circumstances of Karnamaya Mongar's death, Staloski and Telencio left blank the answers to the questions on the evaluation form about anesthesia and post-operative care. They also certified that the building had easy access for wheelchairs and stretchers, which was patently untrue. The three-story building has narrow corridors and no elevator. According to the grand jury report, Staloski and Telencio "inexplicably" decided on March 12, 1992, to approve the clinic to continue operations, citing "no deficiencies."

State health inspectors returned again on April 8, 1993. Because of instructions from Tom Ridge, a pro-choice Republican governor, it would be their final visit for seventeen years—until the raid in February 2010. Once again in 1993, Susan Mitchell was the inspector, joined by her colleague Georgette Freed-Wolf. And once again, nothing had changed. Gosnell was still the only doctor, no nurses had been hired, and the building had become even more cluttered and inaccessible. But Mitchell and Freed-Wolf certified that the clinic was perfectly accessible. They made no notes about cleanliness, broken equipment, or staff qualifications. They did find some expired drugs and some contraventions of the Abortion Control Act regarding lab work and tissue samples, but three months later Mitchell signed off on the clinic's license, stating that all the deficiencies noted earlier had been addressed. Neither Mitchell nor Freed-Wolf had returned to verify that Gosnell had in fact changed anything. The state renewed his operating license through March 21, 1994.

Pennsylvania gave Gosnell carte blanche for the next seventeen years. With every license extension and slipshod inspection, state health regulators sent a message: do what you like, because no matter what you do, we won't bother you, and we don't care whom you kill or injure along the way.

After Ridge's election in 1994, the state Department of Health stopped *all* routine inspections of abortion clinics. Not that it would probably have mattered if the inspections had continued, given the lax standards of Staloski, Mitchell, and their colleagues. About the only value the inspections had was to bump up DOH staffers' mileage reimbursements.

When the Pennsylvania Department of Health ended routine inspections of abortion clinics under the Ridge administration, it was still supposedly committed to inspections in cases of serious complaints about a clinic. Or so officials said.

What follows are some of the complaints filed against Gosnell between 1993 and 2010. It is a litany of shame. None of these complaints triggered an inspection—even the cursory sort of inspection that had taken place before.

In 1996, the Department of Health was informed that Gosnell had perforated a woman's uterus during an abortion. The patient required a radical hysterectomy. No one from the Department of Health visited to examine procedures or standards or to see if the staff were qualified.

In 1997, Dr. Donald Schwarz, a pediatrician at Children's Hospital of Philadelphia, hand delivered a complaint to the Department of Health reporting that several girls he had referred to Gosnell for abortions had returned to him with trichomoniasis, a sexually transmitted parasite they hadn't had before visiting 3801 Lancaster Avenue. Schwarz also hand delivered a copy of his complaint to the Pennsylvania Secretary of Health's office. Nobody ever followed up with him. His complaints were completely ignored. And of course there was no Department of Health visit.

When the grand jury asked the Department of Health to hand over all complaints it had received about Gosnell, Schwarz's was not among them. Who knows how many other complaints state health inspectors "lost"?

The grand jury report made a point of highlighting the Schwarz case: "We heard testimony from DOH officials who should have been aware of Dr. Schwarz's complaint—[Department of Health senior counsel] Kenneth Brody and [health inspector] Janice Staloski, at the least. Yet they made no mention of it to the grand jury. Did they remember the complaint and choose to exclude it from their testimony? Is ignoring complaints of this seriousness so routine at DOH that they honestly do not remember it? Or did the secretary of health never even forward it on for action? Of these possible explanations, we are not sure which is the most troubling."

In 1999, Marie Smith visited Gosnell's clinic for an abortion. She already had a one-year-old at home, and she had high blood pressure. In April, she discovered she was five months pregnant. She consulted the yellow pages for clinics and called Gosnell's Women's Health Society. According to Smith, an employee there told her over the phone that they performed abortions up to eight months. Smith arranged an appointment for the following day. After filling out some paperwork, she saw Gosnell, who inserted some dilators. She was told to return the next night at 7:30 p.m. Nobody at the clinic conducted any blood work, and they performed no ultrasound. Smith was never counseled about other options, or given an explanation of how the procedure would work.

When Smith returned the following night, one of Gosnell's assistants gave her three pills and explained "two of the pills are relaxer pills to relax your body and another pill [is] for the procedure." Once Smith was in the procedure room, an assistant inserted an IV and gave Smith some sort of sedative. She said she remembers nothing after that.

Marie Smith's mother, Johnnie Smith, waiting for her in the clinic lobby, began to wonder what was taking so long. She asked a staffer, "Is everything OK? Where's my daughter?" And she was assured everything was just fine.

Everything wasn't fine. Distressed and fearful about her daughter, Mrs. Smith let herself into the back of the clinic and began searching.

She found her daughter Marie slumped unconscious in a recliner, bleeding. The room was full of other women in the same sorry state. One Gosnell employee was monitoring the post-op room. Mrs. Smith recalls thinking to herself, "This is nasty! What's he up to in here?" She asked the attendant if she could take her daughter home. The attendant said that would be fine, and they left.

Johnnie Smith put her semi-conscious daughter to bed. But Marie Smith did not seem to recover. She became increasingly ill. Her chest became swollen; she vomited green fluid, had a very high fever, and was extremely weak. Her mother phoned Gosnell, who refused to see her. The doctor assured the worried mother that her daughter would be fine and said that her swollen chest was due to lactation. He offered a prescription that would "dry up" the milk.

Marie Smith did not get better. By the end of the week, she was admitted to Presbyterian Hospital. She can remember driving up to the hospital with her mother and seeing the sign for the emergency entrance before she blacked out. She woke in a hospital bed, where doctors told her she was lucky to be alive. They showed her an X-ray and ultrasound that had been taken just after she was admitted. Gosnell had left an arm and a leg of her baby inside her. Marie had become severely infected; she had to remain in the hospital for weeks.

While Marie Smith was at Presbyterian, Gosnell visited her twice. The first time, she refused to talk to him and asked him to leave. She also told Gosnell she would be contacting a lawyer. Gosnell immediately took out his checkbook and tried to pay her to forget anything had happened. She refused his money.

The second time he came to Smith's room, she was asleep. He left a note. "This is Dr. Gosnell. I was here but you were asleep."

Just as she had chosen the wrong doctor for her abortion, Smith chose the wrong lawyer for her lawsuit against him. Not only did she end up with a tiny award—just five thousand dollars for Gosnell's near-fatal abortion—despite the doctor's gross and surely criminal negligence, but her lawyer, Nina Perris, turned out to be a crook who would later be disbarred in a separate case involving forged documents and other ethical breaches. Marie Smith never received even a dollar of her settlement. She did draw some comfort from being able to help in the Gosnell prosecution—she supplied the FBI with the ultrasound images of the fetal remains Gosnell left inside her. Her new attorney is still trying to garnish the five thousand dollars from Gosnell.

Despite a patient's near-death experience because of the doctor's negligence, there was no visit or investigation by the Department of Health.

In 2009, Dana Haynes, a repeat abortion patient at 3801 Lancaster, sued Gosnell for malpractice in a botched abortion he had done on her in November 2006. It was her fourth with Gosnell. Haynes received no counseling for any of her abortions, and Gosnell, as was his normal practice, insisted on full payment in advance. Haynes had asked her cousins, Stephanie White and Monique Carr, to pick her up at 7:45 p.m. after the procedure was done. But when they arrived they were not allowed inside. The door was locked, and a receptionist communicated by intercom that Haynes wasn't ready. So the cousins went to a pizza place across the street. They returned several times and were denied entry every time, even though they could see other people coming and going.

At midnight, the cousins finally decided something must be wrong. They told the receptionist that if they weren't let in they would call the police. Gosnell let them in and admitted their fears were correct. They found Haynes slumped in a La-Z-Boy chair, bleeding and incoherent. She wasn't wearing any pants, or a hospital gown, she was just covered with a blanket. She wasn't hooked up to any monitors, either, and nobody was in the room watching her. When Monique

Carr asked why Gosnell hadn't called 911, he assured her that Haynes would be fine. "She's safe. She's OK. Her condition is not life-threatening." Thankfully, the cousins didn't believe him and insisted on an ambulance.

At that point, Gosnell admitted to the cousins that he had been unable to remove all of the fetus. The grand jury learned that he had made at least two unsuccessful attempts to complete the abortion. Gosnell then gave Monique Carr a jar with the pieces that he had removed. One of cousins handed the jar over to the staff at the Hospital of the University of Pennsylvania, where the ambulance took Haynes for emergency treatment.[9]

Doctors at the hospital told Haynes that Gosnell had left most of the fetus inside her. Not only that, he had also torn her cervix, uterus, and bowel. She required emergency surgery to remove five inches of her bowel and needed a blood transfusion. Haynes had no health insurance. Her hospital bill was twenty thousand dollars.

Shortly afterwards, Haynes's sister-in-law, Kelly Foster, confronted Gosnell at his clinic. Bizarrely, Gosnell offered Foster a tour of the facility, and chatted amicably and at length about himself, his life, his family, and his medical practice. He brought Foster to the back of the clinic, where he showed her the procedure rooms, including some intact aborted babies. Foster had had three abortions herself, at Rolling Hill Hospital in Philadelphia. When detectives visited her, she told them that the memory of those aborted babies upsets her to this day.

She described the Gosnell clinic's terrible stench. She saw blood on the floors, and the equipment looked ancient. Nothing appeared to be sanitized. She noted that people were constantly coming in and out.

"This is a mill," she said.

Gosnell explained that Haynes had signed a medical release and no refund was due. Foster disagreed and insisted Gosnell had a duty of care. He refunded cost of the abortion—$680—and asked Foster to have Haynes contact him before she filed a lawsuit or notified any oversight agency. She didn't agree and never contacted him again.

Haynes did file suit, but she was another victim of Gosnell who chose the wrong lawyer. Her case was dismissed after her lawyers failed to file a "certificate of merit," which is a notification of the expert witnesses who will testify at trial. It isn't entirely clear whether this failure was due to incompetence or because the closing of ranks by Gosnell's colleagues in the abortion industry made it hard to find expert witnesses. But then the lawyers failed to file an extension motion on time, which would have given them more time to search for experts. And once again a documented botched abortion that had almost killed a patient apparently merited no visit to Gosnell from either the Department of Health or the Department of State. In the words of the grand jury, "No one [at the Department of State] thought Ms. Haynes' complaint was worth investigating."

State officials who were supposed to monitor and regulate Gosnell missed many opportunities to inspect and stop America's biggest serial killer. Perhaps the best missed opportunity came in December 2001, when a former Gosnell employee, Marcella Choung, delivered a detailed handwritten complaint to the Department of State about the horrid conditions at 3801 Lancaster. She gave more information about the appalling conditions in Gosnell's clinic in a follow-up interview in March of 2002.

In essence, Choung's complaint was a summary of what the grand jury was to find over a decade and hundreds—perhaps thousands—of killings later. Long before Karnamaya Mongar was to die, Choung described how Gosnell had untrained workers performing specialized medical work. She included herself in this group. Uneducated, semiliterate workers were administering anesthesia and doing ultrasounds; the clinic was filthy, and two flea-infested cats roamed the procedure rooms, where Gosnell would eat sandwiches. The clinic reused single-use medical equipment. An autoclave sterilizer for abortion instruments didn't work properly, and a worker who had AIDs hand-washed the instruments. Gosnell would sometimes have a bowl of cereal as he was performing an abortion.

Choung also alleged that Gosnell performed abortions on children brought to the clinic against their will by their mothers. She said she saw this happen at least four times while she was there. And she claimed that Gosnell was involved in extensive insurance fraud. His staffers had put a false name on a medical file so that the insurance company would pay out despite the patient's lack of insurance.

Choung explained irregularities in the way Gosnell prescribed opiates to his patients as well—information that Detective James Wood would have to discover for himself ten years later.

This is the complete, unedited text of Choung's original handwritten complaint:

> There are 2 cats walking around in this medical office. They are allowed in procedure (abortion) rooms. They vomit up and down the steps. On procedure days, they reuse curettes, but they are disposable. They never get thrown in trash. There are dried up blood stains in the chairs in the recovery rooms. The Dr. will eat in procedure rooms while patient is in there. There are 2 males in the room while procedures are taking place. Many of the patients complain, but nothing is done. The patients are knocked out of medicine. They pay for "Twilight and Custom" anesthetic but only get "Heavy." They (patients) are unaware of this. In one of the charts, a patient used her cousin's insurance to get the procedure done, and they wrote this in the chart. There are minors who don't want the procedure done, and they say it, but the Dr. does it anyway. The Dr. does 2nd tris on Tuesday nights and does not report it to the I.R.S., he (the Dr.) pockets the money.

On Mondays, the office is open to 11 p.m. The Dr. will write notes for patients he hasn't seen in 3 months. He also writes a lot of Percocet prescriptions 90 for the same people like every Monday night. How much pain are they in to use 90 Percocets in a week. The Dr's pediatric room, where they get weighed, is where the cats' litter box is. The Dr. will do their (patients') procedures right after they've been counseled (suppose to be 24 hours after). The person who cleans doesn't take the whole trash bag. He takes what's in the trash bag. Nasty. If a patient vomits, it's in the trash the next day. All in all, this is a nasty facility. When he first got the cats, he had to treat his staff for fleas. Check Shala or Tanya Butler chart. It's probably been cleaned up. She signed 3 different names.

*****Please keep my name confidential. *****

You can ask anyone working there about this complaint, except Jonathan, he is Dr. Gosnell's right hand. I think he should lose his license because he should know better. The things that are going on in this medical office is nasty and could be spreading diseases.

Christine Wechsler was impressed with Choung. "She was amazing, great. She came from Atlanta. We flew her up to talk to us. Now, talk about a good witness. She's really edgy, really pretty, she's like Asian, blue makeup, real character, tons of accessories, cool, and extremely smart, extremely well-spoken, works in the abortion field because she believes in it."

When Choung was interviewed later by the Pennsylvania Bureau of Enforcement and Investigation, she explained the conditions that had forced her to leave Gosnell's clinic. When Gosnell's right-hand man "Jonathan" left for a vacation, the doctor simply told her that she would be on her own and needed to "med up" between twenty and thirty patients. Choung looked at the women in the clinic, who needed expert medical attention from qualified medical personnel. She knew she wasn't even remotely qualified—she knew that giving these women anesthesia would endanger the life of each and every one of them, and as she looked at the faces of the women who were lining up for treatment she wanted no part of it. So she told Gosnell she had forgotten something in her car, walked out of the building, and drove away. She never looked back and never went back to collect the personal belongings she had left behind in the clinic. She made her complaint to state officials the next day.

Here is how the Department of State responded. First, they interviewed Gosnell at a government office in King of Prussia, a Philadelphia suburb. An investigator made a perfunctory phone call to Dr. Warren Taylor, who said he had performed abortions at the Women's Health Society clinic in 2001 and remembered a case where he had refused to do an abortion on an underage girl. He couldn't say for certain whether Gosnell did the abortion himself later. Taylor said that was all he knew. He told investigators that he believed in "Do no harm" and that he considered himself "lily white."

Finally, a DOS functionary interviewed Ronald C. Cohen, a pharmacist at Bell Apothecary, two blocks from the clinic, about the prescription drug claims. Cohen said they hadn't noticed any unusual prescriptions—though they did subsequently stop honoring Gosnell's scripts.

Investigators did meet with Gosnell, but their written report of the meeting concludes with this line: "[Gosnell] indicated he would not be sending a written response to the allegations. He would think about it but probably would not." The investigators, of course, did not insist.

They did not visit the clinic. They did not talk to other members of staff, or to patients. They made no serious effort to establish the veracity of the damning allegations made by a member of staff who had risked her future career by complaining against Gosnell, who was one of the most respected long-standing members of the abortion community.

Instead, on April 29, 2004, attorneys Mark Greenwald and his boss Charles J. Hartwell of the Pennsylvania State Board of Medicine, the Department of State agency responsible for licensing doctors, recommended no further action on Choung's allegations. They stamped the case file, "Prosecution Not Warranted."

And state officials continued to miss opportunities to investigate and shut Gosnell down.

On October 9, 2002, the Professional Underwriters Liability Insurance Company informed the Pennsylvania State Board of Medicine that it had made a settlement of four hundred thousand dollars with the family of Semika Shaw, a twenty-two-year-old mother of two who had died after having an abortion at Gosnell's clinic in March 2000.

In January 2003, the Pennsylvania Medical Professional Liability Catastrophe Loss Fund informed the Department of State that it had paid out five hundred thousand dollars in the same case.

In January 2004, the Department of Health decided further investigation of Semika Shaw's death wasn't warranted. Once again, State Board of Medicine attorney Mark Greenwald handled the case. And exactly as he would with Marcella Choung's complaint later that same year, he stamped Shaw's file, "Prosecution Not Warranted."

Greenwald's case summary noted how Shaw had been taken to the emergency room of the University of Pennsylvania's hospital complaining of pain and heavy bleeding following a "seeming routine procedure." Shaw's surgeons couldn't locate a perforation, and she subsequently died from infection and sepsis. "Although the incident is tragic," Greenwald wrote, "especially in light of the age of the patient, the risk was inherent with the procedure performed by Respondent [Gosnell] and administrative action against respondent's license is not warranted."

Greenwald's report left out two key facts. First, the insurance company report, relying on the autopsy, pointed out that Gosnell's malpractice was responsible for Shaw's death: "Autopsy report indicated perforation of cervix into uterus." Greenwald also failed to mention that the insurance company had paid four hundred thousand dollars in compensation to Shaw's family and the Pennsylvania Catastrophic Expense Fund—in other words, the taxpayers—had paid five hundred thousand dollars. Despite not noting these relevant pieces of information, Greenwald did find space in his report to note that this was Shaw's fifth abortion. It seems that when officials were forced to investigate, information that revealed the truth about Gosnell was ignored or suppressed, whereas information that would make the victims appear less sympathetic was to be highlighted.

And the complaints kept coming, and they kept being ignored.

In August 2003, the Philadelphia Health Department's Environmental Engineering Section received an anonymous complaint alleging that Gosnell was storing aborted fetuses in paper bags in the refrigerators employees used for their food. Mandi Davis, a sanitation specialist (and thus presumably not part of the "abortion establishment" in Philadelphia), wrote a memo to her colleague Ken Gruen, and copied then-Assistant Health Commissioner Izzat Melhem, describing the "rather disturbing" complaint she had received.

Davis requested a site visit. She told Gruen, "I am not expecting a 'wild goose chase' for aborted fetuses." Philadelphia Health Commissioner Donald Schwarz told the grand jury that notations on the memo seem to suggest that somebody from the department visited 3801 Lancaster at some point. But the department could produce no additional documentation. Nor was there evidence that the department took any action against Gosnell for his bizarre and insanitary mishandling of medical waste. He didn't even have an infectious waste plan, as the city health code required.

On August 2, 2005, William Newport, an attorney with the state Bureau of Professional and Occupational Affairs, learned that Gosnell didn't have liability insurance. In fact, Gosnell wasn't insured *at all* between July 15, 2004, and April 18, 2005. A doctor practicing without insurance is simply unheard of. Despite his record of lawsuits and out-of-court settlements, Gosnell courted disaster for himself and his employees by operating uninsured. No action was taken.

In 2005, Derek Layser, a lawyer representing Cassandra Barger, an abortion patient, had sued the state of Pennsylvania for medical malpractice at Gosnell's clinic. Ms. Barger was a recovering drug addict. She had used methadone for two years as part of her recovery but was almost totally weaned off the methadone dependency when she went for an abortion. Ms. Barger made clear in her medical history form at Gosnell's clinic that she was in recovery and using methadone. When the staff brought her into the procedure room Ms. Barger reminded them again of her methadone use. Despite this, Gosnell administered the anesthetic Nubain intravenously. Nubain is clearly contraindicated for people on methadone therapy. Ms. Barger immediately had a reaction and told Gosnell to stop giving her the Nubain. Gosnell ignored her. Ms. Barger pulled the IV out of her own arm and started to convulse. She fell off the operating room table, injuring her head.

While these troubling details are more evidence of Gosnell's appalling treatment of patients, there is an added insult in this case.

Ms. Barger's lawyer Derek Layser filed a medical malpractice complaint and was very troubled when Gosnell himself filed his answer. On September 13, 2005, Layser wrote to Jennifer Bush Archer at the Pennsylvania Department of State, "I am puzzled as to why [Gosnell] is representing himself since all physicians are required to have insurance coverage under Mcare Act. I am requesting that your office investigate this matter on its facts and the issue of Dr. Gosnell's apparent failure to have the statutory insurance coverage."

Gosnell wasn't insured. The Pennsylvania Department of State knew he wasn't insured. Nothing happened.

On May 4, 2006, David Grubb, an attorney for the State Board of Medicine, recommended no further investigation or prosecution in Ms. Barger's case. His supervisor Andrew Kramer agreed and signed off on the decision.

In 2007, Delaware County Medical Examiner Dr. Frederick Hellman complained to the Department of Health about another one of Gosnell's patients, a fourteen-year-old girl. On day two of one of Gosnell's three-day abortions, she had delivered a stillborn baby girl at Crozer-Chester Medical Center. Hellman determined the baby was at least thirty weeks gestational age—it could even have been as much as thirty-four weeks—far beyond the legal limit. Once again, the Department of Health did nothing. The grand jury included a photograph of that baby girl in its final report, and jurors saw the picture during the trial. It is a fully formed baby. It is haunting.

Finally, in 2009, Karnamaya Mongar died after an abortion at 3801 Lancaster Avenue. She was medicated to death by untrained staff. Because of the inaccessible corridors and padlocked emergency exit, valuable time was lost getting her to the hospital. Gosnell duly informed the Department of Health of the death. And the Department of Health responded as it always had. They deemed no further investigation was necessary.

Gosnell must have felt invincible. No matter what he did, there were no consequences. Until, that is, his path crossed that of a tenacious narcotics investigator for the Philadelphia district attorney.

———

Month after month, a steady stream of government regulators who had never regulated Gosnell appeared before the grand jury. They were from the Pennsylvania Department of Health, the Pennsylvania

Department of State, the Philadelphia Department of Public Health, the Pennsylvania State Board of Medicine, the Philadelphia Department of Public Health, and the Philadelphia Health Department's Environmental Engineering Section.

With a few notable exceptions, state and local government officials had completely failed to do their jobs. Official incompetence, bureaucratic inertia, neglect, and the desire to protect abortion from a harsh spotlight whatever the cost caused needless deaths and injuries. The grand jury's conclusion was damning: Kermit Gosnell murdered and maimed with impunity for thirty years because virtually no one did his job properly.

When the staff from the Department of Health and Department of State appeared before the grand jury, they all brought legal counsel. Even the lawyers had lawyers. The final cost to taxpayers was $116,000.

Of all the witnesses the grand jury heard—and they were subjected to some appalling testimony—the panel had special contempt for the Health Department officials who appeared before them. These were the very people paid by taxpayers to inspect, supervise, and monitor health facilities and to take action when they were not up to par. They were paid to protect people, and they failed abysmally.

Worse, when Health Department employees were questioned, almost every one of them pointed the finger of blame somewhere else.

Certain Pennsylvania Department of Health officials involved in the Gosnell case particularly infuriated the grand jury and the prosecution team.

The uncaring attitude of Janice Staloski, head of the DOH's Bureau of Community Licensing and Certification, who was ultimately responsible for overseeing the care in all Pennsylvania abortion clinics, angered and appalled the panel. According to the report, Staloski "readily acknowledged many deficiencies on DOH's, and her own, oversight of abortion facilities," but her "dismissive demeanor indicated to us that she did not really understand—or care about—the devastating impact that the department's neglect had had on the women whom Gosnell treated in his filthy, dangerous clinic."

Staloski admitted that she had inspected Gosnell's clinic in 1992 and done nothing about the failures and deficiencies she saw at the time. Yet she continued to rise through the department ranks and eventually reached a director's position.

Cynthia Boyne, the chief division director for the Division of Home Health, with responsibility for oversight of abortion clinics under Staloski's supervision, didn't think an inspection of the clinic was necessary after Mrs. Mongar died in 2009. Boyne laid the blame for her negligence on the department's senior counsel. Small children show more shame and have a greater sense of responsibility than Boyne or Staloski.

The Health Department's senior counsel, Kenneth Brody, told the grand jury that there was no legal obligation for the department to inspect abortion clinics. This was an odd thing for Brody to say. Until 1995, when the self-described "moderate and pro-choice" Republican Governor Tom Ridge took office, inspections were fairly routine—if completely ineffective in Gosnell's case. Ridge ran as a pro-abortion Catholic Republican—a convenient mix of beliefs that would help his electoral chances in a state that was turning increasingly Democrat.

Ridge's election was catastrophic for the many women and the hundreds of live babies who were injured and killed in Gosnell's clinic. The governor had campaigned specifically on a promise of not wanting to place more barriers to women seeking abortions. Because of that promise, Kermit Gosnell was allowed to continue murdering countless babies and to kill and maim women, safe in the knowledge that nothing he did would get him in trouble. Even as the lifeless bodies of Semika Shaw and Karnamaya Mongar were carried out of Gosnell's clinic and complaint after complaint was received by regulators, the knowledge that the "look the other way" policy was coming from the very top meant there was no oversight. The governor's office put a blanket of invincibility around the doctor and his house of horrors.

J. D. Mullane, a Philadelphia-area reporter who covered the Gosnell case and tweeted out the famous photograph of the empty courtroom to demonstrate the blackout of the case by the national media, is clear about Ridge's culpability. "Ridge is, to me, Gosnell's chief enabler," he told the *Daily Caller*. "[I]t was his administration that decided to halt annual inspections of Pennsylvania's abortion clinics. This happened because the Ridge administration felt shoddier clinics like Gosnell's would be forced to close if inspectors from the state department of health came through and did their jobs."

"Closing clinics would create a 'barrier' for women seeking abortions, and Ridge didn't want that," Mullane says. "Though Tom Ridge is a chatty guy, he has maintained radio silence on Gosnell. Now you know why."[10]

The Susan B. Anthony List, an anti-abortion activist group, was very clear about Ridge's responsibility for Gosnell's decades-long crime spree. "When Governor Bob Casey, a Democrat and a longtime pro-life champion, was replaced by Gov. Tom Ridge, a pro-choice Republican, Kermit Gosnell was given free rein," they pointed out.[11]

And Ridge found willing and able accomplices in the public health bureaucracy. They knew better and still did nothing. Many of them were registered nurses. All of them were health care professionals. But in their neglect, they rendered "health care" and "professional" meaningless. Even before Tom Ridge issued his "hands-off" edict, Staloski had seen Gosnell's clinic. She knew it was substandard. Not only did she look the other way, she allowed him to continue practicing.

Christine Dutton, the Department of Health's chief counsel, incensed the grand jury with her callous justifications for Staloski's indifference. They found it surprising that people working in public health, people who apparently have chosen the health of the people as their calling, should demonstrate such callousness. "Appallingly, the chief counsel...defended Staloski's inaction following Mrs. Mongar's death. Dutton testified that she had reviewed the emails and documents showing that Staloski and her staff were communicating with Gosnell's office to get him to file the MCARE form. Based on these very minimal efforts, Dutton insisted: 'we were responsive.' Pushed as to whether the death of a woman following an abortion should have prompted more action—perhaps an investigation or a report to law enforcement—Dutton argued there was no reason to think the death was suspicious."

And in a throwaway line that incensed the grand jury and infuriates assistant DAs Wechsler and Pescatore to this day, Dutton justified Staloski's gross negligence in Mongar's death.

"People die," she told the panel.

Five years later, "People die" remains fresh in Christine Wechsler's memory. She told us how the grand jury looked completely stunned when they heard Dutton off-handedly say those words. The panel understood that nobody had needed to die at 3801 Lancaster—if Dutton's colleagues had only done their jobs.

The grand jury also discovered that nurses from Jefferson College of Nursing regularly did trainings in Gosnell's clinic. Wechsler questioned a few of those students during the course of the investigation. "I remember lighting up on these nurse practitioner students from Jefferson. 'Why didn't you tell anybody?'" She found it hard to believe that idealistic young nursing students could work in a clinic like Gosnell's and not report him. Wechsler said she wanted to "wring their necks."

So what was their excuse? Speaking to the NAACP in 2000, President George W. Bush described the mindset that, in the name of compassion, tolerates lower standards for minorities as "the soft bigotry of low expectations." He could have been talking about the student nurses of the Jefferson College of Nursing, who told the prosecutors they thought the facility was typical of a poor, inner-city clinic. Wechsler had no patience for their bigotry. "You think that's OK? It's not good enough for you, but it's good enough for them? It was crazy. Jefferson was sending students in there [in] droves. And nobody said a word."

These nurse practitioners were not in the clinic when the abortions were happening, but they would come to the clinic in the mornings—assigned to work with Eileen O'Neill, the unlicensed medical school graduate whom most of the nurses and many of Gosnell's patients assumed was a doctor. To Wechsler, the fact that they didn't even report blood on the floor and flea-infested cats prowling the halls is unforgivable.

We wrote to the Jefferson College of Nursing to find out more about its relationship with Gosnell's clinic. We asked if any students had complained about conditions there. Did supervisors from Jefferson ever visit 3801 Lancaster Avenue? If so, did *they* ever complain about the facility? Finally, we wanted to know whether the school had made any changes in the way it handles student work placements in light of the grand jury's report? Jackie Kozloski from the nursing school's press office replied, "Unfortunately we won't be able to participate in your book project."

That answer isn't nearly good enough. Jefferson College of Nursing is a school in receipt of public money, and the public has a right to have answers to legitimate questions from journalists, as we pointed out in our reply to Kozloski. The Gosnell case involved serious and extensive medical malpractice and resulted in multiple murder convictions. Our questions went to the issue of public health, something one would imagine the Jefferson College of Nursing values. We received no response.

The grand jury did discover a few hardworking, mostly low-level government employees who were diligent, conscientious, and honest. Unfortunately, their superiors were not.

Among the notable exceptions to the cluster of state incompetence was Lori Matijkiw, a quality assurance nurse for the Vaccines for Children Program for the Philadelphia Department of Health. She had been a nurse since 1981, previously working as a school nurse before moving into coronary care and then public service in the DOH. Matijkiw visited the Women's Medical Society on July 17, 2008. Her job was to check the vaccines at the clinic, as Gosnell had enrolled in a federal childhood vaccination program. Matijkiw had made an appointment to meet Gosnell at the clinic, as was standard protocol. He never showed up. The clinic's receptionist said she didn't know anything about an inspection, and she couldn't reach Gosnell by phone. According to Matijkiw, as she waited for the "clueless" receptionist to try to locate the doctor, she took note of the signs taped to the front desk. The papers explained the charges for abortion services and said patients who changed their minds would not get their money back. She also saw a price list for different types of sedation—patients could pay for heavy or light anesthesia regardless of their condition or medical needs. This shocked Matijkiw, and she took a note of everything.

Matijkiw decided that even though the doctor hadn't shown up, she would inspect the fridges where the vaccines were kept anyway. She looked for the logbook that was supposed to show that the refrigerators' temperatures were checked twice a day and that the vaccines were stored at proper temperatures. They were not. The temperature logbook had not been updated for a month and a half. She found expired vaccines.

Matijkiw's report on the varicella vaccine, which is supposed to be kept in a freezer, was detailed and damning:

When I opened the freezer, the woman from downstairs was with me [this was Tina Baldwin, the woman who ultimately pled guilty to corrupting a minor for getting her fifteen-year-old daughter a job in Gosnell's clinic] and there were two containers in the freezer. They were large plastic containers and there were some blue chucks wrapped around them... like a barrier, plastic barrier kind of like when a puppy dog uses a thing on the floor, so there's a barrier underneath and then there's paper on top, so it absorbs any spills....

[T]hese containers which had frozen contents and they were wrapped in some blue chunks and the contents were blood colored. They were dark blood, like dark red colored contents. The varicella was there also. It was in the box, in the manufacture box which is really small... and on the floor of the freezer were some drops of red fluid [...] frozen to the floor of the freezer.

And that wasn't all Matijkiw noticed. "When I walked in the lobby, it was really filthy. I go into a lot of practices and this was really filthy," she told the grand jury. "I've seen many, many different offices. There were two large fish tanks which are very—they were not clean at all, which is very unusual in a practice. There was one large fish tank that just had all these clam—that I remembered had all these clam shells, empty clam shells on the bottom. The water was really murky, there was an odor, and there was a turtle swimming around."

She remembered the smell of the clinic. "It smelled of urine. I didn't see any cats, but I could smell cats."

Matijkiw was so appalled by what she witnessed in the clinic that she immediately called her supervisor from the car, as soon as she left the building.

She then documented her findings in an email to vaccine program manager Lisa Morgan, her senior supervisor, and to Dr. Barbara Watson, medical director for the immunization program. The nurse also met personally with Morgan and Watson to describe the atrocious conditions she had seen. She was so amazed by the clinic that she did a bit of digging herself and found that the clinic had been reported before for similar violations.

Because of Matijkiw's damning report, the Philadelphia city health department suspended Gosnell's clinic from participating in the vaccine program. And nothing more. Matijkiw's supervisors did not contact the Department of Health, the Philadelphia police, the State Board of Medicine—no one. And if that wasn't bad enough, a year later the city department of health was busy trying to re-enroll Gosnell's clinic in the vaccine program.

According to the grand jury report, "A note by one employee in August 2009 recorded: 'Site was told they need to purchase a new unit to store their vaccines completely SEPARATE from all other medical products'—an apparent reference to the containers filled with fetuses. Other than ensuring that vaccines were not placed in the same freezer, the city health department showed no concern about the stored fetuses or the dripping frozen blood observed by Matijkiw."

Matijkiw returned to the Women's Health Society clinic on October 8, 2009. "I was told that the site wanted to re-enroll in the program," she said. She met with O'Neill, one of the two unlicensed doctors Gosnell employed. Matijkiw very quickly realized that O'Neill hadn't a clue about the proper workings of the program aimed at uninsured children under the age of eighteen. O'Neill thought the vaccines could be given to adults.

The grand jury report continues the story:

In addition, Matijkiw noticed that the clinic listed 20 children on Keystone Mercy, a Medicaid health plan. Matijkiw wrote that three of the "children" were almost 19 years old, and one had private insurance through Aetna. She wondered if any of them had ever been in the clinic. She also said that O'Neill was improperly trying to count abortion patients as vaccination patients.

In response to questioning by Matijkiw, O'Neill admitted that she was not licensed in Pennsylvania. She falsely claimed to have had a Delaware license, which she said she let lapse. When Matijkiw asked who in the practice treated children, O'Neill replied: "They don't come in." Yet Gosnell and O'Neill claimed to be providers of children's vaccines.

In a depressingly common refrain, Matijkiw noted that nothing had changed since her first visit. "It was still dirty, still filthy. It still smelled of urine. The fish tanks were still there. The plants, which I didn't mention in the beginning, but there were plants all over the place in various stage of green and brown, being half dead or being alive."

Matijkiw wrote another report for Morgan. This time she also told her boss about something else she had noticed that was a very serious issue: patients being escorted into procedure rooms when Gosnell was not on site. Matijkiw concluded her report, "If Dr. Gosnell was out of the office and [O'Neill] had to call the other physician's assistant on his cell phone and leave a message for his Medical Assistant why were patients in the procedure area?"

It was hard for the grand jury to fathom how Matijkiw's report of very serious breaches of state law did not result in immediate action.

"If nothing else," the grand jury pointed out, "Matijkiw's supervisors should have passed her information about the unsanitary conditions and the fetuses in the freezer to another division within the city health department with jurisdiction over such matters.

"They should also have reported Gosnell and O'Neill to the Department of State's Board of Medicine, based on the evidence apparent to Matijkiw that patients were being treated in Gosnell's absence and that O'Neill was practicing without a license. Yet the city health department did nothing."

The very problem Matijkiw identified—unqualified people treating patients—led to the death of Karnamaya Mongar just one month later. She would very likely be alive today if only Matijkiw's superiors had listened to her and the clinic had been shut down.

A note in the Philadelphia Department of Public Health records from December 2009, one month after Mrs. Mongar died, reads, "Site will not be enrolled in [the Vaccine for Children program] after Matijkiw's visits. We will pick up any wasted vaccines in January. Jim is reporting Dr. to state licensing."

But Jim Lutz, the immunization program's director, never reported Gosnell. And he wasn't the only one who failed. No one else at the city health department reported Gosnell, either. Lori Matijkiw had done her job thoroughly and professionally. She trusted that her superiors would do their jobs. She was dead wrong.

One of the most poignant moments of the grand jury investigation happened during the testimony of a witness we'll call "Sandy."

Sandy was twenty-seven and pregnant with her first child when she went to Gosnell for an abortion. Her pregnancy was far along; Gosnell told her it was twenty-one weeks. That's in the second trimester, when the abortion process requires two or three days, depending on the baby's gestational age.

Sandy started to feel uneasy about her decision when Gosnell started the procedure. On the first day he inserted the laminaria—these are pieces of seaweed (or a synthetic substitute) that expand in the cervix, allowing the baby to come out more easily. The first day, a few of these are inserted. If the baby is big, they are removed the second day and replaced with more.

Gosnell told Sandy it was imperative that she have her abortion right away because she was so big. She was nervous and unsure. She asked Gosnell what happened to the babies when the abortion was over, and he replied, "We burn them."

When Sandy went home, she became more and more uneasy. She began to really acknowledge for the first time that she was pregnant. She spoke to her cousin and told her how she felt. Her cousin phoned Gosnell to explain that Sandy didn't want to go through with the abortion—she wanted a reversal. Gosnell became very angry. He said he didn't do reversals and Sandy wouldn't be getting her money back. She had already paid thirteen hundred dollars in cash. She told investigators, "It was like he was mad that I wasn't going through with the abortion."

Sandy went to the Hospital at the University of Pennsylvania for a reversal. Once she had told all of this to the grand jury, assistant DA Joanne Pescatore asked what happened after that. "Oh, my baby started kindergarten today," she replied. The grand jury burst into applause. The prosecutors believe that was the first time a Philadelphia grand jury had ever applauded testimony.

It was interesting that Gosnell told Sandy that the babies aborted at his clinic were burned. Christine Wechsler says she discovered a lot of addresses for undertakers who did cremation in Gosnell's rolodex. She always wanted to find out why Gosnell had those contacts. She was convinced that he was having the babies burned. It would certainly be cheaper than burying them—and it got rid of the evidence.

———

"People die."

Semika Shaw was dead. Karnamaya Mongar was dead. Dana Haynes nearly bled to death. And Gosnell just kept running his business as usual.

The grand jury sat through a year of these horrific, tragic stories, hearing about the countless complaints. When they got an opportunity to hear explanations from the army of ineffectual government workers, they were very attentive. Two things sickened them especially: the civil servants' appalling attitudes and complete unwillingness to admit responsibility—and the fact that they all lawyered up at taxpayers' expense.

Even the grand jury report, however, is not a perfect examination of how the authorities could have stopped Kermit Gosnell's killing spree. The grand jury appears to have missed the fact that the Philadelphia police department's homicide unit failed to properly investigate Gosnell when it was alerted to the fact that Gosnell had performed an abortion on a woman who was almost eight months pregnant with twins. Although the grand jury proceedings are secret and sealed, in the final report, which is public, there is no mention of a case that could have shut Gosnell down in 2007, thus saving the lives of Karnamaya Mongar and Semika Shaw—and perhaps hundreds of babies.

It has never been reported on until we came across it in our research for this book.

The story starts with a worried husband we will call "Jalil." We know his identity, but have decided to refrain from publishing it to protect his privacy. Jalil, who lives in Virginia, was worried about his estranged wife, "Khalifa," who was almost eight months pregnant with twins. Although they had recently separated after their young marriage went sour and Khalifa had moved from Virginia to live with her brother in Pennsylvania, the couple was still in regular contact.

Suddenly, Jalil couldn't get in touch his wife. For days, he called and emailed without reply. She seemed to have disappeared. He asked the Philadelphia police to make a "welfare check"—a call to her house to see if she was injured or otherwise in danger. Jalil said the police responded quickly. They understood a woman pregnant with twins might have required urgent help.

But Jalil was surprised at what the police reported when they called back.

"They found her at her house and she was ill," he told us. "They said she looked very sick, but they also told me that she was no longer pregnant."

Jalil was shocked by the news that she had lost the babies. But Khalifa was still not answering his phone calls, so he didn't know what had happened.

The next day, his credit card statement arrived in the mail. "It was then that I noticed this really large charge for a medical clinic in Philadelphia. And when I checked it out, it turned out to be Gosnell's abortion clinic. That's when I realized she had aborted the twins even though she was almost eight months pregnant."

Jalil made a complaint to the Philadelphia police homicide unit. Stated simply, he presented the police with a case that had many of the elements that led to Gosnell's trial, conviction, and imprisonment—several years and many more deaths later.

But Jalil claims the police had no enthusiasm for investigating Gosnell and his illegal abortions, despite a credit card statement proving that Khalifa had paid for an illegal late-term abortion.

"The detective who investigated was a cocky little bastard, and I could tell from the start he clearly sympathized with her and her situation," Jalil said. Khalifa told the detective that she had visited her doctor and he told her that the babies were dead in the womb and the pregnancy had to be terminated in an emergency operation before it endangered her health.

"I asked if she at least produced a letter of referral from her doctor that she would have needed to terminate the babies, but the detective just said she can't find the documents but that he believed her story," Jalil told us. "It was clear from the very beginning that he didn't want to do anything."

Confronted with the unbearable loss of his twin babies and a system that didn't seem to care, Jalil struggled to make sense of what had happened.

"I went to the mosque and did my prayers on them. It's like a Muslim funeral. That's all I could do," he said.

Until we phoned him on a quiet Sunday night almost three years after Gosnell was convicted, Jalil had not known that the man who killed his babies was in prison for similar crimes committed years after Jalil first let the police know about his twins.

"It's disturbing that so many were killed at his hands after that homicide detective was alerted," he said.

Jalil believes that Gosnell was not investigated or prosecuted at that time because "he was protected by the corrupt establishment. He was protected by those around him."

Jalil says, with some justification, that the failure by the police to investigate thoroughly was worse than the inaction of the state bureaucrats.

"This was the homicide unit. When they get a lead, normally they leap on it like flies on shit. That's what they do—they hunt killers. But they just ignored this, and he kept on killing."[12]

Despite repeated requests, the Philadelphia police department has not responded to questions about its failure to investigate Gosnell properly years before he was eventually brought to justice. It promised us that it would answer after the pope's visit (explaining that it was too busy beforehand), but since then has repeatedly ignored requests for a comment.

And Jalil was not the only father who found out the fate of his child too late. The FBI asked Gosnell employee Latosha Lewis about another distraught father in an interview they conducted on March 9, 2010. According to a transcript of that interview which the authors have seen, "Lewis was asked about a man who came into the clinic in 2007 who was very upset and was screaming 'You killed my baby.' Lewis vaguely remembered the incident."

No wonder Gosnell was so arrogant. Women died in his clinic. Others were maimed. Still others were infected with STDs. Viable babies routinely had their necks slit and their bodies tossed in the trash. But nothing happened to him, and practically nobody cared, until one undercover narcotics cop heard about Karnamaya Mongar's suspicious death. Thank God Jim Wood cared.

The grand jury report did lead to some accountability after the fact. Governor Tom Corbett sacked the state Health Department's senior counsel, Kenneth Brody, who had told the grand jury that there was no obligation for the DOH to inspect abortion clinics. Also shown the door were former acting Department of State secretary Basil Merenda; Department of Health deputy secretary Stacy Mitchell, who had inspected Gosnell's clinic in 1989 and 1993 and signed off on extensions of its license despite multiple serious infractions of the law; and State Health Department chief counsel Christine Dutton, who had shocked the grand jury with her "People die" attitude.

Janice Staloski and Department of State lawyer Andrew Kramer decided to retire after the grand jury was called.

————

And some who were supposed to be seeking the truth, the facts of the case, were also concerned, perhaps inappropriately, about just how those facts would be used.

Judge Cardwell-Hughes was completely disgusted with the Department of Health.

"The state Department of Health was absolutely irresponsible, uncaring," she told us.

But Cardwell-Hughes, a passionate advocate for abortion, was keen to draw attention away from the abortion establishment closing ranks, protecting one of their own and protecting abortion, regardless of the harm done on the way.

Instead she attributed the lack of action to elitism and racism. "There is just no question in my mind that had this been in a rich suburb, it would never happened. The poor women of color in Philadelphia, they didn't give a squat [about them]," she told us.

As the judge told us, she did not want the grand jury's report to become fodder for anti-abortion activists.

"My fear...the D.A.'s fear....We were all terrified that if this wasn't written very carefully, that this was an aberration, and that the law needed to be improved but that the law didn't need to be eliminated. It was a major concern to me, because Pennsylvania is very conservative and very conflicted about choice."

She described the state of Pennsylvania by quoting James Carville, the famous Democratic strategist who is married to Mary Matalin, the Republican strategist. "He coined this phrase during Clinton's first election. There's Philadelphia, and there's Pittsburgh, and then there's Alabama in between."

"So, my goal was to say this is about a woman's health," she told us. "And no woman should die in the Commonwealth of Pennsylvania because she can't get a safe, clean abortion. That's crazy. That for me was really important and that the report not add fuel to the fire."

"Remember it's my report. I have to sign it. I have to bless it."

Judge Cardwell-Hughes did not elaborate on what she did or would have done if the truth—the facts of the case—clashed with her belief that women in Pennsylvania are entitled to a "safe, clean abortion."

Her determination not to have a report that undermined the current system of abortion may account for the unusual decision not to name the National Abortion Federation representative who failed to report on the appalling and unsafe conditions she found.

The grand jury's report was released on January 11, 2011. The panel recommended that Gosnell be arrested and charged with seven counts of first-degree murder for babies whose necks he snipped; third-degree murder in the death of Karnamaya Mongar; conspiracy to commit murder in "hundreds of unidentifiable instances" of killing babies born alive; two counts of infanticide for failure to resuscitate born-alive infants that could have survived; multiple violations of the Abortion Control Act and Controlled Substance Act; hindering apprehension; perjury; evidence tampering; racketeering; theft by deception; and corrupting the morals of a minor (for employing Ashley Baldwin). Gosnell faced 258 charges in all.

Gosnell told us he views the grand jury report as "salacious."[13] He claims it was false because it relied on testimony from those who had plea bargained and had "the inherent benefit of pleasing those who would negotiate their own fate."[14]

But the district attorney thought differently. He decided that Jim Wood should arrest Gosnell. Because there had been leaks to the press throughout the investigation, the DA's office didn't inform the police department or their contacts at the FBI or DEA. Judge Cardwell-Hughes signed all of the arrest warrants, and Woody made haste to Gosnell's house.

He took Gosnell and his wife, Pearl, into custody at the same time. Their daughter, Jenna, was sent to the neighbor's house next door, where she would spend the next five months.

As he was arrested, Gosnell remained calm—with a half smirk on his face. Wood remembers Gosnell saying, as he was being handcuffed, "So this is what happens, when you try to help people."[15]

But he stopped smirking when he was brought before the judge. He believed that he would simply be charged, given bail, and released; but he was informed that no bail was possible in a capital murder case.

"His face dropped, he was shocked, he didn't expect that," says Wechsler.

Gosnell might have been planning to run, as he had done after the "Mother's Day Massacre" nearly forty years earlier, when he injured nine women with an experimental abortion method that involved inserting multiple razor blades into the uterus.[16] In interviews with the authors, he spoke of his regret about not keeping his assets liquid.[17]

But Jim Wood thinks he probably would have stayed.

"He has an enormous ego. He thinks he is innocent. He would have stayed to fight," says Wood.

Placing Gosnell in handcuffs was "one of the things that I felt good about," Woody said.

"It's ceremonial, more or less. That's one of the things, when you are a cop. You do the job. You chased somebody. You catch them. Your cuffs go on them. That's your arrest. I made sure my cuffs are going on this guy."[18]

FOUR

WILLING ACCOMPLICES

"Those two. If you ever meet them, you wouldn't let them cut your grass, let alone give stuff to patients."
—DETECTIVE JIM WOOD, on Sherry West and Lynda Williams

"Those Baldwins. They loved that money."
—FORMER PHILADELPHIA ASSISTANT DISTRICT ATTORNEY CHRISTINE WECHSLER,
on Tina and Ashley Baldwin

"We had, like I said before...we had to prevent life. We had to kill. It's as simple as that."
—STEVE MASSOF

Gosnell wasn't alone in his house of horrors on Lancaster Avenue. He could not possibly have carried out his crimes without accomplices. He had plenty of willing assistants. Several were arrested with him and went to prison, too.

Why do seemingly ordinary people commit extraordinary crimes? Why did so many "good Germans" carry out the barbaric wishes of Adolf Hitler? Why did Russians slaughter tens of millions of their countrymen at the behest of Stalin? Why did millions of people worship Mao during the Cultural Revolution, and turn Cambodia into killing fields on the orders of Pol Pot?

Where does naiveté end and moral culpability begin? Criminals often attract their intellectual inferiors and manipulate them into abetting their crimes. John Allen Muhammad, the Washington, D.C. sniper who killed ten people in October 2002, trained seventeen-year-old Lee Boyd Malvo to shoot innocent victims from the trunk of their car. Muhammad got the death penalty and Malvo was sentenced to life in prison because the jury didn't believe he was as culpable as his mentor.

Charles Manson didn't kill anyone. But he manipulated his followers into committing several heinous crimes, including most notoriously the brutal 1969 massacre of pregnant actress Sharon Tate and four others in the Hollywood Hills. Manson exercised power through charm, charisma, ideology, sex, and drugs. While his "family" was out killing, Charles Manson was home smoking dope, having sex, and thinking about "Helter Skelter"—the revolution he had long predicted. As the murderous dictators of history have noticed, a good smattering of "revolutionary" politics helps motivate followers to do terrible things—all in the name of helping the less fortunate.

Gosnell's employees weren't exactly the Manson family, but many of them did adore him, and he did have (or try to have) sex with a number of them.

Just like Manson, Gosnell also supplied his accomplices with copious amounts of drugs.

And remember, Gosnell and his employees were also deeply involved in the politically charged world of abortion—which supplied their criminal enterprise with a sense of mission. Many involved in abortion feel they are part of a political movement helping the less fortunate. It is a moral crusade. Unfortunately, history has shown time and again that people can do terrible, terrible things in the name of the greater good.

The doctor did choose a specific type of person to work for him. His employees were people who would carry out his orders and would not question him. All of them seemed to have broken or unfulfilled lives. They were beset by addiction, depression, mental illnesses, childhood abuse, and neglect. Appalling dysfunction was the perfect employee profile for a Gosnell staff member.

SHERRY WEST AND LYNDA WILLIAMS

Everyone at the clinic called Sherry West and Lynda Williams the "Delaware girls" because they drove in together from that neighboring state every morning for work. The women were an incendiary mix of mental health problems, tragic lives, and ongoing criminal fraud, deception, and addiction. On top of this, they weren't very bright. Oh, and they were arrogant and bullying towards anyone they thought of as inferior whenever they thought they could get away with it. These qualities made them terrible to work with, and eventually the Delaware girls' character flaws were to prove fatal to one of their patients.[1]

Lynda Williams, with an eighth-grade education and a phlebotomy certificate that qualified her to draw blood, had worked at the Delaware clinic where Gosnell also did abortions, but she had been fired from there on account of her erratic timekeeping and unexplained absences and the management's suspicion that she was helping Gosnell syphon patients from their clinic over to his Lancaster Avenue clinic in Pennsylvania so that he wouldn't have to pay a cut to the Delaware management. They couldn't prove he was doing it, but they took the opportunity to get rid of their most troublesome employee—so in 2008 Lynda Williams moved to Gosnell's Lancaster Avenue clinic.

Williams was born on October 18, 1968. She seems to have a permanently tired look. There was a dullness about her behavior that may have been partly due to her low intelligence—or to the large number of drugs she consumed.

In many ways getting into the Philadelphia clinic—being closer to Gosnell, who was a respected member of the community—brought some stability to Williams at the lowest point in her life. The year before she started in Philadelphia, her husband was murdered, leaving her with three young children to raise. She is bipolar and suffers from depression and anxiety. Assistant district attorney Joanne Pescatore described Williams as "pathetic," but she didn't mean it in a derogatory way. "She was used and abused by Dr. Gosnell," Pescatore said. "This woman probably can't add. Probably can't read. She was the anesthesiologist who was in charge of mixing the concoctions and giving the anesthesia to the patients while the doctor wasn't there"—a reluctant anesthesiologist. In her interviews with detectives, Williams said she didn't like giving injections because of how the needle felt when it entered the skin. On the other hand, as she would later testify, "I only do what I'm told to do."[2]

But in truth Lynda Williams didn't even do what she was told. Despite fellow employee Ashley Baldwin knowing more about the medication—even drawing up a color-coded document to help staff— Lynda treated Ashley with contempt and bullied her whenever she got the chance. Lynda paid no attention to Ashley's drug guide or Gosnell's more complicated "cheat sheet," which he had posted on a wall. According to Baldwin, Williams would give patients drugs according to what she thought they needed, with no input from the doctor.

Sherry West, a fifty-five-year-old white woman with a plethora of mental health problems, had been one of Gosnell's patients for more than twenty years before he hired her in October 2008.

So Gosnell knew about Sherry West's significant mental health issues—including anxiety attacks and depression—and about her Hepatitis C, because of which she had lost her job at the Veterans Administration in 2007. Losing that job had prompted a massive nervous breakdown, and she was being treated by a psychiatrist who had put her on Prozac.

Sherry wanted an off-the-books job that would allow her to fraudulently claim disability benefits from the Veterans Administration. So when Gosnell came along with the offer of a cash job and lots of free drugs as needed, she signed up immediately. Working for Gosnell had the added bonus of allowing West to almost forget she had Hepatitis C, because she never wore surgical gloves or took other precautions against infecting patients, and Gosnell never asked her to. The doctor didn't act like her condition was serious, and that allowed West to convince herself that it was no big deal.

Sherry West had an aggressive attitude that made her unpopular at Gosnell's clinic, but she didn't care. Philadelphia homicide detective Jack McDermot remembers her very well. On the door of her apartment in Delaware she had a large sign on her front door: "BEWARE: Woman in Menopause." Inside, the atmosphere wasn't much more welcoming. One detective remembers coming inside and meeting her brother. The police officer reached out to shake his hand but was aggressively informed by the brother that he didn't shake hands with cops.[3]

Because Gosnell was running a pill mill operation, both of the Delaware girls had access to all sorts of prescription drugs that otherwise might have been hard to get. Gosnell kept West and Williams both well supplied with Xanax, OxyContin, promethazine, and Percocet, which they regularly took on the job. Williams also became Gosnell's patient. Even though he had no special qualifications to treat anyone for mental illness, he prescribed her a cocktail of drugs including Depakote, Seroquel, and Celexa, which she took twice a day.

Although the Delaware girls drove in to work together and spent all their working days with each other, Sherry West did not see Lynda Williams as an equal colleague. Sherry really liked bossing Lynda around, swearing at her if she thought she was moving too slowly. This abuse started with making her do errands: going to the shops, carrying files to the front desk. Eventually it would take a darker turn, with West ordering Williams to "snip" the babies who were born alive.

Detective Jim Wood was scathing in his assessment of the Delaware girls' capabilities. "Those two. If you ever meet them, you wouldn't let them cut your grass, let alone give stuff to patients," he said.

Their incompetence was bound to kill someone sooner or later—and that's how Karnamaya Mongar died.

At the clinic Sherry West administered anesthesia, conducted ultrasound exams, and monitored heavily sedated women in the recovery room. Lynda Williams cleaned, answered phones, sedated patients, and did ultrasounds, too. Ordinarily, an ultrasound tech has at least two years of training through an accredited institution. Gosnell taught Williams how to use an ultrasound machine over the course of a few days at the Atlantic Women's Medical Center in Delaware. Williams and West also received "training" at Gosnell's Lancaster Avenue clinic from equally unqualified employees including Tina Baldwin, Kareema Cross, Latosha Lewis, and Ashley Baldwin—who was barely sixteen years old.

And Gosnell taught Williams how to murder babies by snipping the backs of their necks with scissors after they were born alive.

Both women helped deliver babies that "precipitated" into the clinic's toilet. West called them "specimens" instead of babies because, she said, "It was easier to deal with mentally."

At trial, Sherry West testified about one born-alive infant that became known as the "crying baby."

"I can't describe it," West said. "It sounded like a little alien." She said the baby was between eighteen and twenty-four inches long, and was one of the biggest she had ever seen delivered alive. "It wasn't fully developed…It didn't have eyes or a mouth but it was, like screeching, making this noise," she said. "It was weird…it really freaked me out. And I said, 'Call Dr. Gosnell,' and I went back out front."

Williams also described the horrific murder of another baby— "Baby D"—born in the toilet—who struggled and moved its arms as she killed it. "The baby precipitated into the toilet. I took it out of the toilet and put it into a bowl and I used surgical scissors to cut the back of the baby's neck, just like Dr. Gosnell showed me to do," she explained. "Before I cut the neck, I saw the baby's arms moving. This was when I took it from the toilet and put it in the bowl and then I went to put it in a milk jug to take it upstairs. Before I put it in the milk jug, I saw the arms moving, and that's when I cut the back of the neck," she said. And she would plead guilty to third-degree murder in the death of another fetus—"Baby C," who was breathing outside the womb and moving its arms for about twenty minutes before she snipped its neck with scissors, as she had seen her boss do.

West and Williams were exactly the type of employees Gosnell liked—people who were desperate for a job, or just plain desperate. He paid between eight and ten dollars an hour in cash, as well as bonuses of up to thirty dollars for every abortion they assisted with. The money added up fast.

Gosnell kept ignoring complaints about the Delaware girls from other members of staff—that they were dangerously incompetent (in a clinic that was already a dangerously incompetent house of horrors).

In testimony before the grand jury, Latosha Lewis complained that Sherry and Lynda were always "just goofing off and playing around" when they should have been working and that they didn't seem to care about the effects of the drugs they gave patients—that their work "seemed like it was a game to them."

That "game" ended in the death of Karnamaya Mongar. The callous, untrained Lynda Williams gave Mrs. Mongar lethal doses of anesthesia—to the point at which the patient wasn't moving and Williams had to tell Gosnell that her color was "funny." And then

Sherry West accompanied the patient's family to the hospital in their car. She falsified Karnamaya Mongar's medical file and lied about the drugs Mongar had been given[4]—so that the hospital did not have information critical to the attempt to save her life. Lynda Williams and Sherry West would both plead guilty to third-degree murder in Karnamaya Mongar's death.

We saw in chapter one how on the night of the February 18, 2010, raid Lynda Williams admitted to the police that she had medicated Mrs. Mongar when Gosnell wasn't even in the clinic—and also spilled the beans about the doctor's falsification of fetal ages in violation of Pennsylvania law.

And yet when the police showed up on that night, both Lynda and Sherry obviously wanted to protect their boss. The Delaware girls were naturally loyal to Gosnell. He had given West a job when no one else would. He had kept Williams on the payroll after her shenanigans got her fired from her previous job and despite erratic behavior following her husband's death. Given the Delaware girls' appalling level of personal dysfunction and their bizarre dependency on Gosnell, perhaps it's not surprising that their statements to the police were a mixture of damning admissions and false statements meant to cover up Gosnell's illegal activities.

Both Lynda Williams and Sherry West lied for Gosnell. The two of them even visited Gosnell at his home after the raid to check on him—and to get their stories straight.

"I was concerned about my disability benefits being cut off if I was making too much money," West later told the court. That said a lot about West's priorities. When her longtime doctor, employer, and friend was under police scrutiny for murdering women and babies and trafficking in drugs, West's foremost concern was whether she could continue to rip off the welfare system.

Williams was remarkably talkative the night of the raid, and as we have seen she did reveal key facts about Karnamaya Mongar's death and Gosnell's illegal practices. But it would later emerge that she had also lied at length. Detectives told her she was not under arrest and didn't have to continue talking, and she said she understood but wanted to continue. She showed them the logbook that recorded the drugs that were given to Mrs. Mongar. Later that night detectives found her crying in a recovery room. Once again, she insisted on talking and showing them exactly what Mongar had been given. Williams was the one who explained to the investigators how Gosnell manipulated ultrasound images to make fetuses appear younger than their actual gestational age.

But Lynda Williams also lied to the police, saying that one of Karnamaya Mongar's relatives had told her Mongar tried to abort the baby by taking drugs *before* she went to Gosnell. That was completely untrue. And she lied repeatedly. In some demented way, Williams saw Gosnell as a lifeline and believed she needed to protect him by lying to the police. In her chaotic, drug-addled, mentally unstable universe, she needed the stability that Gosnell offered.

At the end of one of Williams's original interviews, a detective asked if she had anything more to add.

She chose the opportunity not to defend herself, but to defend Kermit Gosnell.

"Just want this to all end," she answered. "He done nothing wrong."

In addition to the murder charges in the deaths of Karnamaya Mongar and "Baby C," Lynda Williams was also charged with violating the Controlled Substances Act; conspiracy to violate the Controlled Substances Act; conspiracy to commit murder; conspiracy to violate the Abortion Control Act; and thirteen counts of violating the Abortion Control Act by assisting in abortions past the gestational age limit. She was sentenced to five to ten years in prison.

Assistant district attorney Ed Cameron wanted to see Williams go away for twenty years. "She is an adult, she is a mother herself," he argued. She drugged Mongar to death and snipped the neck of a baby she knew was alive. Cameron was particularly angry that she had treated the crying baby so callously.

"This was a living human being in front of her, a living human being who was crying," he said.

Judge Benjamin Lerner, who presided over Williams's case, disagreed with Cameron about the length of her sentence but shared his disgust at her actions. "You were a functioning, responsible adult human being," Lerner told Williams at her sentencing hearing. "You chose to do terrible things."

Sherry West was charged on ten counts, including third-degree murder in Karnamaya Mongar's death; violating the Controlled Substance Act; conspiracy; tampering with or falsification of evidence; tampering with records; hindering apprehension; obstructing administration of law; abortion at twenty-four or more weeks; racketeering; and corrupt organization. Like Williams, West was sentenced to five to ten years in prison.

LIZ HAMPTON

Liz Hampton, friends with Gosnell's wife from their time together in foster care, worked for Gosnell on and off for twelve years before the law came down on his house of horrors. That made her one of Gosnell's longest-tenured employees. She knew him very well. She even cleaned Gosnell's mother's house as a side job. The old lady treated her very kindly; it was a taste of a real family life she had never known. "She was very nice. Beautiful woman. Heart of gold," Hampton told us. "I would go clean for her, and she would have lunch for me. She would have me sit down with her. I'm like, I'm here to clean but she just wanted to talk." In 1999, Hampton became a tenant in that house, where she lived with her common law husband Jimmy

Johnson, who was also the maintenance man at the clinic; her daughter; and four grandchildren. Every month, Hampton would hand over her eight hundred dollar disability check to Pearl Gosnell, the doctor's wife, and Mrs. Gosnell would then give her back two hundred dollars in cash. This fraud (receiving a disability check when she was perfectly fit) continued until Hampton got out of prison—but we're getting ahead of ourselves.

We interviewed Hampton at the office of her attorney Murray Dolfman, a sprightly elderly fellow straight out of central casting for the wise old lawyer who has seen it all. He has been practicing law for over fifty years and still finds it exciting. Our interview had hardly gotten underway when Hampton burst into tears. Dolfman was not concerned—he'd seen all this before. She pulled tissues from a box he had pre-emptively placed on the desk beside her. She never quite stopped crying the entire time we talked. She explained that she cries very easily. There was no doubting that—though some of her tears didn't seem all that genuine to us.

Hampton had a tough childhood—she was in foster care until the age of fourteen. It was there that she met the future Mrs. Gosnell. Hampton told us that she used to call Pearl Gosnell her sister and love her "unconditionally." The girls lost contact after leaving the foster home, and their lives took off in what appeared to be very different directions.

Hampton became an alcoholic often prone to violence, no stranger to the court system. "I've always been in trouble for drinking. I always got locked up when I was younger for fighting," she told us.

Pearl, on the other hand, ended up married to a doctor who owned seventeen properties, including a beach house. He was one of the most respected members of Philadelphia's African American community. The two women met again by accident in a grocery store in

1994, and out of the blue, Pearl asked her childhood friend if she would like to come to work for her husband. "It sounded like everyone's dream," Hampton recalled. "A doctor, you know, working for a doctor."

Liz Hampton was excited. She had worked for years at a moving company, where she spent her days lifting and moving furniture. "The first thing that came into my mind was, wow, no more labor work, no more picking furniture up," she told us. "I actually thought it would be cool."

At the Lancaster Avenue clinic, Hampton was paid ten dollars an hour under the table to answer phones, clean procedure rooms, and sterilize instruments. But that wasn't all. Steve Massof, an unlicensed medical school graduate who was working illegally as a doctor at Gosnell's clinic, testified during the trial on April 4, 2013, that when some patients would start to give him or Gosnell trouble during an abortion—as he put it, "when patients would maybe get resistant during procedures"—Hampton would "help to physically hold them down."

Hampton now claims to hate Gosnell, whom she calls by his middle name, Barron. She wonders whether the difficulties between them might be connected to their astrological signs. They are both Aquarius. His birthday is February 9 and hers is February 10. She described him to us as "a mad, mad, bad, evil, conniving, selfish, inconsiderate bastard" and claims she only kept working for him out of necessity. "Whatever Barron threw at me, I dealt with because he was paying me and I had to live," she said.

And yet, however much Hampton claims to have disliked her boss, she was willing to perjure herself before the grand jury to protect him. In her trial testimony she told the court, "I storied a lot."

The prosecutor asked what exactly she meant by that.

"I lied," she answered.

When the police and FBI first questioned her, Hampton lied about what she knew about the circumstances of Karnamaya Mongar's death. She lied about Mrs. Mongar's treatment, claiming that Mongar's daughter spoke English fluently, and backed Williams's fabrication that Mongar had taken a lot of drugs in an attempt to abort the baby herself. Hampton repeated that lie to the grand jury, which is why she ended up being charged with perjury, along with false swearing, obstructing the administration of law, and hindering apprehension or prosecution.

Hampton agreed to release her August 11, 2010, grand jury statement to us. In it she lies to the grand jury. She says that when she went upstairs to tell Mrs. Mongar's family that Mrs. Mongar was "having problems" they responded "we told her not to take the drugs" and later, "They told me that they told their mother not to take the drugs. She was trying to abort the baby." All of this was a lie.

In her interview with us, Hampton was obviously anxious. She wanted to make sure we knew two things: that she didn't work in the back where the procedures were going on and that Gosnell was a horrible man. Unlicensed "Dr." Steve Massof, however, gave evidence that Liz Hampton did sometimes assist with the abortions. And Lynda Williams told investigators that Hampton would "hand Gosnell instruments" when she herself wasn't able to assist him. The initials "L. H." were found on Karnamaya Mongar's file indicating that Liz Hampton had administered Cytotec, a labor-inducing drug— apparently because Ashley Baldwin had to leave early that day. Hampton also testified at trial that she got a twenty dollar bonus for every second-trimester abortion. The only employees who received those bonuses were involved in the procedures. It appears from the bulk of the evidence, however, that Liz Hampton did spend most of her work day in the "front of house"—assisting in the abortions only if the clinic was shorthanded.

On April 3, 2013, Hampton described her cleaning duties in court, telling how she disposed of the fetal remains in the bottles attached to the suction machine. Assistant DA Joanne Pescatore had asked what she did with the bottle's contents.

"I would pour it in the drain, in the sink, and then I would turn it on," she answered.

"[Turn] the garbage disposal on?" Pescatore asked.

"Yes."

As Hampton tells it, she once temporarily left the clinic after she happened to be in the procedure room when she saw a baby being stabbed with a pair of scissors. She immediately left the building, crossed the street to a bar, and got drunk—breaking her sobriety.

This story may be true, or Liz Hampton may have been more involved in Gosnell's house of horrors than she lets on. She lies often but also appears—at least sometimes—to want to tell the truth and move on with her life.

It wasn't clear when Hampton was telling the truth and when she "storied," and she offered all kinds of justifications for her lies. "I was scared of him," she told us. "So I was just trying to think of something. I didn't know.... Maybe to help [the police] more."

According to Hampton the other workers idolized Gosnell. "They were Barron's little girls. All of them were his little girls. If Barron said jump, they would jump. He would come in the office. Everyone would be like, 'my Barron,' 'my doc.' They had names for him. One called him Unc. One called him Dad. They were very friendly with him."

But Hampton thought Gosnell was arrogant. "I started working, answering phones, signing people in. And his attitude I didn't like. It was like, 'I'm superior. You're nothing.' This is how I got treated," she said.

Gosnell didn't like it when Hampton described herself as Pearl's sister. The idea that his wife would be the sister of someone like Liz Hampton infuriated him. "He looked down at me personally when I first started working. He told me to tell everybody I was Pearl's cousin. I'm like, 'I'm not going to do that. We're sisters. We grew up from babies.'"

She says Gosnell dominated all the staff—except for her. "He had everyone under control." But Hampton claimed she put him in his place. Apparently Gosnell liked to grope his staff—several of his former employees told us the same—but Hampton wasn't about to let him grope her. "When I started, I was coming down the hallway, and Barron was behind me. I couldn't hear him because of the carpet. He came [into] the office, and he put his hands on me."

"I turned around I told him, 'Don't you ever put your f---ing hands on me again.' From that point on, we didn't get along."

Hampton told us that she believed Gosnell had two men come to the clinic to scare her and her husband, the clinic maintenance man. One night she was on the phone and when she turned around, one of two strangers had a gun to her head and shouted at her to hand over the money. There wasn't any money, she explained, because it was an "elder's night"—a night Gosnell would see older patients—so there was no cash in the clinic.

"Jimmy was down in the basement…and he heard me talking. I talked extra loud so he could hear me. I'm like, 'I don't have any money. There's no money.'"

"Jimmy heard me. He came up. As he was coming up the hall, the guys stood behind the door. When he got to the edge, he put the gun to him and made him lay on the floor," she said.

Gosnell was upstairs, apparently heard what was happening, came down, and tackled the armed intruder. The two men ran off.

But suspiciously, Gosnell didn't want to call the police. Hampton said the two men also knew the crazy layout of the clinic, which made her suspect that Gosnell had arranged the robbery. She also told us about an incident in prison that suggested Gosnell and his wife were behind the apparent robbery attempt.

Liz Hampton and the other clinic workers were held in the same women's prison after their arrests and during the lead-up to the trial. Liz shared a cell with her childhood friend Pearl. The Gosnell group was held in protective custody at first, because prison authorities feared the other prisoners might kill them. Even criminals believe baby killing is heinous.

"Everyone wanted to kill us," Hampton said. "The first day we went to court, as we walked into the prison...the guards, the girls— they knew before we even got there what we were there for. When we walked into [the] prison doors, people were screaming, 'Baby killers!' 'They're baby killing bitches!'

"I'm like, 'I didn't kill no babies!' I don't know. And it was like me talking to the wall because no one wanted to hear what I had to say. As we were in the prison for a while, guards got to know who did what. Prisoners got to know who did what. So in about the third month, I didn't have a problem with anyone.

"When they finally let us all out of [protective custody], we all got together. We were sitting and talking, and Pearl says, 'Yeah, if my brother Toothy was still living, I would have him f--k people up. Barron and I already had someone come in the office and correct two people.'" When Hampton heard this, she realized that Pearl was probably talking about the "robbery," slapped her hands on the table, stood up, and went back to her cell.

Their time together as cellmates ended soon afterward. "Pearl was telling everyone I was a drunk," Hampton said. "Pearl was telling them I was mentally ill....The whole time I was sitting in that room with Pearl, Pearl deceived me. I would have to cry myself to sleep. I don't care what time I woke up, Pearl never slept. She never slept. I had the top bunk bed. She had the bottom. And I would always look down. She would just be lying there. She never slept.... She never ate.

"It got to the point where I had to tell the guard, 'Get me out of this cell or I will kill her.' About half an hour later, they took me out."

According to Hampton, Pearl tried to get her to lie at trial. "Pearl was telling me that we're family, that we have to stick together. If [the prosecutors] asked me if she worked [at the clinic] on Sundays, she wanted me to say no." Hampton refused. She was already behind bars for lying, and she wasn't about to do anything that would lengthen her stay.

Hampton says she resents how Gosnell never seemed the least bit repentant for what he'd done. "He's spiteful," she told us. "He was Barron. He knew, he just knew, he was sitting on top of the world. Like he made a comment one day on the news—'I will prevail.' I didn't actually know what that meant. And I'm like, he just thinks he's over everybody. Like all he has to do is open his mouth. Like he's candy."

Those who defend abortion often accuse *anti*-abortion activists of wanting to control women's bodies, but interestingly Liz Hampton says it was this exact impulse that drove Kermit Gosnell: "I actually think it was…like I have control over you, too. I have control over your body. If he could control your body, he would control your mind."

Hampton said it was her tough upbringing that left her immune to both Gosnell's charms and his bullying. "I was very strong about that controlling," she said. "You're not going to control me. All my life, I've been put in foster homes, pushed around….I refuse to let anyone control me."

"I'm my own woman now. I have my own voice. I'm not going to allow anyone to control me."

Up to a point.

"If I don't have to. Like the courts, I had to. I have to do what they told me. And I'm doing what they told me."

"I was brought up not to hate. But I hate him," Hampton said. "I hate him for what he did to other people. I hate him for ruining so many women's lives. I hate him for ruining *my* life. It's very hard for me to get a job. People have offered me jobs, but under the table. I won't take it. It's against the law."

Hampton received probation for the perjury charge. She says the entire ordeal has left her "scared to even breathe too hard about anything." She told us, "Today, if I hear a car stop in front of my house, I'm jumping up to see if it's the police."

Hampton is seeing a therapist, which she says helps a lot. She needs medicine to help her sleep at night. She understands that her life isn't entirely her own. "I'm in the hands of the DA. I'm in the hands of the court. The least little thing could get me locked back up."

"I don't ever want to, this is why I stopped drinking," she told us. "I found out that was my problem. I stopped. I don't want to ever go back to jail."[5]

ADRIENNE MOTON

"I'm so glad I got arrested," a tearful Adrienne Moton told the court the day of her sentencing in May 2013. "I don't feel like I got arrested. I feel like I got rescued."

Moton had been charged with murder, conspiracy to commit murder, conspiracy, and racketeering for her role in killing an infant born alive at Gosnell's clinic. "Baby D," as the victim was known, was delivered into a toilet and appeared to swim. Moton described removing the baby from the toilet and severing its spinal cord with surgical scissors. She testified during the trial that she had snipped the necks of at least ten babies during her time at the Women's Medical Society.

When Moton first met Dr. Gosnell, she was still in high school—a friend of Gosnell's niece Safona Willis. Willis lived with the Gosnells, and Moton spent many evenings hanging out with her at the Gosnell's house on 646 North 32nd Street.

Moton got pregnant in her junior year at high school. Pearl Gosnell was the first to notice. She told Moton she was much too young to have a child and arranged for her to have an abortion at the clinic. Moton had no way to pay, so she persuaded her boyfriend to mend a fence at the Gosnell's house in trade. Shortly afterwards she became pregnant again. She paid Gosnell for her second abortion by babysitting his children.

Moton moved in with the Gosnells when she turned eighteen and was still a senior in high school. She was having problems with her parents and called Gosnell her uncle. And the Gosnells took care of her. They bought her clothes and kept her fed, so she felt she owed a debt to them. After she graduated high school she attended the local Pierce College where she studied computers but left after a few semesters when she became pregnant again. This was her third pregnancy and she was just nineteen. On this occasion she kept the baby—a girl.

The Gosnells were accommodating at first, but when Moton's daughter was five months old, they asked her to leave. Moton was forced to go and live in a homeless shelter. Pearl Gosnell initially told investigators that this was because the baby made too much noise, but the truth was much more sinister—and revealing about the true nature of Kermit Gosnell and his claims that he was always trying to help vulnerable women.

Moton's world was turned upside down when her boyfriend sexually assaulted a child who was closely related to her—a child staying in Gosnell's house. Devastated and angry, she started to phone the police, only to be stopped by Gosnell, who tried to dissuade her from reporting the assault. Perhaps worried about what they would uncover once they started investigating, Gosnell told her he didn't want the police around his house. So she couldn't report the sexual assault of a child. Moton defied Gosnell and reported the assault, and her ex-boyfriend is now serving a lengthy prison sentence.

For this she was thrown out of her home with the Gosnells.

Her options were limited. "The thing was, you either go to school or the Army," she told us. "I wasn't ready for either." At the shelter she met another man, fell in love, and married. But it didn't last long. She took temp jobs at Verizon Wireless and Wells Fargo, but nothing ever seemed to work out.

By 2005, Adrienne Moton was desperate and in need of money. Like most of the clinic employees, she had no qualifications to work in a medical facility. Gosnell knew it, and offered her a job anyway.

Much like West, Williams, and Hampton, Moton did just about everything at the clinic. She was also paid under the table and testified that Saturdays were often busy days, which meant she could make as much as $120 in cash bonuses for assisting with second trimester abortions. It was great money for the young woman.

We asked Moton how she rationalized what she was doing at the clinic.

"At first, I was like, okay," she said. "Then I became so numb. I was all over that place. I was just loyal to him. He helped me through high school. They bought my clothes. They helped my daughter. I felt like I owed him."

She also told us that she focused on helping the women. She could empathize with them because she'd had two abortions herself. She tried not to think too much about the babies.

But Moton clearly knew that what she was doing was wrong. Yes, she could say she felt indebted to Gosnell and, yes, she also wanted to help women who were going through what she had gone through. But she was also earning a very attractive wage that she couldn't have made anywhere else. There may also have been another reason Moton stayed. Investigators suspect she and Gosnell were having an affair. They looked at their phone records and saw many, many lengthy phone calls at odd hours in the night—suggesting a more-than-employer-employee relationship. Moton denies they had such a relationship, but she does say that Gosnell had many affairs with other coworkers.

Ultimately, however, Adrienne Moton's guilty conscience prevailed, and she testified against her boss. She knew that what she was doing was very wrong. She did the right thing, and it saved her from a lengthy prison sentence. It also helped ensure the conviction of America's biggest serial killer.

During the trial, Joanne Pescatore spoke very emotionally about the significance of a picture Adrienne Moton took of the infant who became known as "Baby Boy A"—and how it sealed Gosnell's fate. The murder of "Baby Boy A" proved a turning point for Moton. This baby was so large—between eighteen and twenty-four inches long, by Moton's reckoning—that she snapped a picture on her phone before Gosnell took him out of the room in a shoebox.

Moton said she knew she was taking a picture of a young human being—in fact, that was why she took the photo.

"It was a big baby boy. He had that color, that color that a baby has.... I just felt he could have had a chance....He could have been born any day."

"I took the picture," she told us. "I remember coming home. I showed my mom. I said, 'The Doc has lost his mind. This is ridiculous.'"

She knew the photo represented a madness that was present in 3801 Lancaster Avenue, and she also had a feeling that it was going to be important some day.

"I never got rid of that phone. To be honest, I just couldn't get rid of it. I had a feeling that this was going to come to surface. I just didn't know when. So when the police came, I gave them the phone, I said, 'There's a picture in there. Do whatever you have to do with it because now I'm free of it. I'm free.'" Investigators needed to send the phone to the FBI in Quantico to recover the image.

By the time Moton testified on April 18, 2013, she hadn't seen Gosnell in several years. She couldn't believe how relaxed and jovial he looked. "He looked at me. The crazy thing was, when we were going on a break, they put me in a cell first. As he was walking past, he screams out, 'Everything's going to be all right, it's all going to be okay,'" she recalled. "Then when lunch was over, they brought me back upstairs. He was in a cell, they brought me past him, he's banging on the glass giving me a thumbs up."

Pescatore recommended a sentence of three to six years for Moton. She explained that, unlike the other workers at the clinic, Moton had admitted what she had done was wrong and shown tremendous remorse. It helped, too, that Moton had left Gosnell's clinic almost two years before the February 2010 raid.

Moton's father, Gregory, appealed to Judge Lerner to show leniency. He testified that his daughter's character and general attitude toward life had improved. Pescatore fought back tears as she listened to the man speak on his daughter's behalf. When Lerner sentenced Moton to time served—twenty-eight months—plus three years probation, her father and sister Rhonda shouted "Hallelujah" from the gallery.

Moton regrets her own abortions. Her entire attitude has changed. She would never recommend anyone have an abortion, she told us, "because I am a Christian, and babies are a gift from God. My thing is...if you can't take care of it, there are so many people out there that wish they could."

Spending more than two years in prison changed Moton in lasting ways. She couldn't stand the dark. She would stay awake until sunrise and only then go to sleep. If she slept in the light, it seemed to help with the nightmares. The nightmare was always the same—it was the baby that she had taken the photo of, Baby Boy A.

"I always saw this baby," she told us. "Just standing there, looking at me, just standing there. I would still see that baby in my dreams.

He would just be standing there looking at me. I've caught myself a couple of times just saying sorry, sorry, that's all I could do."

It took Moton two years to learn to sleep in the dark again.[6]

TINA BALDWIN

Tina Baldwin was a terrible mother.

Baldwin was a Gosnell employee like any other, inasmuch as she was wholly unqualified to do ultrasound tests, insert IVs, administer anesthesia, and assist with abortion procedures. She had done all of those things for nine years, up until a month before the February 2010 raid, when she decided to leave the Women's Medical Society to care for her cancer-stricken mother.

Baldwin was as greedy as anyone who worked at the clinic. She made sure she worked the front desk on nights when drug dealers would come to pick up their bogus prescriptions. They left generous tips.

What set Tina Baldwin apart from the rest was the fact that she got her fifteen-year-old daughter Ashley a job at the clinic. The grand jury was as disgusted with Baldwin for exposing her teenage daughter to the charnel house as they were with Gosnell for operating it.

For her role in Gosnell's illegal prescription drug and late-term abortion business, Tina Baldwin was charged with conspiracy and racketeering. For bringing her underage daughter into the business, she was charged with corruption of the morals of a minor. Ashley Baldwin was not charged.

Assistant district attorney Christine Wechsler said both Baldwins were "all about the money."

"[Tina] was a nut for roping [Ashley] into that," Wechsler told us.

"Those Baldwins. They loved that money," she said. "Tina moved to the front, and all she was doing was taking tips off of those drug dealers. She loved it. She was so happy to get to the front, but then she serves Ashley up to the back. But it was like you graduated. Your reward for doing the dirty business back there and making some extra money was to come up front."

Tina let no opportunity to make money pass her by.

Unlicensed medical school graduate Steve Massof found out that Tina was selling the free samples that pharmaceutical reps would drop off. Also, a lot of the patients' personal money, which she was responsible for keeping safe, seemed to go missing. He told Gosnell, but Gosnell did nothing.

A certain callousness runs through Baldwin's testimony, both to the grand jury and at trial. She tried to cast Gosnell in an unfavorable light when she described the way he treated his patients, but she just ended up sounding contemptuous and cold.

"One of the things I did when he was in one room, we were always in another room setting it up and getting the patient ready. And I would go to him, 'Dr. Gosnell, do you want me to medicate this patient?' He would say yes or no. Nine times out of ten, if the patient was white, he didn't want [me] to medicate the patient. He wanted to meet her, talk to her, get a little history on her. If the patient was African American or from Africa, I would say—we used to call, *repeat offenders*—it really didn't matter. He would say, 'Go ahead, med them, go ahead.'"

Had Baldwin ever asked Gosnell why he treated black and white patients differently?

"He said, sorry, but that's how it is."

Baldwin worked the night Mongar died, but her plea deal allowed her to escape murder charges. James Berardinelli, Eileen O'Neill's attorney, highlighted Baldwin's culpability in a line of questioning at Gosnell's trial on April 11, 2013.

"In fact...you did give the doses of Restoril that, combined with the Demerol, put Ms. Mongar in a coma, didn't you?" he asked. "You gave her the three doses of Restoril that we saw. The Rs on the chart there, the Rs?"

Baldwin answered: "Yes, I did."

"You aren't licensed to give narcotics in any way, right?"

"No, I'm not," she replied. "I was doing what my boss told me to do."

"You were doing what Dr. Gosnell told you to do, correct?"

"Yes," she said.

Baldwin was sentenced to thirty months probation for conspiracy, engaging in a corrupt organization, and corruption of a minor.

KAREEMA CROSS

Kareema Cross was twenty years old when she began working for Gosnell in 2005. She drew blood, did ultrasounds, and eventually even injected labor-inducing drugs to patients vaginally. And in a depressingly familiar pattern, she was no more qualified to do the work than her coworkers were.

Cross didn't like Gosnell. He was mean to her. She complained that he would often yell at her, and she didn't like that. She came to understand that something was very wrong at 3801 Lancaster Avenue.

On October 22, 2008, Cross took a series of pictures that would later be used as evidence in Gosnell's trial. In one there is a container on a filthy floor. The container is full of surgical scissors in a green sterilizing liquid. In another there is a dried bloodstain. Another shows a cat in the procedure room. But the most chilling of the lot are a series of five. Some are out of focus and overexposed, but it's possible to make out what they depict: rows and rows of severed baby feet in jars. Some of the feet appear to be very large. Gosnell, as we have already seen, told Cross that he kept the feet in case of a DNA request—something that nobody ever asked for in Kareema Cross's four years working at the clinic. Yet Gosnell kept the feet.

Cross was not charged with any crime, and she cooperated fully with the investigation. She told police and later the grand jury that she was aware of more than one hundred abortions that Gosnell performed after the legal limit, at twenty-four weeks or older. She told detectives about minors who were brought to the clinic against their will by their mothers. If Gosnell sensed the girls might not want the abortion, he would give them a pill. After they had taken it, he would tell them that it was a poison, and their child was already dead so there would be no turning back. In fact, Cross said, she saw many babies born alive after these mothers were induced.

Like Adrienne Moton, Cross took a picture of "Baby Boy A." She also told detectives that she saw lots of babies born with their eyes open, alive, breathing, and with color.

She stopped working at the clinic in 2009, shortly before she gave birth to her daughter.

That was before the investigators raided the clinic, but after they began their investigation of Gosnell. The same day that FBI and DA investigators interviewed clinic front desk worker Latosha Lewis about Gosnell's pill mill operation and Lewis became an informant, Cross called the FBI offices with a tip. She said she had information about prescription drug dealing on the premises. The agents suspected that Lewis had told Cross about what she was doing, and Kareema had decided to get in early to cut the best deal she could. Cross used a false name but didn't really try to hide her identity. She left her real phone number, and when detectives called her back, the call went to an answering machine that said, "This is Kareema Cross." DEA agent Steve Dougherty checked the clinic's employee files and realized Cross worked there. When he brought her in for questioning, she was very cooperative. Ultimately, her testimony would be pivotal in sending Gosnell to prison for life.

LATOSHA LEWIS

Latosha Lewis—Tosha—was the Gosnell employee who became a confidential informant when the three amigos were investigating the clinic as a pill mill. She had started working for Gosnell in 2000. Lewis had a basic training certificate from the Thompson Institute that qualified her to take vital signs and prep patients for exams, which was more than many of her coworkers could say.

Lewis worked staggeringly long hours. Her shift typically began at 10:00 a.m., but she often stayed until 2:00 or 3:00 in the morning assisting with procedures.

The difference between Lewis and Gosnell's other untrained workers was that Tosha was actually aware of her own incompetence. She finally refused to administer anesthesia to patients because she was certain somebody would die. Lewis had had a few near misses with patients she had over-medicated. One case in particular really scared her: "I was the person who had given her too much and I was concerned whether she would come up from anesthesia," she testified at trial.

Lewis did not snip the necks of babies. She did witness babies "fall out" of their mothers almost every night she worked in the clinic. She told investigators that this happened a lot when Gosnell wasn't there. When she realized a baby was about to come out she would take the mothers to the bathroom where they would sit on the toilet for three to four hours. Lewis would rub their backs. The light in the bathroom was on a timer, and after a while it would go out, and she would stay in the dark with the mother sitting on the toilet. She would tell her that it was okay, and that someone would come and help soon. She said she never touched the baby if it fell out. She had had an abortion herself, and that memory prevented her from ever touching any of the babies at the clinic, she said.

Lewis explained that because the anesthesia was being administered by unqualified staff, women very often woke up on one of the chairs outside the procedure room, would feel their baby falling out of them, and would ask "Did my baby just fall out of me?" Lewis said the staff would lie and say what they felt was the laminaria coming out.

Christine Wechsler had a certain respect for Lewis. "Latosha is very smart," she told us. "She's very bright, very well-spoken, very street smart. This girl has been around the block. She knew exactly what was going on."

Lewis did Karnamaya Mongar's pre-examination. She couldn't weigh Mongar because the clinic's scale was broken.

Lewis was also supposed to be the custodian of the files at the clinic. But at the trial she admitted that the records weren't kept very well and that whatever was in them was likely not a complete record of all the drugs a patient had been given. She testified that some patients had received the labor-inducing drug Cytotec as many as eight times.

Lewis ended up pleading guilty to drug distribution charges in connection with Gosnell's pill mill operation. Because of her coop-eration with investigators, she received a sentence of one day in prison and twenty-four months supervised probation.

MADELINE JOE

To Kermit Gosnell she was his friend of over thirty years. All the other staff just called her "The Bitch."

Madeline Joe spent seventeen years at the Women's Medical Soci-ety, but she knew Gosnell much longer. She and her boss were very close, and he had been her OB/GYN—even though he was never certified as one.

Joe was supposed to ensure the clinic stayed in compliance with Pennsylvania's Abortion Control Act. That meant she had to send reports about each abortion to Harrisburg every month. The problem was, she rarely received the files on second trimester cases. She was also in charge of keeping the clinic's payroll, which was quite a trick since so many of Gosnell's assistants were paid under the table. And she was supposed to handle the clinic's fraudulent insurance claims—which is one reason she was charged with conspiracy and violating Pennsylvania's corrupt organization statute.

The staff who felt loyalty toward Gosnell blamed Madeline Joe for a lot of the chaos and problems at the clinic. It is true that she was nasty and incompetent. When in a bad mood, she would walk through the clinic lashing out at staff in front of patients. Sometimes she would even tell the patients that the women administering the medications and drugs were unqualified and incompetent. The bewildered patients just assumed Joe was an irrational member of staff rather than the only person in the building telling the truth. The staff particularly hated her because they thought she told tales to Gosnell about what went on when he wasn't there.

Certainly whatever Madeline Joe did and however she spent her time, it wasn't in following procedures and regulations.

When the police returned with another search warrant after the February 2010 raid, they found boxes and boxes of unopened mail from various state departments in Harrisburg. Joe wasn't the only person who didn't do her job. The bureaucrats at the State Department of Health and the Pennsylvania Department of State would write to her, but they never followed up when their letters went unanswered.

Madeline Joe was charged with corrupt organization and conspiracy; she received four years probation.

RANDY HUTCHINS

Randy Hutchins needed to pay off a drug debt. But he ended up helping bring down a prescription drug trafficking ring.

Hutchins had known Gosnell for years. His brother had worked for the doctor in the late 1960s and early '70s. Then in the 1980s

Hutchins went to work for Gosnell as a physician's assistant—a rare example of an employee at Gosnell's clinic who was actually licensed for the job he was doing there.

Unfortunately, Hutchins also had an expensive cocaine habit. Gosnell fired Hutchins after discovering he had stolen money from him to buy cocaine. Later, according to Hutchins, he went into a special rehabilitation program that allows medical personnel with drug habits to keep their licenses, and he has been clean since 1991. The program required Hutchins to write to everyone he stole from, detailing how much he had taken and apologizing for his actions.

Then in 2009, Hutchins got a call out of the blue from his former boss. Gosnell reminded him that he still owed several thousand dollars of the money he stole and told him that he could pay the debt by coming to work at 3801 Lancaster. Once the debt was paid off he could start earning money. Hutchins had three jobs already, but he was going through a painful divorce and needed money for lawyers and child support. So he said yes.

It turns out that Gosnell was ripping him off. Hutchins had forgotten just how much he had stolen from Gosnell, but investigators eventually found the letter he had written the doctor as part of his rehabilitation program. In reality he had only stolen eight hundred dollars, but Gosnell told him he owed five thousand dollars.

Gosnell needed Hutchins's help. He explained that a doctor friend had recently been arrested for selling drugs and that he was worried he'd be next. He wanted Hutchins to make sure that didn't happen.

Hutchins asked Gosnell directly, "Are you selling narcotics?" The doctor assured Hutchins he wasn't, he just wanted to make sure that somebody would keep all of his paperwork in order.

Hutchins's job was managing the chronic pain patients. He worked at the clinic on Mondays, Tuesday, and Fridays. His hours were, by any reckoning, very odd. His shift began at 8:00 p.m. and ended when the last patient left, which could be as late as 5:00 a.m. Hutchins told investigators he saw anywhere from twenty-five to thirty patients a night. All of them paid their $155 office fee in cash. (Gosnell wouldn't accept credit cards at the pain clinic.)

Hutchins was supposed to take a history of each pain patient, do a short physical exam, and then write down what pain medication the patient wanted. Gosnell would then decide whether to prescribe the medication the patient requested.

Pain clinics have a reputation for acting as covers for illegal prescription drug sales, and Hutchins quickly became suspicious about what was going on at Gosnell's office. The same patients would come back over and over. Spotting the liars was easy. He saw women walk in wearing five-inch heels and complain of back pain. Hutchins started to make a notation on their files: FOS—as in "Full of Shit." These were the addicts and dealers. He said he didn't know how Gosnell treated those with the FOS annotation on their file. The answer was simple. The doctor gave them drugs—lots of drugs—and charged them a lot of money for the service. Hutchins told investigators he estimated that 60 percent of Gosnell's chronic pain management patients were FOS.

When the girls downstairs were busy, Hutchins would occasionally help them do ultrasounds. Unlike the rest of the staff, he was actually a qualified sonographer. But he says he stopped doing the exams when he realized that the ultrasounds that showed women to be past twenty-four weeks were being destroyed and redone to show a younger baby, to make the abortion look legal. He also denies ever assisting with the abortions. In a written interview with detectives that the authors have seen, however, Madeline Joe listed him as "physician's assistant, assists Dr. in abortions" —though it is possible that Joe, who worked during the day, was not clear about the duties of the various staff who worked during the night.

Eventually, Hutchins resigned—he said he didn't want to be part of the Gosnell enterprise. It's true that he also had a heart attack at around the same time, so he may really have quit for health reasons. One week after he left the clinic, a friend phoned Hutchins to ask if he was OK. Sure, why? What's up? He hadn't heard the news that the Lancaster Avenue clinic had been raided. Hutchins had gotten out just in time.

PEARL GOSNELL

Pearl Gosnell was the proud wife of Dr. Kermit B. Gosnell, until she wasn't. "I am the wife of Kermit Gosnell," she told Judge Lerner at her sentencing hearing in May 2013. "I am not happy about that now and I haven't been for a long time."

Pearl was Gosnell's third wife and is the mother of two of his six children, now all adults. Both of her children testified in court to her good name.

Pearl started working at the Women's Medical Society clinic in 1982. She married the doctor in 1990. After the wedding, she didn't work as much, but she would often come in to the clinic to drop off supplies such as paper towels and toilet paper.

But Pearl Gosnell also assisted her husband with the "difficult" abortions that Gosnell scheduled on Sundays—when all of the other staff were off. The grand jury's assessment of the Sunday abortions is chilling: "Gosnell made little effort to hide his illegal abortion practice. But there were some, 'the really big ones,' that even he was afraid to perform in front of others. These abortions were scheduled for Sundays, a day when the clinic was closed and none of the regular employees were present. Only one person was allowed to assist with these special cases—Gosnell's wife. The files for these patients were not kept at the office; Gosnell took them home with him and disposed of them. We may never know the details of these cases. We do know, however, that, during the rest of the week, Gosnell routinely aborted and killed babies in the sixth and seventh month of pregnancy. The Sunday babies must have been bigger still. But we'll never know." Apparently the doctor surreptitiously disposed of these babies' remains as well as the files.

Pearl avoided life in prison because her husband destroyed the records.

At her sentencing hearing, Pearl called her husband "cowardly" for not apologizing or admitting what he had done and for not taking the stand at his own trial. "I'm sorry for my part in this horror," she told Judge Lerner. "My husband is in jail forever, which is where he should be."

Part of Pearl's animosity can surely be explained by the fact that her husband refused a plea deal that would have allowed her to keep the family home and avoid jail time. Together the Gosnells owned seventeen properties, a Dodge Durango, a Ford F-150 pickup truck, a Ford Expedition, and a motorboat.

Pearl's husband was also a cad. There were the late night, all night phone calls to Adrienne Moton, the constant groping of female staff members, and the rumors of affairs with some.

And then there was Jennifer Leach. She was a striking-looking twenty-eight-year-old woman who had a time card as if she were an employee of the clinic. And although she was forty-one years younger than the doctor, she was also Gosnell's mistress. Leach testified to the grand jury that Gosnell was paying her three hundred dollars weekly for "psycho-social counseling," despite the fact that she had no training as a counselor. Frequently she didn't even show up at the clinic on the single day a week she was supposed to. Leach had originally been a patient of Gosnell's when she was seventeen, and she told the grand jury that she had a years'-long on-and-off "fling" with the doctor that ended only a week before her grand jury testimony. Investigators believe Leach's eleven-year-old child is Gosnell's, but she denies this.

So Pearl Gosnell has many reasons to be angry with her husband. "You can tell from the arrogance that he displayed—turning down the deal, as well as refusing to speak—he's left Pearl holding the bag in terms of talking to the public and apologizing," defense lawyer Michael Medway told the Associated Press. "Her name is still Gosnell, unfortunately," he added. "I guess it's like being Mrs. Frankenstein."

At sentencing, Judge Lerner told Pearl, "You were his partner," and pointed out that she benefitted from all the money earned at the "foul operation masquerading as a medical facility." Pearl Gosnell was sentenced to seven years and twenty-three months in prison after pleading guilty to racketeering and to performing an abortion past Pennsylvania's gestational age limit.[7]

STEVE MASSOF

Steve Massof hated the flea-infested cats that roamed about Gosnell's clinic. They repulsed him. "There was always cat excrement all over the place," he testified. "It was dirty, but the smell was the worst—of cats, and cat excrement, and cat urine."

But apparently Massof wasn't repulsed at severing the spines of live babies.

The unlicensed medical school graduate compared his involvement in Gosnell's crimes to the frog in the slowly heating water. "I was just put into a lot of situations that, you know I didn't want to be in, it all started gradually." For an educated man from a nice home this explanation sounds ridiculous. He could have walked away at any time. He didn't.

At trial, Massof explained to the stunned jurors and the judge exactly what he had done: "What I would do is I would run around with a basin, scissors, and I would cut the umbilical cord and cut right back on the base of the skull," he said "The base of the skull where the base of the skull meets the neck. If you want to humor me, you could place your hand right there and you could feel it's very fleshy and supple. Do you feel right there? You just keep your neck—and that is the exact spot." The judge interjected. "For the record, the witness is indicating and pointing to the back of his neck and pressing in on the back of his neck just below his scalp."

Massof wasn't like the other workers at the Women's Medical Society. He was intelligent and university educated, with a solidly middle-class background. In 1993, he had enrolled in the St. George's School of Medicine on the Caribbean island of Grenada. (Students who cannot get into a U.S. medical school often choose to go to the West Indies, where the academic entry requirements are not as tough.) After graduating in 1998, Massof took two U.S. medical licensing exams and a clinical skills analysis test, but he failed to land a residency. Without a residency, he couldn't become a doctor.

His career going nowhere, Massof worked as a bartender and a cook for a few years. Then his brother-in-law Kenneth Gordon thought he could do him a good turn. Gordon was a sales rep for a pharmaceutical company, and Gosnell was one of his accounts. Gosnell had complained about having too much work and really needing help, and Gordon knew that Massof was desperate for clinical experience. So Gordon introduced Massof to Gosnell in 2003, and soon afterward Gosnell offered him a job. He had a keen eye for the desperate.

Massof didn't start snipping the necks of babies until Gosnell showed him the technique in 2004. When he was interviewed by the Philadelphia police department homicide division on July 2, 2010, at his home he said the job started out fine. "I was an 'extern.' It's between a med student and a resident physician. I had taken my medical boards and I was working there to gain experience. When I started there, I saw patients before Dr. Gosnell would arrive. Dr. Gosnell would review my work, and after he had confidence in me, he asked me to come in earlier. Then I saw patients on my own. Dr. Gosnell reviewed the charts when he got in. But he started coming in later and later. He came in at 7 pm or 8 pm most nights."

Initially, Massof worked from 4:00 p.m. until 9:00 p.m., or whenever Gosnell decided to show up. But very quickly Gosnell saw that Massof was useful and asked him to come in during the daytime. So the medical school graduate started working Monday to Friday from 2:00 p.m. to 9:00 p.m. As the work mounted, Massof would come in on Saturdays as well. He would get pre-signed prescription pads from Gosnell, and when Gosnell was not at the clinic he pretended to be a licensed doctor and prescribed medicines to patients, who were none the wiser.

Things quickly "evolved," and soon Massof was helping Gosnell with procedures. At the trial, Massof testified that he was curious about the abortions. "I had an interest, I wanted to see what the procedure was like and I was very inquisitive," he said. "So that was one of my interests too.... I started helping moving patients around in the procedure area."

He helped Gosnell to falsify the ages of the babies by manipulating ultrasounds. "Instead of pressing [the transponder] tightly to get the most accurate reading, you could just raise it up a little bit.... And like anything that's farther away that you see visually, it gets smaller. They would then qualify to have their procedures done at the clinic."

Most weeks he took home between four hundred and fifty and five hundred dollars under the table. He got thirty dollars cash for every second trimester abortion he helped with.

Massof testified that he believed 40 percent of the babies aborted at the clinic were over the gestational age limit for legal abortion in Pennsylvania.

The trouble with late-term abortion patients, Massof said, was they often wouldn't have all the money they needed to pay. So they were already very late in their pregnancies, but might spend a week or longer trying to scrape together the cash. "It would get up to the 27th week, and that was very important because that is what we know as the week the lungs are mature to function on their own outside utero," he explained.

Massof's casual descriptions of illegal abortions were completely bereft of any sense of shame. If anything, he showed only a cold clinical intellectual curiosity. Gosnell had found a perfect accomplice in Massof—a man without a moral compass.

At trial, Massof described how Gosnell had tried unsuccessfully to use the drug Digoxin to kill the babies in utero. Digoxin is a drug commonly used in legal abortions performed before twenty-four weeks. An injection of the drug into the heart of the baby will kill it quickly. Massof would follow the needle on the ultrasound and let Gosnell know how he was doing. "I would look and see if the heart was beating," Massof testified. "If it was beating, I'd say there was rhythm. If it wasn't beating, then I would say there was no rhythm, *good shot*. Most of the time, it was failure in the procedure. The heart was always beating."

The phrase "good shot" to describe a successful killing seems an odd choice for a medical professional—or even a human being.

As Massof testified, Gosnell tended to have many more bad shots than "good" ones. On one occasion he completely missed the baby and injected the mother. After she went home, she had to be rushed to the hospital.

Massof's testimony was particularly horrific because it was the most candid. "Literally…it would rain fetuses," he said. "Some days I would come up, I'd be called—a scream, and I would go running, and fetuses all over the place and blood."

One of the jurors said that Massof's testimony was among the most disturbing at the trial, both on account of its content and because of the manner in which it was delivered. "We thought he might have been high. He seemed to be enjoying giving evidence," the juror said.[8]

Steve Massof openly admitted to killing babies born alive.

During the prosecution's examination, assistant district attorney Ed Cameron asked Massof what he would do after a baby would "precipitate." "We had a pair of surgical scissors and I would take the surgical scissors and I would…snip the back of the neck so that you are snipping right at the top of the spinal cord. We call it a transection," Massof explained. "But it's literally a beheading because what you're doing is you're separating the brain from the body. In other words, if you cut off the head, the body dies. That's plain as it gets."

The prosecution wanted to know why Gosnell had instructed Massof to cut the neck. His answer was simple and appalling: "We had, like I said before…we had to prevent life. We had to kill. It's as simple as that."

Massof quit the Women's Medical Society in 2008—not because he grew a conscience but because of a bad joke. Ashley Baldwin's father threatened to kill him for joking about his daughter's flatulence. "[Ashley's] father just briefly threatened to beat me within an inch of my life because I had made a remark about her prom dress because Ashley was very gaseous around the clinic. I used to playfully call her Fartzilla and she had a prom dress, she was graduating and it had a train and I said, 'Please remember if you fart with your train it will flap in the wind.' And suddenly her father was threatening to beat me within an inch of my life."

"So based on this," Ed Cameron asked, "your employment terminated in 2008 after her dad threatened to kill you basically?"

"I ran quickly," he replied.

Murdering babies was one thing. Being murdered by a local thug was another matter. But what's really amazing about Massof's testimony is the impression he makes, of someone who joked around and had a good time at work—when his job wasn't keeping him busy beheading babies.

Ironically, Massof expressed regret that he had to leave the clinic. He was sorry because, he said, he "felt a responsibility for the patients."

But obviously not for their babies. Massof described one baby that moved. He said it made him "almost jump out of my skin." It was an abortion in the larger procedure room. He saw a leg jerk and move. He described it as a flex—the baby seemed to move its leg to its chest. Dr. Gosnell was moved only to pick up a "very sharp pair of scissors" and stab the baby in the back of the neck, severing its spinal cord.

Although Massof couldn't attest that that baby took a breath, he testified that he saw plenty of others that quite obviously had heartbeats and respiration. He could see their chests move up and down. Massof described them as "pulsations, rhythm, heart" clearly visible beneath the babies' often translucent skin. Perhaps most horrifically, he sometimes saw the babies' hearts beating *after* their spinal cords were cut: "The pulsations would slow down and stop. Not immediately, not right on the spot. But they would slow and then stop totally…sometimes it would take a minute." Death was not instantaneous. It took time for the baby to go "flaccid."

Massof was charged with two counts of murder, conspiracy to commit murder, conspiracy, violations of the Controlled Substances Act, racketeering, and theft by deception. He pled guilty to two counts of third-degree murder, along with criminal conspiracy and racketeering.

Judge Lerner sentenced him to six to twelve years in Somerset State Prison. At his sentencing, Lerner told Massof, "As evil as Dr. Gosnell was, as charismatic as he may have been, he didn't do this alone…. He couldn't do this without the assistance of someone like you."

EILEEN O'NEILL

Like Steve Massof, Eileen O'Neill is a medical school graduate. Also like him, she is not a licensed doctor, but she posed as one in the clinic, seeing patients and prescribing medicine.

She wore a white lab coat, and when patients called her "doctor," she didn't correct them. Her room on the second floor of the clinic was an oasis of cleanliness and order in the chaos that was 3801 Lancaster. On the night of the raid, O'Neill fled out the back door of the clinic, fearing detection of her fraudulent medical practice.

On one occasion, when she asked Gosnell for a raise, he said, "You can't do anything without me. You're a glorified secretary."

She graduated from the University of Texas at Galveston in 1995. She got a Graduate Medical Trainee license in September 2000, but she said she allowed it to expire because of PTSD and some personal issues connected with her sick mother and her boyfriend.

O'Neill was tried alongside Gosnell. She looked uncomfortable every day, embarrassed to be there. Her lawyer, James Berardinelli, brought in multiple character witnesses, including O'Neill's own elderly mother, her two brothers, and an award-winning doctor who said "I wish I could hire her now!" Each supported O'Neill's claim that she had nothing to do with the horrors occurring everywhere else in the building. And Berardinelli's strategy succeeded; O'Neill was sentenced to only six to twenty-three months of house arrest.

But the sympathetic, above-the-fray O'Neill portrayed by her character witnesses is a stark contrast with what is known about her past. Before coming to work with Gosnell, O'Neill worked at Delta

Women's Clinic of Baton Rouge. Delta employed her as an abortion-ist despite the fact that she had been dismissed from the Louisiana State University Medical School residency program in Gynecology and Obstetrics for failing meet their minimum standards.

When O'Neill was interviewed by the FBI in March 2010 and they asked her why she had run out of Gosnell's clinic the night of the raid, she initially lied to them. She said she needed to leave to help her mother, who had broken her hand. But when FBI agent Jason Huff said they had evidence suggesting she left because she was worried she was in trouble, she agreed. She also admitted she had been the defendant in three medical malpractice lawsuits involving abortion procedures in Louisiana.

One of those lawsuits, in particular, stands out for its horror.

In August 1998, Denise Doe (a pseudonym) went for an abortion in Delta Clinic. Her finances were not good, her marriage was in trouble, and she had two children already. She noticed blood on the floor of the clinic. She was not asked for her past medical history. She waited seven hours to be called for her procedure.

Eventually O'Neill came for her. Denise felt excruciating pain almost as soon as the procedure started.

She screamed. O'Neill snapped, "If you don't lie still and shut up.... you're going to die right here on this table." Nursing assistant Markethia Clarke corroborated this story in a sworn deposition on July 22, 1999.

Forty-five minutes later, O'Neill came out of the procedure room and told Denise's mother, Jane, (a pseudonym), "Something has gone wrong." Jane insisted on seeing her daughter, and she found her crying and dripping with sweat, with blood draining from her vagina. There was a clear bucket positioned at the foot of the table where her daughter lay. It was half full of blood and had a clear tube hanging on the side.

Jane was told to take her daughter to the nearest hospital and come back in a week to "complete the procedure." At the Earl K. Long Hospital Denise was given an ultrasound. Her baby was still alive.

Denise's condition deteriorated. She was moved to University Medical Center, Lafayette. Tests showed that her baby was eighteen weeks old and that Denise had a severe bacterial infection. When her condition deteriorated and fourteen hours of triple antibiotics failed, doctors performed a septic abortion, a suction D & C procedure. On September 15 Denise had a hysterectomy.

Delta Clinic sounds a lot like Gosnell's clinic. Delta, however, is still in business today.

Delta Women's Clinic was owned by Philadelphia native Leroy Brinkley, who also owned the Atlantic Women's Clinic in Delaware. He's the reason O'Neill got the job with Gosnell.[9] When we called the Delta Women's clinic to find out if Leroy Brinkley was still the owner, our call was transferred and the woman who spoke refused to answer the question and hung up on us.

O'Neill was charged with theft by deception, conspiracy to commit theft, racketeering, conspiracy related to corruption, perjury, and false swearing. Found guilty of conspiracy, participation in a corrupt organization, and two counts of theft by deception, she has successfully appealed her convictions and is currently awaiting a retrial.

FIVE

"THE INDIAN WOMAN"

*"Gosnell's contempt for the law and his patients cost
Karnamaya Mongar her life. Her death was the direct
result of deliberate and dangerous conduct by Gosnell
and his staff. They consciously disregarded the unjusti-
fiable risk that their conduct would cause death."*

—GRAND JURY REPORT

Gosnell's staff called her "the Indian woman."

Karnamaya Mongar had never been to India. But Gosnell's
assistants working the day she walked into the Women's Medical
Society clinic wouldn't have known that because they didn't ask where
Mongar was from or anything else about her background, for that
matter. They glanced at her and looked at her brown skin, tiny frame,
and the Asian-style Kurta dress she was wearing and decided she must
be from India.[1]

More crucially, nobody bothered to ask about her medical history.
The utter lack of concern—the almost casual indifference toward
Mongar's background and health—proved fatal for a woman who
had arrived in the United States only recently full of hope after leaving
behind a life of poverty and violence.

Karnamaya Mongar was an ethnically Nepalese woman born on
April 30, 1968, in the tiny kingdom of Bhutan, which occupies a

mountainous region of South Asia nestled between China and India. Mongar was born into difficult circumstances—Bhutan is tiny and poor—and Bhutanese politics made her life even more difficult. She was born in Bhutan, but her ancestors had migrated there from the neighboring country of Nepal generations earlier. The Nepalese, who are predominantly Hindu, had been welcomed for more than a century, living peacefully alongside the native Buddhist Bhutanese for years. But their numbers had spiked in the 1960s, raising tensions.

In the 1970s, with a keen eye towards Western fads, Bhutan's absolute monarch King Jigme Singye Wangchuck began promoting the Kingdom of Bhutan as a "Buddhist Shangri-La." The king also announced that the prosperity of his country would henceforth be measured in terms of Gross National Happiness, as opposed to Gross National Product. And he decided that the happiness of the kingdom's Hindu minority would not be counted in his new index. Bhutan's cheerleaders in the West were quiet as ethnic Nepalese faced greater discrimination, oppression, and then massive ethnic cleansing. The kingdom's Nepalese minority made up roughly one third of the kingdom's population in the 1980s. This was too much for King Jigme, who ordered a census that categorized them as "illegal immigrants," even though many were fourth-generation Bhutanese. Some one hundred thousand people were expelled or fled for their lives. Proportionally it was one of the largest, and unreported, mass deportations in history. Karnamaya Mongar was among those expelled. In 1989, when she was just twenty-one, she fled Chirang Lami Danda, her home in southern Bhutan, and arrived at the Timai refugee camp in Nepal. She would spend the next twenty years there, first living in a wooden hut with a thatched straw roof. (Eventually, the straw was replaced with corrugated iron.)

The conditions were poor, but at least Mongar was surrounded by family. "Our whole family was there," recalled her daughter,

Yashada Gurung. "My parents, other children, my father's family members, my mother's. Everybody was there."

Although she had escaped from discrimination and violence, Mongar's life was not free from tragedy. She had four children—two boys and two girls—but shortly after the family arrived in the refugee camp one of her sons became ill and died.

In 2009, after twenty years in a refugee camp, Mongar's family was accepted into the United States as part of a refugee resettlement program. It was through this program that she arrived with her family to live in Woodbridge, Virginia.

At first life in America was good. Mongar and her husband found a large support network, with nonprofit organizations and family members helping them adjust to a new life. "There was a refugee settlement organization here in the United States, they helped us with everything. There were caseworkers assigned to us, they helped us with our housing and other things," her daughter said. "And there were other family members who had come previously, other relatives, cousins, they also helped us."

Mongar's house in Woodbridge was crowded with her husband and her children, along with her daughter Yashada's husband and his mother. But Mongar was happy to have the help and the company. In her four months in the United States, she hadn't learned much beyond the most rudimentary English. "She had learned some but...very few words," her daughter Yashada Gurung testified during Gosnell's trial. "We would tell her, like, 'good morning is this' or 'bye bye' or 'thank you'—those were her only words."

In early November 2009, Mongar thought she might be pregnant. A home pregnancy test confirmed her suspicion. Her daughter was happy, but Mongar was alarmed at the prospect of raising a child in a country in which she had barely settled and where she didn't even speak the language. Mongar wanted an abortion, but Yashada wanted her to keep the child. "I did tell her, let's keep the baby, like it's already there," Mongar's daughter said.

But her mother decided the family simply could not afford another mouth to feed so soon after arriving. "We just came to this country," Yashada Gurung testified. "We didn't have anything, we were on food stamps and they would give us food stamps only for a certain [length of time]. We had to work; everybody had to work." Gurung explained that the refugee resettlement agency only covered the first three months of the family's expenses. After that, they were on their own. "Mom said this is not a good idea, we are new to this country, we don't know anything. So she said [she] wouldn't be able to support the baby."

––––––

Fear led Mongar to choose an abortion, and it brought her to the front door of the Women's Medical Society on November 19, 2009, and into the hands of Kermit Gosnell and his untrained, unsupervised, and—in the words of one prosecutor—"psychotic" staff.

Mongar couldn't get an abortion in Virginia because she was over fourteen weeks pregnant. Two clinics in Virginia turned her down, and then she went to a third in D.C. The receptionist took one look at her and surreptitiously handed her a handwritten post-it sticker with Gosnell's name and phone number on it.

It's a five-hour drive from northern Virginia to Philadelphia. Mongar was accompanied by her sister, her daughter, her daughter's mother-in-law, and Damber Ghalley, a distant relative and close friend of the family who was so protective of Mongar and her children that Yashada Gurung considered him an uncle. Ghalley drove the car.

The car ride was quiet, and the purpose of Mongar's visit was not discussed. Bhutanese women do not discuss their medical issues in front of men. Ghalley waited in the car while the four women went into the clinic at 2:30 p.m.

Mongar was greeted by Randy Hutchins, the former cocaine addict who was working at the clinic to repay money he had stolen from Gosnell years earlier. By all accounts, the treatment Mongar received from Hutchins was medically sound. But Mongar was given no counseling, as Pennsylvania law required.

Mongar returned the next day. The first people she met were Tina Baldwin and Liz Hampton. They were untrained and unqualified, but at least Baldwin was experienced. Unfortunately for Mongar, however, Baldwin wanted to leave work early that day, so she asked Hampton to start medicating the "Indian woman."

Hampton claims it was the first time she had ever given abortion-inducing Cyotec to a patient. She remembers the scene vividly: "[Mrs. Mongar] was sitting in a gray chair," she said. Hampton immediately gave her the drug to open her uterus so the abortion could proceed.

Later, Mongar suffered another tragic misfortune—falling into the hands of Sherry West and Lynda Williams, the "Delaware girls" whose incompetence Gosnell had been warned about repeatedly. Ashley Baldwin had complained that they were lazy and slapdash. Kareema Cross had warned Gosnell that Williams was careless and dangerous in the way she dispensed medication. But he ignored the complaints. That night the Delaware girls arrived around 7:00 p.m. and started "to med up" the patients so they would be ready when Gosnell showed up later.

At the trial, Dr. Andrew Herlich, a University of Pittsburgh anesthesiologist who is now president of the Pennsylvania Society of Anesthesiology, called the clinic's practices "reprehensible." Patients at the Women's Health Society were presented with a form explaining how anesthesia worked. We have reproduced it in its entirety. It is difficult to believe it was written by anyone with better than an eighth grade education:

You have already decided that a procedure is best for you. Now you need to choose the type of pain relief. It will probably be best to pay the extra money and be more comfortable if some of the following conditions are true for you:

1, The decision to have the procedure is a difficult decision.

2, Medication is usually necessary for your menstrual cramps.

3, Your **decision has been forced** by your parents or partner.

4, Your **family members** and **friends** don't like pain. [Emphasis added]

Not only were Gosnell's employees encouraging patients to decide, without even the advice of a doctor, what kind and quantity of anesthesia they could have; this document was an admission that a number of the women and girls getting abortions at the clinic were there involuntarily—"forced by your parents or partner."

Mongar was a diminutive woman. Williams fed her sedatives orally and intravenously without regard to her height or weight (which, in any case, the clinic didn't know—as we saw in the previous chapter, Latosha Lewis had been unable to weigh her because the clinic's scale was broken). At first Yashada Gurung was in the room with her mother. She testified that Mongar received five or six different sedatives and at least one IV injection. Williams inserted the IV *after* Mongar was already asleep. But Mongar kept waking up and, with her daughter translating, complained that she was in pain. So Williams phoned Gosnell at home to ask what to do. Gosnell didn't ask for a patient history or details about her already heavily sedated condition. He simply instructed Williams to give Mongar a "local" consisting of Demerol and Promethazine. At the trial, Williams testified that Gosnell preferred those drugs over Nalbuphine because they were cheaper.

And yet the drugs didn't reduce Mongar's pain. She continued to complain of severe cramping and discomfort. Williams phoned Gosnell a second time, but he didn't answer. Worried that Gosnell would get angry with her for calling again, and believing that Mrs. Monger was in "severe pain" because she continued to "squiggle around," Williams decided to give her another "half a local."

At first, Williams said, Mongar appeared "fine." But after a short while she looked uncomfortable again. Williams called the doctor a third time. He answered the phone and gave Williams a short, pointed response that meant a death sentence for "the Indian woman": "He told me to put her in the room and med her up," she told the court.

So Lynda Williams administered "twilight" anesthesia—75 milligrams of Demerol, 12.5 milligrams of Promethazine, and 10 milligrams of diazepam (Valium).

When Gosnell arrived at the clinic around 8:00 p.m., Yashada Gurung was asked to leave her mother, and West walked Mongar into the procedure room—and to her death.

The only question Gosnell asked was whether Mongar had been given her meds. She had. She had been given so much that they were going to kill her. Gosnell checked Mongar's heartbeat with his stethoscope and her pulse with his fingers. He made no notations in her chart. He started the abortion.

Halfway through the procedure, Lynda Williams, who was operating the ultrasound machine "to ensure he got everything out," became concerned. She testified that she normally monitored patients by looking at the veins on their neck, to make sure they were pulsating. Williams only became alarmed when she noticed Mongar's color had changed. She looked "grayish," and her breathing had slowed down. As soon as she noticed, she alerted Gosnell.

"I told Doc," Williams testified. "I said, 'Doc, her skin color is kind of funny looking and she's not breathing right.'" But Gosnell ignored her warning and continued with the abortion. Only after he finished did Gosnell check her pulse. Then he became concerned.

In a crucial piece of testimony that everyone except for one juror believed was an outright lie,[2] Williams said that Gosnell immediately began performing CPR and shouted to get Eileen O'Neill, one of the two unlicensed medical school grads that most patients assumed were doctors. There's no other evidence that Gosnell ever started CPR. It wasn't until Williams went upstairs and brought O'Neill down to the procedure room that serious attempts to revive Mrs. Mongar actually began.

Twenty minutes after Lynda Williams had alerted Gosnell to Mongar's grayish color and faint pulse, the doctor told his staff to call an ambulance. Williams made the 911 call.

Seven other women were awaiting abortions that night. West testified that none of them was hooked up to a pulse oximeter to monitor their vitals. Williams told the court that it wouldn't have mattered anyway because the pulse oximeter never worked. They had tried using it once with a patient, Williams said, and it "pinged" but didn't function. So the clinic's patients were monitored by "looking at them and asking them questions, talking to them." Gosnell didn't know his patients' blood pressures or their weight because he never bothered to replace the clinic's broken equipment. The women who came to see him, many of whom had mental illnesses and drug addictions, were simply sedated by untrained staff—and then Gosnell went to work.

Meanwhile, Yashada Gurung waited in the reception area with the turtles for about four hours. It felt like an eternity. She began to worry. Nobody would tell her anything about her mother.

The ambulance siren alarmed her. Anxious, she asked someone what was the problem. It was "the Indian lady," she was told. This chilled her. Could it be her mother? But nobody came for the family. Surely if there was a problem she would have been told by now. Fifteen minutes later Liz Hampton approached Gurung and told her that her mother's situation had deteriorated and that she would need to be taken to a hospital.

Paramedic Chris Smith and his partner Dana Kozma received the emergency call shortly after 11:00 p.m. It was a "code blue"—cardiac arrest—at a medical clinic on 3801 Lancaster Avenue. A fire truck was already on scene, which was a relief because a code blue always requires more than two people. One person performs CPR and another manages the patient's airway, while a third administers medicine. Then they have to put the patient on a gurney and transport her to the hospital, often while CPR is ongoing.

Lieutenant Don Burgess of the Philadelphia fire department, who was performing CPR on Mongar when the paramedics got to the clinic, testified that when he arrived Gosnell had appeared "confused and discombobulated." (Ashley Baldwin remembers Gosnell as unusually quiet. "The doctor said nothing, he had a blank stare.") Burgess thought something just wasn't right about the entire scene. For him it was strange that the clinic was open so late at night, and that building itself was like a maze. And Burgess was astonished that when he eventually found the procedure room with Mongar inside, no one was performing CPR on the dying woman.

When paramedic Chris Smith arrived, he noticed that Karnamaya Mongar's legs were still in the table's stirrups and she was naked from the waist down—no one had even covered her up. Smith also noticed that no IV was attached, something that he would have expected in a clinical setting. What Smith didn't know was that the scene, as shocking as it still was, had been staged to make things look better than they were. Sherry West told how when she was called back as the emergency started, Mongar's legs were flat on the bed and out of the stirrups. But Gosnell put her legs back into the stirrups before the emergency personnel arrived—possibly to make it appear as if the emergency had just happened and they had immediately called 911, rather than waiting as long as they had.

Between Burgess and the paramedics, emergency personnel worked on Mongar for about twenty minutes before they decided she needed to go to the hospital. They asked the staff to show them the quickest way out of the clinic.

In the meantime, Williams had moved Mongar's family to the second floor. They were in a state of panic, and nobody had told them what was going on. Eventually Yashada Gurung was brought back downstairs and led to the small procedure room, where she could see that her mother was being moved by the paramedics out to the ambulance.

But getting Mongar there wasn't easy. The corridors were so narrow that the gurney became stuck in places. And as the police would discover the night of the February 2010 raid, the clinic's main emergency exit was padlocked shut and nobody could find the key. Firefighters used bolt cutters to open the door.

Outside, Yashada Gurung started crying hysterically on the sidewalk. Damber Ghalley, the family friend who had driven Mongar to the clinic and who spoke the best English of the group, asked Gosnell what had happened. Gosnell said that he had completed the procedure and that Mrs. Mongar's heart had simply stopped beating. Sherry West rode in Ghalley's car to the hospital with the family. Ghalley recalled how West was upset in the car but assured the family that everything would be fine. "Maybe, she was trying to calm us down," he said. "And she was saying her own mother passed away shortly before that."

After Mongar was transported to the hospital, the staff returned to their normal duties. Gosnell still had more abortions to perform.

As Liz Hampton described it, "We all went back to doing what we do."

————

Mongar arrived at the Hospital of the University of Pennsylavania's emergency room shortly after midnight on November 20. She was attended by Dr. Raina Merchant and Dr. Nafis Ahmed, with assistance from head nurse David Gaines. Because Mongar was relatively young and in cardiac arrest, the ER aggressively fought to save her life.

But their efforts were not helped by the deceptive patient chart that Sherry West presented to them, which did not accurately represent the medication Mongar had been given. When paramedics had asked for the chart back at the clinic, according to the grand jury report, "West grabbed the chart and took it herself to the hospital. By the time the file was turned into hospital doctors, it had notations about medications that Ashley [Baldwin] said had not previously been there.... The notations were totally inconsistent with all of the other evidence...and grossly understated the amount of medication that was given." And West compounded the lies in the chart by telling hospital staff that Mrs. Mongar had been taken ill while she was watching TV in the recovery room after her abortion. The self-serving fabrication, cooked up by Lynda Williams, that Mongar had given herself drugs in an attempt to abort the baby herself before she arrived at Gosnell's clinic, also muddied the waters.

HUP head nurse Gaines recalled the night Mongar was brought in, and how there were so many circumstances that just didn't add up, making her case more difficult to treat. "If it was an abortion case, we were assuming she was in maybe some type of shock from bleeding, maybe some hypovolemia," he testified. "That's what we prepared for, and it's a different approach that you take, as opposed to coming in with some type of cardiac issue. And I know that I was surprised, as well as the doctor, because we didn't see any blood. There was no blood from the vaginal area. That's the first thing we do, is examine everybody to make sure there's no missed injuries. And we put her on a cardiac monitor and we didn't get a profusing rhythm so we continued CPR."

At trial, HUP's Dr. Merchant explained in detail how the ER staff tried to save Mongar. "We treated the cardiac arrest, so we immediately assisted with the breathing. She was intubated.... We immediately continued chest compressions. We provided medications, epinephrine and atropine to restart the heart. We consulted the obstetrics and gynecology resident to evaluate the patient, perform an ultrasound and exam. We also consulted the [cardiothoracic] surgeon about putting the patient on bypass."

The team worked on Mongar for almost an hour. They weren't going to give up. They just couldn't let someone her age die of a heart attack. "She kept going in and out," nurse Gaines explained. "We had some activity." But he admitted they couldn't be certain what that activity meant. "A lot of times, epinephrine will be the cause of the activity, not the person sustaining. As soon as you take them off, the activity pretty much dwindles away." But despite the setbacks they kept treating her, hoping for progress. "She was young, so we worked on her quite a bit more than we normally would," he said.

And then there was a breakthrough—they finally got a pulse. "Once she regained a blood pressure and a pulse," Dr. Merchant explained, "then we immediately started therapeutic hypothermia"— that's a process in which doctors literally pack people in ice to lower their blood temperature. In many cases, it's the only way to improve brain activity after major cardiac arrest.

Mongar was transferred to intensive care, but it was too late.

Her family waited anxiously all night at the hospital for any news about her condition. A staff member told them that she was in very serious condition and that they should pray for her. At times they were hopeful. "We were there, like, the whole night and then my uncle went and.... saw my mom and then he came back and told me they are giving her oxygen," Yashada Gurung recalled. Ghalley assured her that her mom was going to be fine, the doctors were doing their best. But their best couldn't save Karnamaya Mongar. By morning, the doctors who had fought so hard to save Mongar's life gave Gurung and her family the bad news. There was nothing more to be done. She would be taken off life support.

Gurung begged them to keep her on the machines in hopes that she might recover. But the doctors persuaded her it would be a futile effort. She phoned her husband in Virginia and told him to bring the family to Philadelphia as quickly as he could to say their final goodbyes. She and the rest of her family paid her mother one last visit. Karnamaya Mongar was declared dead at 6:15 p.m. on November 20.

Meanwhile, back at the clinic, the imminent death of the patient didn't disrupt Gosnell's pursuit of profit and pleasure. After he had finished the remaining abortions, Gosnell filled out dozens of phony prescriptions for the drug dealers and made a few calls to his mistress, Jennifer Leach. Gosnell was not a stickler for rules, including the one forbidding doctors from having sexual relations with patients, which Leach had been since she was seventeen years old. (As we have seen, he then put her on his payroll, but she did practically no work.) Starting at 2:09 a.m. the night of Mongar's botched abortion, Gosnell called Leach twelve times throughout the early morning and into the day. He spoke to her another six times the day after. Leach told investigators she couldn't recall what they had discussed, but she was certain he didn't tell her the shocking news about the death of one of his patients.

Sometime the next morning, Ghalley saw Gosnell arrive at the hospital to pick up West, who had stayed with the distraught family all night. He asked Gosnell what had happened. "I went to his side, you know, by the car and ask him. He say the same thing, 'Everything was done, procedure was done fine, and I didn't do anything wrong. I would be able to answer any questions anywhere.' That's what he said," Ghalley recalled.

That was the last Mongar's relatives heard from Gosnell—until they received a bizarre, self-serving, and strangely self-obsessed "sympathy letter" from him a few months later. The night of the February raid, Gosnell told Detective Wood he had written an apology to Mongar's family. Wood recovered a copy of the letter, dated November 27, 2009, from a shoulder bag in Gosnell's truck. He had typed two pages:

November 27th 2009

To the family of Karna Mongar,

I am apologetic that all that I have to offer you is my sincere grief and condolences for the loss of your wife and mother and loving family member. I am filled with remorse and severe recrimination.

I hoped to have an explanation as to why her heart stopped beating. At one time, I thought that I had an understanding of how I could have caused her cardiac arrest. But my associate pointed out to me that even if a perforation had occurred and nerves were damaged during the surgery, nothing affected there could have caused such a result. The heart has its own internal stimulus for the heart to beat. And there was no perforation. I have enclosed a copy of my report to our Pennsylvania State authorities. And as stated, there were no problems or difficulties or even minor delays during her surgery....

Still, I am filled with self-doubt and fears and feelings of guilt. I happen to be extremely well trained and experienced in the provision of abortion services. During my Gynecologic training at Thomas Jefferson University Hospital, we provided abortions and challenged the laws against abortion which were later overturned. In 1971, I was the second physician in the united states [sic] to provide legal abortions under Roe vs Wade Supreme Court decision [in fact Roe v. Wade wasn't decided until 1973]....

My training included the methods and knowledge of physicians who provided these services when they were considered illegal. I am a Clinician who has provided training for Gynecology specialists to improve their ability to perform second trimester terminations.... and never have I experienced such an event as with Mrs. Mongar.

I share my experience not to brag or to inflate myself.

I am the father of three daughters and my standard of care is always to provide the level that I would want my daughters to receive, I assure you that Karna Mongar received the same care that I would have provided to my family, but never, ever, will I allow myself to be complacent. If there could be any consolation, there will be better care for other women.

This weekend I am away with my family. One moment I feel confident that I did everything possible and the next, I am very down....

One moment I am fearful for the security of my family and the future of my community endeavors. The next moment, I believe my community work to be commendable. I live and work in an underprivileged neighborhood. As I continue to reinvest in community projects (right now we are working on aspects of prison release), I am not a wealthy individual. My lower fees are a reflection of what my neighbors can afford. But please let me know if there is any way that I can compensate in any way for your loss. Incidentally, I have not touched the monies you paid. An envelope with her name contains the money from the credit card. Another envelope contains the cash monies that you paid.

It is myself who has suffered a similar loss to your own. On Christmas Eve all too recently, I found my mother at the bottom of her steps, twisted and stiffened in death. She had fallen and broke her neck.

The directory in the office, you will see that we exist in loving memory of Cornelia K. Gosnel [sic]. Had my mother survived, you would have met and known her, as she was our evening receptionist. She was the person who comforted those in crisis and those from distance and fearful.

I share my loss to share with you that I know your loss. I feel your loss, My heartache is with your own. My strength in loss is that the depth of loss reflects the degree of love. I believe that we are fortunate to have such love and that the loss of it is extreme.

Your family will continue to be in my prayers. Please excuse me if my letter and my feelings could be better expressed, as I have not been myself and thank you for allowing me the opportunity of expressing myself.

Sincerely, Kermit Gosnell, MD

The day after Mongar died, Gosnell instructed the staff to clean the clinic thoroughly.

"After Mrs. Mongar died, we cleaned real good," Liz Hampton said. Her husband, Jimmy Johnson, repainted the building. Gosnell even bought some new chairs for the reception area. It was one of the only times staff could remember that place ever being cleaned.

Gosnell expected regulators and investigators from the state Department of Health to come calling. After all, a woman had died.

But he needn't have worried. Nobody in Harrisburg cared.

SIX

THE BABIES

Gosnell was charged with seven counts of first-degree murder and two counts of infanticide, and conspiracy to commit murder. But from the evidence, it's fair to assume that he murdered hundreds—perhaps thousands—over the course of his career.

So why was Gosnell charged with only seven murders and two counts of infanticide?

First of all, there's the statute of limitations for infanticide—which is only two years in Pennsylvania. Sometimes the law can be maddening and nonsensical, and this is clearly an example of both.

There is no statute of limitations for murder. But Gosnell could be charged with only seven homicides because, although he may have been a very bad doctor and a worse human being, he was a very good destroyer of evidence. Kareema Cross, the clinic employee who supplied investigators with photos of Gosnell's macabre collection of baby feet, told them that she had seen medical files from the clinic in Gosnell's house during Thanksgiving dinner in 2007. Detectives were also told that Gosnell was angry that clinic maintenance man Jimmy Johnson had lost his driving license because of a DUI conviction. The doctor had wanted Johnson to rent a truck to remove all the files he was storing in the basement of his clinic and take them to his house, where he planned to destroy them. Several staff members told police and the grand jury that Gosnell routinely took patient files home and did not even keep records of most of his late-term abortions at the clinic.[1]

According to the final grand jury report, "Tina Baldwin explained that Gosnell took second-trimester files home 'if there were difficult cases or some cases where he thought they shouldn't be in there.' [Steve] Massof told us that Gosnell always took files home, so 'I think he has them. If he hasn't destroyed them, he has them.' A subsequent search of Gosnell's home and car turned up only some of these files. One of the files seized from Gosnell's car was partially shredded."

We know, too, that somebody removed hundreds of files from the clinic after the initial February 2010 raid. Because the first raid was only focused on Gosnell's pill mill operation and Karnamaya Mongar's death, investigators couldn't remove any evidence of other crimes. As we saw in chapter one, Latosha Lewis had shown FBI agent Jason Huff a shelf filled with files on second trimester abortion cases, and the investigators took photographs, but the files were gone when the police returned in April with another set of warrants that would have allowed them to take those files.

It also appears that Gosnell removed all of his files from the Wilmington, Delaware, clinic where he had worked part time. The clinic sacked him after he lost his Pennsylvania medical license in the wake of the February raid. But Gosnell kept his keys, and the clinic's managers never bothered to change the locks or the building security code. When prosecutors subpoenaed Atlantic Women's Services for Gosnell's files, they received a grand total of three. Everything else had mysteriously vanished.

There was one more reason Dr. Gosnell wasn't charged with more murders. Originally prosecutors thought they might have enough evidence to charge him with dozens—maybe up to one hundred—but this plan provoked strenuous objections from the leadership of the Philadelphia police department and its political allies.

Philadelphia has had a reputation as a violent, murderous city but in recent years the murder rate has been in decline—a source of pride for the police and the city's politics. Charging someone with a hundred murders, even if some of them were old, would have spiked the statistics and made it look as though crime had come surging back in Philadelphia. No city in the United States wants the distinction of being the murder capital of the country. It's bad for business, for tourism—and for re-election. The plan to charge Gosnell with a large number of murders was quietly dropped.

———

Gosnell turned almost no one away from the Women's Medical Society clinic. This is not meant as a compliment. Repentant Gosnell employee Adrienne Moton testified he would perform abortions on any girls or women with no concern about the age of their babies. The only times she could recall Gosnell refusing to perform an abortion was when somebody's Social Security number couldn't be verified. In those cases, Gosnell was worried that the "patient" was an undercover cop.

The seven babies Gosnell was charged with murdering were identified in court only by letters of the alphabet. Their stories were told by the few who witnessed their short lives and horrific deaths. Some of those same witnesses were also the babies' murderers.

Baby Boy A was born and murdered on the same day—July 12, 2008. He was so large, even in a clinic where late abortions were not unusual, that two clinic employees snapped pictures of him on their cell phones.

The frozen remains of Baby Boy B were found the night of the February 2010 raid. The grand jury included a photograph in its final report. It shows a long gash at the back of the baby's neck.

Lynda Williams slit the neck of Baby C after Gosnell delivered the baby alive. Williams testified the baby moved and breathed for twenty minutes before it was killed.

Baby D was delivered into a toilet and was attempting to swim. It was struggling to live. Adrienne Moton picked it up from the toilet bowl and severed its spinal cord.

Baby E was the baby that cried—the one Sherry West said "sounded like a little alien." Two of Gosnell's assistants heard it, Gosnell went into the procedure room alone, and the crying stopped. When he emerged, the baby was dead. He put the body in the trash.

After Baby F jerked its leg to its chest, Gosnell cut its neck with scissors.

Baby G breathed. Gosnell snipped its neck.

The two cases of infanticide involved two babies discovered frozen in containers during the February 2010 raid. The first, a twenty-eight-week-old boy, had a surgical incision at the base of the neck. The medical examiner found that the baby had been viable. The second was a twenty-six-week-old girl the medical examiner also determined to be viable. Her remains had been frozen in a distilled water jug.

We know the most about the stories of two babies—Baby Boy A and Baby Girl Manning—because their mothers testified at Gosnell's trial. Gosnell was charged with first-degree murder in the case of Baby Boy A. Baby Girl Manning, stillborn after a botched abortion at 3801 Lancaster Avenue, was the twenty-six-week-old girl. Because the medical examiner could not determine a cause of death, Gosnell could not be tried for her murder so instead was charged with infanticide.

At the trial, twenty-one-year-old Shayquana Abrams, the mother of Baby A, testified about her baby boy. In 2008, Abrams, who goes by Shay, was seventeen, a junior in high school living in Chester, Pennsylvania, with her aunt Vicky Berry, a nurse. When Shay thought she was pregnant, she took a pregnancy test. And when it turned out to be positive, she started searching online for abortion clinics. She felt she couldn't have the baby because at seventeen she already had a ten-month-old baby, which her family was looking after. She didn't tell anyone, and nobody suspected because she was very thin and didn't show.

Shay's best friend told her that if she went to Delaware, she wouldn't have to tell her aunt or her mother about the pregnancy or the abortion. The friend recommended the Atlantic Women's Medical Clinic in Wilmington, where Gosnell worked.

Abrams thought she was quite far along in the pregnancy—four months, most likely. She didn't realize it was closer to seven months. She met Gosnell at the Wilmington clinic, where he performed an ultrasound but did not show her the images.

In court, Abrams was handed her own medical file, tagged as prosecution exhibit C 504. In it were three ultrasound pictures. All had the same date—July 10, 2008. The first one was time-stamped 14:31; the second, 14:33; and the third, 14:36.

Only one of the images had a gestational age noted under the time. It said 24.5. But all of the ultrasounds show a measurement of the baby's head—the biparietal diameter (BPD), which helps determine gestational age. The first ultrasound had a BPD of 74.8; the second, 75.8. These measurements meant the child would be almost seven months. This was not the answer Gosnell wanted. So he fiddled with the ultrasound until he got a fraudulent BPD number of 61.8, which would give the appearance that the baby was only 24.5 weeks.

But this was a fraud compounded by an error. The law in Pennsylvania prohibits abortions after twenty-three weeks and six days.

The limit in Delaware is even earlier—twenty weeks. Every time that Gosnell noted 24.5 on a patient's file, he was admitting to a crime.

But apparently he didn't know that. Dr. Gosnell was horrified when investigators told him the gestational limit in Pennsylvania was just twenty-three weeks and six days. He seems to have got it into his head that he could do legal abortions on babies as long as he wrote 24.5 on the chart. So his falsification of the sonogram images was all for naught.

Gosnell's nurse in Delaware gave Abrams medicine to dilate her cervix after Gosnell recorded the gestational age as 24.5 weeks. Surely she knew he was breaking Delaware law. But Atlantic Women's Medical Clinic wasn't exactly a center for medical excellence, either. It was owned by Pansy Myrie, an entrepreneur who operated two abortion clinics in Delaware and two in Louisiana. Myrie was subsequently found to be passing herself off as a gynecologist in her clinics' advertising when, in fact, she has no medical training.

Dr. Karen Feisullin, an obstetrician-gynecologist at Abington Hospital, explained the BPD numbers in detail when she appeared as an expert prosecution witness. Assistant district attorney Ed Cameron handed her Baby Boy A's ultrasounds and asked her to assess the age based on the images. The original measurements, over 74 millimeters, meant the baby was actually nine or ten weeks past the legal limit in Delaware. And even the sonogram taken after the camera was backed up to make the baby appear smaller yielded a measurement that made the abortion illegal. "The first one is twenty-four weeks, six days. That was the 61.8. The 75.8 is thirty weeks, zero days. And the 74.8 millimeter one is twenty-nine weeks, four days," she answered.

"So based on the law, an abortion could not be done on any of those?" Cameron asked.

"Correct."

Gosnell told Abrams that she was twenty-four weeks pregnant. He said the abortion would take three days and cost twenty-five hundred dollars.

She'd already been given two pills to start her dilation. The second day, Abrams testified, she was told she'd have to come back "for him to do something to my cervix." And the third day, "they were going to remove the fetus," she said.

Gosnell sent Abrams on her way. The nurse told her that if she experienced any pain from the dilation, she should take some Tylenol. She received no counseling beyond that. She went home and began to have severe cramps.

The next day, Friday, July 11, Abrams returned to the Wilmington clinic to have her cervix softened. A nurse injected her, although where on her body became a matter of dispute. Abrams testified it was in her cervix. Gosnell's defense attorney argued it was in her stomach, an injection of Digoxin that killed her baby before birth.

Abrams said she felt nauseated almost immediately, had difficulty breathing, and was in terrible pain. Gosnell was not there. For the rest of that day, Abrams said, she felt the baby moving, and pushing down on her cervix. "That's how I felt, like, the baby was pushing down on my cervix trying to come out," she testified. If she had been injected with Digoxin, it clearly had not worked.

Abrams started crying on the stand when she was asked to remember those three days in 2008.

The Delaware clinic nurse told Abrams she would need to go to Philadelphia for the final day. "Philadelphia was where he finished these type of procedures," she told Abrams.

Pescatore led Abrams through a series of questions asking her to describe how long after she left the Wilmington clinic she felt her baby move.

"After you got that needle in your stomach or, you told the detectives, your cervix, did you feel the baby moving at all?"

"Yes."

"How much more movement did you feel after you got that needle?"

"I felt movement Friday and I felt movement Saturday. I still felt movement on Saturday."

"By movement, what do you mean? What did you feel?"

"The way a baby moves, like, a regular movement, a regular baby movement."

"And you had been pregnant before, so you know how a baby moves around inside you. Is that right?"

"Yes."

"Is that what you were feeling when you went to Dr. Gosnell's clinic in Philadelphia on that Saturday?"

"Yes, I was still feeling it on Saturday."

Her aunt Vicky drove Shay Abrams to 3801 Lancaster Avenue that morning. The girl was in so much pain, her aunt had to sign her in. Shay described the pain as worse than when she gave birth to her daughter. She felt like she was in labor, "like I was about to have a baby."

Kareema Cross was working the reception desk.

She testified that she had a very clear memory of the day. Cross remembered because of Abrams's aunt, who worked as a registered nurse at the same clinic as a friend of hers. And she remembered because Abrams's baby was just so big.

Cross gave Abrams a pill and told her it was to help with the pain. Then she was directed to an upstairs waiting area, where some other women were also waiting for abortions.

For over four hours Abrams sat and waited. In that entire time, no doctor came to check on her. But Gosnell's assistants gave her pills—at least four—that might have been for pain or might have been for some other purpose. Nobody bothered to tell her. She wasn't worried because she thought the people giving her the drugs were actual nurses. She became very sleepy and dozed off now and then on the recliner in the room.

Abrams waited eight hours before Gosnell arrived. He was running late. Somebody told her the abortion would start. She was so out of it from the medication that her memory became fuzzy and uncertain after that. She woke in a recliner chair, but in a different room. Four or five other women were with her. The procedure was done. It was almost 11:00 p.m. Abrams had been at the clinic for more than twelve hours.

According to Cross, Abrams was heavily sedated when she was taken into the procedure room and "the baby just came out." Gosnell was in the room. The baby was about eighteen inches long.

Gosnell put the baby boy in a Tupperware container. He was still breathing.

Gosnell did not cut the baby's neck straight away. He was so big that his arms and legs hung over the sides of the container.

Cross testified about what happened next.

"He put it in a shoebox and the baby was hanging over the shoebox, but the baby somehow, some way came together," she said.

Pescatore asked Cross to show the court what the baby did.

"The baby just came together and the picture, it shows that the baby was just in a shoebox like this," Cross replied.

Judge Minehart wasn't quite following. "When you say, 'came together,'" he interjected, "what do you mean?"

"Because when Dr. Gosnell put the baby in the shoebox," Cross repeated, "the baby was hanging over the shoebox."

Pescatore asked Cross to stand up in the courtroom and show how Baby Boy Abrams curled up in the container. She crouched into a fetal position. The jury was stunned.

When the lights in the courtroom were dimmed and the photograph of Baby Boy Abrams was finally shown, there was silence.

"What happened to that baby?" Pescatore asked Cross.

"The back—the doctor snapped, cut the back of the baby's neck," she said.

Baby Abrams was born, then he curled up in a fetal position before he was stabbed to death by the doctor and was moved in the Tupperware box to the next room. No one really cared where he ended up. This carelessness would come back to haunt Gosnell.

Adrienne Moton usually called ahead before her shift began to ask how many abortions were on the schedule so she'd have some idea of what kind of day she would have. That night, Cross answered the phone and told her about the enormous baby boy that had just been aborted.

"I said, okay, I'm on my way," Moton testified. When she arrived, she found the baby at her workstation, in the Tupperware container. She was furious.

"I literally went off and I cussed everybody out because I did not want to see that," she said.

Cross and Moton both took pictures—pictures that ensured Gosnell's conviction five years later. Cross called Ashley Baldwin over to see. While Cross, Baldwin, and Moton were shocked by the sight of Baby Boy A, Gosnell found the situation humorous. He joked to Cross, "The baby is big enough that it could walk to the store, walk to the bus stop."

Moton testified that the baby boy was so big that even Gosnell "looked guilty." It was rare for his staff to see a baby so large. Gosnell and his wife usually took care of the bigger ones on Sundays.

"He just got this guilty look on his face, and he's trying to explain himself to me," Moton recounted. "I said, 'Nuh-uh, you don't got to explain nothing to me.' I just looked at him like, are you serious?"

Moton said she had seen big babies aborted plenty of times at the clinic, but Baby Boy A was different. "The ultrasound said 29.4

weeks. But he seemed bigger than that to me. He could have been due any day. That's how big he was to me."

———

Abrams's aunt paid $2,450 for the abortion, in cash, and helped the girl to the car. Shay Abrams was in tremendous pain. When they got home to Chester, she became very ill.

"In the next couple days...I started bleeding really heavy, and I was real sick to my stomach," she testified. "It was to the point where I was, like, crawling around, and I was throwing up like every five to ten minutes...."

Abrams went to see her primary care doctor, who took cultures and advised Abrams to go back to Gosnell as soon as possible. Gosnell also took cultures, but he never got in touch with her about her test results. Very quickly, her own doctor phoned and told her to go to Crozer-Chester Medical Center right away.

Doctors at Crozer discovered that Shay had an abscess the size of a grapefruit and a blood clot in her heart. She spent two weeks in the hospital.

Shay Abrams's health has never been the same. She suffers from shortness of breath and is constantly stressed. She became pregnant again, and her new pregnancy was deemed "high risk" following the abortion. Abrams's son has health problems, including a compromised immune system. She says she can't stop thinking of the abortion, and how it could have killed her and left her daughter without a mother. "Just knowing that, today, I wouldn't be able to be here for my daughter and I wouldn't have my son."

In his defense of Gosnell, Jack McMahon introduced reams of consent forms that Abrams had signed at the clinics in Delaware and Pennsylvania, showing she had given consent to the procedure. One form also indicated she had consented to be given Digoxin, which, if administered properly, would kill the baby in her womb.

"You agreed to an injection, a needle that would kill the baby inside your uterus; correct?" McMahon asked.

"Yes."

"And you agreed to that and a needle was given to you; right?"

"Yes."

"And as this says," he asked, holding up one of the forms, "that will make the baby not viable, correct?"

"Yes."

"No further questions."

But there was a big problem with McMahon's defense. As Gosnell injected Abrams, he didn't do another ultrasound. Normally, abortion doctors will use the ultrasound to make sure they inject the fatal drug directly into the heart of the fetus. When the Digoxin is injected correctly, the baby should be guaranteed to die. But without an ultrasound, it's practically impossible to ensure the baby's heart has been pierced.

And Abrams was confused. She couldn't say for certain whether the Digoxin injection was to her abdomen or her cervix. But she was very clear on two other details: the injection was given without the use of an ultrasound; and the baby didn't die. Baby Boy A was indeed alive. He was moving long after Shay was given the injection.

The life of Baby Boy A was short and violent. But even though he lived for just twenty minutes after he had been born, his brief struggle for life had a meaning and a purpose. When he curled into that fetal position and Gosnell's staff saw him do it, he helped put America's biggest serial killer in prison for the rest of his life.

In 2007, Shanice Manning was fifteen years old, living in Secane, just outside Philadelphia. She was in eighth grade but had an eighteen-year-old boyfriend named Andre. In March of that year, she realized she was pregnant. She was skinny, just like Shay Abrams. And she did a good job hiding her pregnancy with big sweaters and continuing with all her regular activities, running track and playing sports. She waited until September to tell her mother. By that time the baby had started to kick.

Her mother was upset. She was a single mom, too, having gotten pregnant herself at sixteen. She wanted a better life for Shanice, and in her world that meant Shanice having an abortion.

"I wanted to keep my baby, but I was only fifteen," Manning told the jury. Her boyfriend and his mother met Shanice and her mother at 3801 Lancaster Avenue on September 7, 2007. Instead of following the law and waiting the prescribed twenty-four hours to begin the abortion, Gosnell immediately did an ultrasound and inserted laminaria sticks to start dilating the cervix.

One of the saddest parts of all the trial testimony was Manning's description of her conversation with Gosnell that day. It has stayed with her. It has also stayed with everyone else who was in the courtroom.

Joanne Pescatore asked if she had spoken at all with the doctor before he did the ultrasound or inserted the sticks.

"Yes," she replied. "I asked him what's the sex of my baby, and he told me, if I'm good enough, I can know. But he never told me."

"Why did you want to know the sex?" Pescatore asked.

Manning struggled and became emotional with her answer. "Because I just—because I like could have—that could have made me think like, well, I don't know—I just wanted to know."

"Could have made you think what, Shanice?" Pescatore asked gently. "It's okay."

"I still wanted to keep her," she answered. "So, like, if I think…if I would have known more about the situation, I would have definitely made my decision on what I wanted to do and I would have talked it over with my mom, because my mom asked me, like, are you comfortable? Are you sure? So…"

Pescatore asked her, "Were you comfortable or sure about your decision?"

"No," she replied.

Manning signed the twenty-four-hour counseling form *on the same day* that Gosnell inserted the dilators and started the abortion. She was told to return the next afternoon to have more laminaria sticks inserted, which took about twenty minutes. And she was told to return again the following day.

That was a Sunday. The clinic was closed, but she was instructed to enter through the side door at 8:00 a.m. The only people there were Gosnell and a woman Shanice hadn't seen before who was wearing ordinary clothes, not a nurse's uniform. Gosnell did not introduce Pearl as his wife.

Nor had Manning been told before she arrived what she could expect to happen. Gosnell explained now. "Gosnell told me that he got to put a needle in my belly to break down the baby," Manning testified. But she did not know what that meant. "He put the ultrasound to my stomach; and then the other hand, he put the needle to make sure—I think he was looking for the baby's head," she said. "I believe he was looking for the baby's head."

"Did he say that?" Pescatore asked.

"Yeah. Well, he was looking for like—'cause he couldn't find the baby. So like when he started to look for it, he found her and he just put the needle…"

"So he was both operating the ultrasound and putting the needle in your belly at the same time?" the prosecutor asked.

"Yes."

"Did he explain to you what was in the needle that he was injecting into your belly?" Pescatore asked.

"No," Manning answered.

That Sunday session also took about twenty minutes. Manning and her mother were sent home and instructed to return the next day.

"What was supposed to happen the next day?" Pescatore asked.

"I was to finish the procedure and get rid of my baby."

They got back in their car and drove home. Within ten minutes, Manning was in agony. She had not been given any painkillers.

That night she started to have contractions. Manning said it "felt like my pelvis was going to break in half, I hurt so bad."

Her boyfriend—who was her ex-boyfriend by then—rubbed her back and put hot towels on her to try to ease the pain. At 3:00 a.m. she woke in her mother's bed with severe cramps. Her water broke. Her mother told her to get into the bathtub. Shanice stood there hunched over while her mother frantically called Gosnell. He never picked up.

Shanice's mother drove her to Taylor Hospital, but the attending nurse said they didn't do deliveries. They called an ambulance, and Manning was taken to Crozer Hospital.

Her mother told the admitting physician about the abortion, and he replied that she was too far along to be having an abortion. That was the first time Shanice heard this. She became very upset.

"Why were you upset?" Pescatore asked her.

"Because if I would have known how far along [I was]" she replied, "I would have kept my baby."

The staff at Crozer couldn't find the baby's heartbeat. The baby was dead and would still have to be delivered. A nurse removed the laminaria sticks, and the baby was delivered a few minutes later, stillborn.

"Then what happened?" Pescatore asked.

"They made me hold her then…"

Recounting that in court, Manning broke down. Judge Minehart instructed the bailiff to give her some water. A minute later, she was ready to continue.

"I held her," she said. "Later on I wanted to see her one more time before I left the hospital, but I never seen her again."

Dr. Frederick Hellman, Delaware County's chief medical examiner at the time, conducted Baby Girl Manning's postmortem the next day—September 11, at 11:00 a.m. He recorded that the baby was well formed: thirty-seven and a half centimeters long, or about fifteen inches, and weighing 945 grams, or a little over two pounds. He judged she was approximately twenty-eight or -nine weeks old. The grand jury included a photograph of the baby in their report. It's a haunting, unforgettable picture of a perfect baby girl with a head of dark hair.

Hellman was unable to determine a cause of death, but he was certain Gosnell had broken the law. He reported Gosnell to the Pennsylvania Department of Health.

We have seen the letter Kermit Gosnell sent to Irene Lafore, the medical/legal investigator at the office of the medical examiner, County of Delaware (in Pennsylvania), in which Gosnell states that the "gestational age of the pregnancy was considered to be 24 and 1/2 weeks based on a biperietal diameter of 61mm."[2] In writing this, Gosnell was admitting to an illegal abortion.

The Pennsylvania Department of Health did nothing.

SEVEN

GOSNELL ON TRIAL

It was a trial full of surprises. But maybe the most surprising thing for Kermit Gosnell's prosecutors was that there was a trial at all. They were confident that the evidence against Gosnell was more than enough to convict him. The grand jury report was damning, and the witnesses against him would be compelling. "We thought he was going to plead," assistant DA Christine Wechsler told us.[1]

But in the face of all reason, Gosnell wouldn't back down.

He rejected one plea deal that would have meant he would spend the rest of his life in prison but would have spared his wife Pearl from incarceration and allowed her to keep their family home. At the very least Gosnell's teenage daughter Jenna, whom he claimed to be very close to, would have had her mother and a familiar place to live during her high school years. But it was not to be—the prosecution had not accounted for Gosnell's narcissism. He turned the offer down flat.

But that was a pretrial offer. The prosecution felt confident that Gosnell would have second thoughts when he walked into the courtroom and saw twelve jurors staring at him somberly. And he would be foolish not to think twice about a deal when he saw the list of expert witnesses the government had lined up against him. But Gosnell never wavered. He rarely lost his cheery, relaxed demeanor. On the first day he arrived in court, he was smiling, greeting strangers like old friends, complimenting and trying to flirt with the female security staff.

Still, even then, the prosecutors felt confident that Gosnell and his lawyer would hear their opening argument and realize he didn't have a chance. "After openings, it was like there was no way he was going to endure it," Wechsler said of the mood on the prosecution team.

But, as she came to believe, Gosnell simply had to be the center of attention. His desire to appear as the smartest guy in the room overpowered all reason and good sense. In the end, that's why Gosnell decided to go to trial. "He was that much of an egomaniac and wanted the show," Wechsler said.

The trial began on March 18, 2013.

Gosnell insisted he was innocent. He proclaims his innocence to this day. And he was certain he would be acquitted of all charges once the jury had heard all the facts.

In retrospect, Gosnell's confidence may not have been entirely misplaced. His was a unique case. The prosecution couldn't be certain that the jury would understand the born-alive law, which was largely untested. Perhaps the jurors would simply ignore the evidence and acquit Gosnell based on their pro-abortion beliefs.

That possibility wasn't far-fetched. Judge Caldwell-Hughes had already ensured that the grand jury report was written in a way so that it did not indict abortion alongside Gosnell and his associates.

And the Gosnell jury was very pro-abortion. Philadelphia is a liberal city. Just about everyone involved in the jury selection was pro-choice. In the tribal politics that exist in America today, the prosecution and defense probably believed that "their people"—pro-choicers—could be trusted to put politics aside and come to a fair verdict. Of the empaneled members, at least nine told NBC 10 News that they were pro-choice and two had said they were neither pro-choice nor pro-life.[2] It seems to be a feature of American life that liberals rarely view themselves as ideological—but their opponents always are. One source close to the prosecution, who asked not to be named, said the legal team did not deliberately exclude jurors with pro-life opinions but they didn't want jurors who might view the women who had abortions unsympathetically. Though they didn't explicitly say so, both the prosecution and the defense clearly assumed that pro-lifers could not be trusted to be fair and objective jurors, and so through jury questionnaires and questioning by lawyers they ended up being kept out of the process.

The prosecution knew almost from the outset they would need to present a case that focused on Gosnell's crimes and skirted the rather obvious argument that he was simply providing a service that most of his patients wanted. Wechsler shared with us her frustration with her supervisors at the district attorney's office who questioned why the city should spend taxpayer dollars putting a man on trial for murdering babies that their mothers didn't want in the first place. "It was ugly. There was a lot of fighting back then," she told us. "It was love/hate. Everybody hated the case...because it was a headache, because it was controversial." On the other hand, "They loved it when they got good press out of it and there was good press out of it."

But as the trial approached, there was more hate for the case than love. Just before the trial, Wechsler remembers being grilled by a new supervisor with some blunt questions: Was there even a case? Could she really make a jury care that a crime had taken place? "I remember one of my bad days... [with] him saying to me, 'You tell me why I should give a damn about these dead babies. Their own mothers don't want them. Are you going to be able to sell that?'"

Confronted with such aggressive and undiplomatic language, Wechsler's first reaction was to dismiss it as the uncaring comments of someone who didn't understand the case. "I was like, I hate you—you are such a man! You can't say that!" But her supervisor was asking the question that would concern the jury and that so many in the pro-life movement fear to ask. If this was murder, then why weren't the mothers prosecuted, too? Weren't they at the very least accessories to the crime? In America and most other parts of the world, if you are the getaway driver during a robbery when someone is murdered, then you are just as guilty of the murder as the gunman. It's a joint enterprise in the eyes of the law.

And many of these women were more than getaway drivers. They were paying for the killing. Wechsler understood the hurdle she needed to jump. "You realize you have to focus on more than just dead babies that are 'throwaways'—that people consider as throwaways," she said. They had to make the evidence of Gosnell's guilt so overwhelming, that the jury would ignore the possible culpability of the women in the crime.

In the end, though, it wouldn't be Wechsler's fight to finish. After so many years of being given "every dead woman and child in the city," Wechsler was looking for a change. She was the mother of four children, and she had given birth twice around the time of the investigation and the trial. Her daughter Georgia was six months old in February 2010, when the three amigos and their joint task force raided Gosnell's office. She had her son, Timothy, in August 2012, just seven months before the trial got underway. Wechsler had been active in the pretrial hearings and motions, but she needed a change.

"I was done. I was spent," she said. "I had little kids, and this is so unhealthy for a thirty-year-old woman to be doing. I lived in an alternate universe." She told us how she would go to kindergarten and be a mom for her oldest child, Billy, and then drive straight to the medical examiner's office where "everything is death and dying."

She had a job offer from the governor's office in Harrisburg "that you don't really say no to." Between that and a city wage tax that was threatening the viability of her husband Tim's custom prosthetic limb manufacturing business, relocating from Philadelphia made a lot of sense. "My husband was going to divorce me," she joked. "Especially if I stayed, and gave up the opportunity in the governor's office, to try a case that was probably going to go away before trial anyway."

Still, it wasn't easy for Wechsler to walk away from a case that she had worked so hard on—this was a case she had cut open babies' skulls for—and in which she had uncovered arguably America's biggest serial killer. Resigning from it was a tough and long thought-out decision.

Wechsler felt more comfortable about her departure when her colleague, Ed Cameron, assured her before the trial was set to begin that the case would be in good hands. "Ed came and said to me, 'I'll try it for you. Just go.... Take the job. This is better for your family.'" Cameron was an able and tenacious lawyer. And Wechsler's co-counsel Joanne Pescatore was already on top of the case. At any rate, as Cameron told Wechsler, nobody would remember who tried the case anyway. People would only remember the outcome.

In addition to the benefit of a pro-abortion jury, Gosnell was lucky in the judge assigned to the case. In Philadelphia, as in most of the country, judges are selected at random to avoid any appearance of favoritism or conflict of interest. The prosecution team was dismayed to learn that Judge Jeffrey Minehart would preside over the case. Minehart was a former prosecutor; before he was appointed to the bench, in fact, he had been Ed Cameron's supervisor in the DA's office. But the two men never had more than a friendly working relationship. On the other hand, Minehart and Jack McMahon, Gosnell's lawyer, were drinking buddies. And Minehart had a reputation among prosecutors for being too easy on defendants and allowing defense lawyers entirely too much leeway. No one connected to the investigation would say so on the record, but some were genuinely concerned that the judge's friendship with the defense attorney would hurt their case.[3]

And McMahon is no run of the mill trial lawyer. He's widely regarded as the best defense lawyer in Philadelphia. McMahon is a formidable and tenacious advocate—a former prosecutor himself—who is never intimidated and has a sharp eye for weaknesses in the prosecution's case. Jim Wood told us if he ever found himself on trial, he would want McMahon defending him. In fact, McMahon's next big case after the Gosnell trial involved six of Woody's fellow Philadelphia police officers facing corruption, racketeering, robbery, and civil rights charges. They were accused of beating up drug dealers and stealing hundreds of thousands of dollars in drugs, cash, and luxury goods, including Rolex watches. The prosecution produced a string of witnesses who detailed criminal activities on the part of the officers. In the post-Ferguson environment of distrust toward cops, a jury might easily have been receptive to those stories. But McMahon systematically destroyed the credibility of the prosecution's witnesses, who were mostly criminals, through skillful questioning and biting sarcasm. All six officers were acquitted.

With Gosnell, McMahon was defending a doctor in a case that depended on unsure and untested scientific evidence and testimony from witnesses who were also co-conspirators and whose own prison sentences depended on their cooperation with the government. Just as in the later police corruption case, McMahon could attack their credibility and claim their testimony was self-serving, to ensure they received shorter prison terms.

In that light, perhaps Gosnell's decision not to accept a plea deal wasn't as unreasonable as it appeared.

———

Another big surprise was the dearth of reporting on the case. The prosecution believed the media would turn out in force for the trial. They had reserved Room 304 on the second floor of the Philadelphia Justice Center—one of the largest courtrooms in the building. But they were wildly overestimating the media interest. Very few journalists turned up, and those who did tended to be local reporters from the *Daily News* and the *Inquirer.* The empty courtroom—along with the horrific images that dominated the proceedings—lent a weird atmosphere to the case. It had the feeling of being utterly removed from the real world. The jury was seeing images that were difficult to digest or comprehend, and the lack of significant media coverage or public interest also lent an air of unreality to the proceedings. Until the press was shamed into covering the trial, Room 304 was a strange and surreal place.

Between the judge and the jury box, just above the witness stand, was a rogues' gallery of mug shots of clinic staff. This was to help the jury put faces to names when Gosnell's employees were mentioned in testimony. But McMahon also tried to use the photos to push the impression that a lot of the evidence against Gosnell was coming from people who were also in the criminal justice system, who would say anything to avoid going to jail or to get a lighter sentence.

The prosecutors also had a major setback with their plan to take the trial jury on a field trip to 3801 Lancaster Avenue so they, like the grand jury, could see firsthand the degradation of Gosnell's clinic. Anyone who visited could not fail to be horrified by the smell of stale urine, the bloodstained walls, and the dirty and broken equipment. Pescatore and Cameron also wanted the jurors to see the room Gosnell set aside for his white patients—the only consistently clean and sanitized room in the building.

Unfortunately, the building had been left unattended and unheated during a harsh Philadelphia winter, and the inevitable happened. A pipe burst and the building was flooded. Several ceilings had collapsed before anyone noticed and shut the water off. At that point, the building was too dangerous for visitors.

Despite the setbacks, Pescatore felt confident as she stood up to deliver her opening statement. The prosecution had the bodies, they had the files, and they had the testimony of Gosnell's accomplices, but most importantly they had the photos of the babies—all looking older than twenty-four weeks, and most with stab wounds in back of their necks.

McMahon made a valiant defense, but the photos were deeply affecting—and effective. He tried with some success to portray Gosnell as just another abortionist in a bloody but legal business carried on out of the public eye and the public mind. But even if Gosnell was no outlier, as McMahon argued, the jury had a difficult time seeing past those images.

Juror Sarah Glinski told ABC News that having to view the pictures of the dead babies was the hardest part of the case. "Seeing those photos and just having to say to myself, 'This did happen to those kids. There were children that died at the hands of this man.' That was what was hard for me. To admit that that kind of evil exists in this world," she said.[4]

Joe Carroll told us that seeing the photographs was a turning point for many of the jurors. "The boy," he said, referring to Baby Boy A, "just that big baby…I mean, that was really, really disturbing just to see that. It was…that was pretty overwhelming. That's when we, as the jury…we all went back into the jury room, looked at each other, and like…" He trailed off. "That's probably the point I said this guy is guilty," Carroll said.[5]

But Pescatore had quite a bit of ground to cover before she could show the jury those pictures. Confronted with a jury she knew to be almost exclusively pro-abortion, Pescatore stuck to the line that so many had repeated and maybe some had actually believed. "The first thing I want you to be assured of, ladies and gentlemen," she began, "is that this is not a case about abortion." This was a case about "the murder of seven born-alive infants at 3801 Lancaster Avenue, the murder of Karnamaya Mongar, a native of the Bhutan back in November of 2009."

And yet a case that was "not about abortion" kept coming back to abortion. Pescatore addressed the problem of the mothers who were paying Gosnell to be rid of their babies. "I want your focus to be on the murder of those babies," she told the jurors. "Not that they were there to be aborted, not what their mothers had in mind when they came to that location—what happened when those babies were born alive. That's what your focus needs to be."

Gosnell, explained Pescatore, was "a wolf in sheep's clothing." Though the Women's Medical Society "sounds good and looks good on the outside," inside Gosnell was running "a charnel house," "a house of horrors" where babies' spinal cords were routinely snipped.

She warned the jurors they would need to sit and listen to a difficult case. "It's going to be graphic…horrible to witness…horrible to hear. And it's going to be even worse to see." Pescatore described how Gosnell went about casually killing the babies born alive and would callously dispose of their remains in empty limeade bottles or kitty litter containers. "They were treated like trash," she said. Pescatore talked about the bloodstained blankets and recliners, the single-use instruments that Gosnell used over and over, and the cats—the filthy, flea-infested cats that roamed the clinic freely and used the entire building as a litter box.

Gosnell's approach to medicine was "really simple," Pescatore said: "Keep your volume high, expenses low, and maximize your profit." Later on, she repeated the point. "This case is all about the money—two hundred and forty thousand dollars was found at his house." Pescatore noticed some of the jurors react with surprise. "You're looking at me like you're shocked," she said. "Well, don't be. Two hundred and forty thousand dollars. You can make a lot of money doing abortions. I told you, women are desperate, especially when they're past the legal limit in most states."

Pescatore pointed out that Gosnell's Women's Medical Society had become the go-to clinic for women who were too far advanced to have legal abortions. "These women came from all over the country. Even Puerto Rico, but you know word gets around. It's not a big community if you need to get it done where you can get it done, and these women came up with the money. Shayquana Abrams? Her abortion cost twenty-five hundred dollars. She was twenty-nine weeks pregnant. She got it done."

She got it done. Though Pescatore and Cameron weren't keen to call attention to the women who sought Gosnell's services, the jurors couldn't help but blame them, too. After the trial ended, journalist J. D. Mullane spoke with three jurors. "It was interesting to learn," Mullane wrote, "that they felt the women who procured the late-term abortions at his clinic should have been charged with murder, too."

"You know when you're expecting a baby at that late date," Joe Carroll told Mullane, "there's no excuse."

There were women from many backgrounds and many parts of the United States who went to Gosnell, but most of his patients were local, minority, and poor. Many were very young, drug addicts, or otherwise broken. Many were ok with aborting their children at six, seven, or even eight months; and many were ok with doing it multiple times. Some appeared to use his clinic as a form of after-the-fact contraception.

The repeat customers were one of the main planks in McMahon's defense of Gosnell. How could the clinic really be a house of horrors if women kept returning for repeat procedures, he argued.

Many of the women regretted their abortions.

Christine Wechsler interviewed many former patients of Gosnell's, and she saw some patterns. "After this broke, I would spend days upon days just talking to women who were in their 30s, who had undergone procedures in their teens, when their grandmother and mother dragged them in. They were crying about who they are now."

Many of the women whose babies Gosnell aborted have changed and grown and are struggling with what happened to them when they were only teenagers. "I'm surprised, they grow up to be church people, to be like those faith-filled Christian women that learned from their being young. But they were always on their own too," Wechsler said.

Davida Clarke's story is harrowing. She was a young African American mother with one child, a daughter. Speaking in the *3801 Lancaster* documentary, she admits she started hanging out with the "wrong crowd." She says she was raped and in 2001 she had an abortion at the clinic. She was six months pregnant. "I remember it like it was yesterday. There was a fish tank in the waiting area. Then you had a receptionist that was like all she wanted was your money immediately.... They finally called my name. I went upstairs. I remember walking through looking and seeing some women that looked half dead in these bloody recliner chairs. There was blood all over the floor. I just kept on. I didn't see [Gosnell] until I was hooked up with IVs and when they put the heart monitor around me. That's when I decided I can't do this.

"I just…I can't do it. And he's like, 'Stop being a little baby.' And he's pounding on my legs. 'Stop being a little baby. Stop being a little baby.' Now, I'm outnumbered. All these women came in. I'm tied to the bed. Next thing I know, I was out of it."

When Davida woke up, she was very groggy, she was in a recliner beside another girl, she couldn't work out where she was for a while, but one thing she knew straight away, she wasn't pregnant anymore. "I knew I wasn't pregnant anymore. I was crying. I kept saying, 'I want my baby. I want my baby.' They just ignored me."

A month after the abortion Davida was diagnosed with a venereal disease, which she is convinced she contracted during the abortion because the place was so dirty. The abortion has changed her life. She says that since then she has had four miscarriages and has been unable to bring a baby to full term. "I can't have babies as a result. I'm married. I have a daughter that wants a brother or sister. I can't give her that. I want a child. I can't have that. Every year that goes past I think of my baby that I would have had."[6]

Robyn Reid was fifteen in 1998 when she was forcibly brought to the clinic for an abortion she didn't want. Her grandmother was insisting she had to have the abortion. Reid planned to tell the doctor that she didn't want to go through with it and then, with his help, escape the clinic.

But Gosnell was having none of it. He shouted at her, "I don't have time for this!" Reid told the *Daily News* the doctor ripped off her clothes, slapped her, forced her onto a bed, tied her down and pumped so much anesthesia into her that she lost consciousness.[7]

Another patient who spoke to the 3801 project anonymously had multiple abortions at Gosnell's clinic. She's one of the repeat customers that McMahon used in his defense as evidence of the good work that Gosnell did, but her story is not much of an endorsement. Her first pregnancy was by a man who quickly skipped town for Jamaica. She felt alone and believed that her only choice was an abortion.

When she became pregnant again she returned to Gosnell's clinic. "I asked them is it okay that I get another abortion.... Fine. Fine. They even had this woman sit down with me, and she told me that women in Brazil have at least twenty-one abortions. They are still able to conceive. That was it for me. That was where I basically said this must be okay. It was a norm for me after she had coached me into believing that that was the norm. In the next fourteen years of my life, I had eight abortions. I look back at it, God, what was I thinking?...I was led to believe that it was okay every time I came in there, it was okay. It was okay to treat it as a form of contraception. Once I started getting older, I really thought I found the right person. We just could not conceive." Her doctor said it was because her body was so damaged by the multiple abortions. "My body was so ravaged from abortions."[8]

We spoke to a patient named Pamela, who was thirty-five with a college degree when she had an abortion in Gosnell's clinic in 1997 even though she was seven months pregnant. "I didn't think I was going to be able to take care of him, even though I have a degree, I'm a chemical engineer, I got into a low place," she said.

Pamela says she was referred by a local Philadelphia doctor. She took her five-year-old son to the abortion. He sat in the waiting room with her sister.

"It was all very fast, they didn't even give any counseling. It was all about the money, he just got rich outa that," she said. "The way people got there was that people were in a bad place and he did late term abortions," she added.

Like many other patients, Pamela woke up during the procedure and remembers graphic and disturbing details. "I can still see it in my mind clear as day. It was such a dirty, raggedy room. I woke up. He started beating on me with his fist to go back to sleep 'Lay down! Lay down! Stop kicking me,' he yelled, and I was helpless and he was yanking, yanking, yanking on the baby."

She saw Gosnell holding her baby. "When he took the baby out, he had this mad man look on his face; he was crazy, really crazy." When we asked her what he did with the baby, she said, "I don't want to talk about that bit right now." She was charged twelve hundred dollars.

After the abortion she saw Gosnell and he laughed about hitting her.

She wonders why none of the neighbors ever reported the clinic to the police. "I wondered why nobody heard because the window was open, as you walk up the steps there's like a window that opens.... I woke up screaming, but I don't understand why nobody ever complained about the screams. I don't know how it went on for so long; there had to be bloodcurdling screams coming from there all the time, because I woke up with blood curdling screams."

When Pamela saw the raid on his clinic on the nightly news she thought, "They've finally got him! It should have been sooner; how did he not get caught earlier?"

She says she went into early menopause shortly after and blames the abortion. She would have liked to have had another child. Her opinion of abortion has changed. "I don't think it's such a good idea, women have so many other different options, like open adoption."[9]

Pescatore promised the jury they would get a "whole education" about abortion, and they surely did. They heard from doctors who explained obstetrics, gynecology, anesthesia, toxicology, "and the abortion procedure itself." What Pescatore didn't say—because she had no idea—was that the evidence would shake the beliefs of many jurors who professed to be pro-choice but hadn't given much thought to the particulars of what choice really means. And it wasn't just the jury that would re-examine their basic assumptions about abortion. Prosecutors, several journalists, and even Gosnell's own lawyer experienced changes of heart and mind. Not all of them ended up in the pro-life camp, by any means, but almost everyone emerged from the Gosnell trial more skeptical about abortion than when they started.

"Almost everyone who was in some way pro-choice, who spent significant time at the Gosnell trial, was less pro-choice at the end," reporter J. D. Mullane said when we spoke with him. "This change was probably because they were for the first time hearing about the reality of abortion from experts under oath. The witnesses may have been lobbyists or pundits or ideologues or all three—but they were not allowed to be such in court. They had to tell the truth and they had to tell it in detail."[10]

Ironically, in a trial that featured so many graphic, gory images projected on the courtroom wall, it was an expert witness's testimony about the realities of abortion that elicited the only audible gasps from the jury box. Dr. Charles Benjamin, an OB/GYN with thirty-three years of experience, was asked how many abortions he had performed over the course of his career. At least forty thousand, came his matter-of-fact reply. The jury was shocked. The prosecution and the defense got a glimpse of how difficult it would be to read the jury in this case.[11]

But Pescatore wasn't leading a seminar on the morality of abortion. She wanted the jury to focus on the legal requirements for abortion providers in Pennsylvania. "The number one thing is the twenty-four-hour waiting period," she told them. "It's not like you can walk in and say, 'I want an abortion,' and you get it. A woman has a right to go in and be counseled before she has an abortion." But Gosnell had flatly ignored the twenty-four-hour waiting period. He ignored the law, Pescatore said, out of simple greed.

"Money. That was the only law that Dr. Gosnell knew," she said. "You went to 3801 Lancaster Avenue where no laws were followed. None, zero."

The facts would show that Gosnell didn't do "normal, legal abortions" largely because it was both cheaper and easier for him to induce labor, wait for the woman to give birth, and then kill the baby outside of the womb with scissors.

Pescatore explained that it didn't matter if the babies weren't viable outside the womb—that is, if they would have died eventually even with medical attention. Once those babies were born alive, she told them, the law was clear: it was murder to hasten their deaths with a snip of the neck. "You see, if a baby is born alive, it's alive and you and nobody else has the right to take some kind of a step to kill it, whether it's twenty-three weeks, twenty-four weeks, nineteen weeks, whatever it is," she said. "You're a doctor. You have to do the minimal to keep that baby alive. If the baby is alive and you don't want it to be, that doesn't mean you have the right to take a pair of scissors and plunge it into its neck and sever its spinal cord, what they did on an everyday basis."

"They called it snipping, and he told all those workers that it was okay. Well, it's not okay. It's not okay in this state and in any other state. If a baby is born outside of its mother's womb, you can't kill it. If it moves or breathes or has a pulsating umbilical cord or heartbeat for a second, a minute, you can't kill it. That's murder. That's a human being," she said.

As the trial progressed the jury would come to understand the crucial distinctions in the law. The question of Gosnell's guilt or innocence hinged on whether or not those seven babies had breathed or moved before Gosnell or one of his assistants killed them.

Gosnell's employees testified that they would sometimes ask the doctor why he plunged scissors into the back of those babies' necks. "To ensure fetal demise," he replied.

"Are you kidding me?" Pescatore exclaimed. "To ensure fetal demise on a live, breathing, moving infant."

Pescatore described how Gosnell created false medical files. Given Pennsylvania's prohibition of late-term abortion, Gosnell needed to record a gestational age that aligned with the law, she explained. By manipulating the ultrasound and teaching his staff to do the same, he could make the babies seem smaller than they were. Pescatore explained that the trick was to move the transducer further away and "magically" a fetus that was twenty-eight, twenty-nine, or thirty weeks along was 24.5 weeks. "Magically."

Despite his mistake about the gestational age limit on legal abortions—as we have seen, Pennsylvania actually forbids them at twenty-four weeks—Kermit Gosnell still believes himself to be a very clever man. Just ask him. When we spoke to him at Huntingdon Prison, he casually dropped references to just how clever people say he is.[12] But arrogance leads to hubris, and hubris leads to stupid mistakes. The doctor was charged with two hundred counts of falsifying documents. In the unregulated world of Pennsylvania abortions after Governor Tom Ridge established the Department of Health's hands-off policy, Gosnell's crimes were tolerated—even when his law-breaking was brought to the attention of the authorities by other doctors. And Gosnell thought he could get away with admitting his crimes to a cop he believed was not as smart as he is. "He actually tells [Detective Wood] that night that 10 to 20 percent of the fetuses that are in the refrigerator, they're past 24 weeks," Pescatore informed the jury.

Gosnell's magical ultrasounds created a big problem for the defense. Every time he had indicated a fetus was 24.5 weeks, rather than under twenty-four weeks, in gestational age, it was a handwritten admission of guilt.

Gosnell explained away the discrepancy when we interviewed him. It was a simple matter of statistics, he said. The explanation allowed him to boast just how clever and multi-talented he was and made all the faked but still illegal ultrasounds perfectly legal. "I took every available statistics class at Temple," he told us. And because of that, he explained, he automatically rounded figures down. He claimed that a baby that was 24.5 weeks on an ultrasound was statistically twenty-four weeks old—and therefore within the legal limit.[13]

It's a fairly ridiculous explanation, but it does highlight the capricious absurdity of the law. Leave aside the question of whether life begins at conception; those who believe that also believe all abortion is wrong, period. But for those who don't believe that, the question of when life begins remains—and the question of legality, to what point it should be legal to abort the baby. Various state laws treat second- and third-trimester abortions differently. In Pennsylvania, it's legal to destroy a fetus at twenty-three weeks and six days, but a felony to destroy that same fetus one day later. Put another way, it is legal to abort a child one minute before the twenty-three-week, six-day cutoff but illegal to do so one minute later. The fetus has not changed or gotten older in any significant way, but one abortion is a legally protected right, and the other is a crime.

The jury never heard Gosnell's lame statistical explanation. He never took the stand, so all the jurors had to go on were hundreds of handwritten admissions of guilt and one statement to a police officer admitting he'd broken the law. Even the greatest lawyer in the world would have difficulty overcoming that.

———

Pescatore described the seven babies that Gosnell was accused of killing.

It was a long and disturbing description for the jury. And it was an account that did not escape McMahon's skillful questioning and probing.

Pescatore tried to draw jurors' thoughts away from the mothers who wanted to kill their babies and direct their attention to the brief lives of the babies Gosnell had murdered. She wanted to drive home their fleeting humanity.

She also needed to prove that they had been alive—at least for a few seconds—after delivery. That wouldn't be easy.

"Do you know what Gosnell said about Baby Boy A? He said the baby is big enough to walk me to the bus stop. That baby, that beautiful baby—that was born alive. Baby Boy A, that he took a pair of scissors and plunged into its neck."

Baby B was the twenty-eight-week-old recovered from the clinic. "He's got a hole in the back of his neck that has to be three to four inches," she said. "Just ask yourself the common sense question: if that baby is not born alive, why are you snipping its neck?"

"You know that baby was born alive," Pescatore told them.

Pescatore ran through the list of murders quickly.

"Baby C. Lynda Williams killed that baby. Baby D is the baby Adrienne Moton killed, that was swimming in the toilet. Baby E. Ashley Baldwin heard the baby whine, and Gosnell killed that baby. Baby F. Steve Massof saw the baby's leg jerk. Dr. Gosnell snipped the neck. Baby G. Steve Massof saw what he called a 'respiratory excursion'—breathing. Gosnell snipped that neck."

Appealing to a jury's emotions is a well-trodden path for both prosecutors and defense lawyers. But it can be risky. Before the jury headed into deliberations, Judge Minehart would instruct them that "you know it must be true" is not sufficient for a conviction. Pescatore's opening was not above emphasizing details that had nothing to do with the charges against Gosnell but would resonate with jurors.

Pescatore explained to the racially mixed jury how Gosnell treated his white patients better than his black patients. "Can you imagine that in this day and age?" she asked. Gosnell's employees would testify that he needed to be consulted on everything that happened to the white women, and "if he wasn't, there was hell to pay.... He even put them in cleaner offices," Pescatore said. "He had conversations with them. He treated them like they were real people." And the minority women? "They were just left in these rotten recliners, drugged up, he never met them, overmedicated. He didn't have five seconds for them," she told the jury.

After highlighting Gosnell's shabby, second-rate treatment of his black and brown clients, Pescatore segued into Karnamaya Mongar's death, which she framed as an act of depraved racism. In fact, Gosnell's slow and haphazard reaction to Mongar's deteriorating condition was depraved, but it was probably more about self-preservation than an irrational dislike of her skin color. Mongar's death threatened his murderous, money-making racket. That needed to be preserved at all costs.

Pescatore told the jury about the circumstances of Mongar's arrival in the United States as a political refugee. She described how the untrained and unlicensed staff dispensed anesthesia with no monitoring equipment, how Lynda Williams noticed Mongar's color had changed and that she wasn't breathing right, and how Williams told Gosnell and Gosnell ignored her. Pescatore laid out in detail Gosnell's inept, panicked response. His unlicensed colleague Eileen O'Neill tried to help, but Mongar was unresponsive. They called 911. The paramedics couldn't get the gurney into the building—and the building shouldn't have been allowed to operate as a clinic for precisely that reason. And by the time Mongar did arrive at the hospital, Pescatore told jurors, it was too late for her.

Then Pescatore raised the issue of the severed feet.

"I don't know how to explain to you what you're going to see when you see those feet," she told them. "You're going to see five jars of baby feet that were at this facility. Because you see, during some of the procedures, he would chop off the baby's feet and save them in jars in a cabinet labeled with their mother's name and the date.... Mr. Cameron and I have asked every expert we've ever talked to—two abortion doctors—what is this? Who does this? Why would this be done? Nobody can tell us," Pescatore said. "They never heard of it. Disturbing. That's an understatement."

Pescatore came as close as possible to describing America's most prolific serial killer as a serial killer without actually using the words. "Trophies," she said. "Was he keeping trophies for what he had done?" Pescatore did not—and could not—say that only serial killers keep trophies. But she hoped the jury would get the hint. The assistant DA felt confident as she sat down and the court took a short break. She had laid out in emotional terms the lives of Gosnell's victims; she had graphically described the squalor of Gosnell's clinic; and she had exposed his racism and greed. She was more certain than ever that Gosnell had miscalculated badly by rejecting the plea deal.

Jack McMahon's job was to demolish the case Pescatore had laid out. It was clear from the start that McMahon wouldn't allow the prosecution to get away with anything. His strategy throughout the trial was attack first and ask the judge's permission later.

McMahon began by attacking Pescatore's boss, Philadelphia district attorney Seth Williams, for giving a dramatic press conference the day Gosnell was indicted. Cameron leapt to his feet with an objection. Judge Minehart called for a sidebar out of earshot of the jury, where McMahon snapped loudly—perhaps for the jurors' benefit, "For God's sake! Already, he's trying to stop me. I didn't say a word during their opening statements."

Such theatrics characterized McMahon's defense; they were central to his strategy of positioning his client as a victim of the establishment. Cameron's immediate interruption meant the defense attorney could play up the apparently unreasonable, overbearing behavior by the prosecutor from the outset. McMahon wanted the jury to know that Cameron and Pescatore were trying to shut down a good doctor and the good lawyer representing him.

When McMahon resumed his opening statement, he returned to the subject of Williams's press conference. That was the beginning, he said, of an ongoing injustice suffered by Gosnell. Whereas the district attorney was free to comment on the case, he and the doctor were under a gag order. McMahon claimed that the prosecution's liberal use of the "First Amendment's freedom of speech" had trampled Gosnell's right to a fair trial. "This is my first opportunity to present to you a different version [of the facts], a version that hasn't been portrayed in the media, a version that hasn't been put on television," he said.

And the defense attorney was only getting started. The prosecution's approach to the case was unprecedented in his long career, McMahon said. "There has been an incredible rush to judgment like I have never seen before in any criminal case. He's been tried, convicted, and told by everyone in this room, press included, that it's a house of horrors and he's terrible."

Just because a lawyer says it doesn't make it true. McMahon, who is bald, told the jurors; "I could walk into a courtroom and say that I have a full head of hair. That doesn't make it true." If the clinic was such a terrible place, he asked, why had the Department of Health not shut it down in the course of thirty-one years? If the Women's Medical Society clinic was really as bad as the government said, surely the government would have intervened long ago. It was a good point—though one that the grand jury had already comprehensively answered.

McMahon would make a similar point as the trial was winding down. He asked the jury to consider testimony they heard from one of Gosnell's repeat patients. "Monica Moran…said she was going there, and she came back time and time again for her treatment. Do you think she would have come back to a house of horrors over and over and over again?"

Nice euphemism, "treatment." It was another good point, though. But just what kind of person went to 3801 Lancaster Avenue for an abortion over and over? We've heard from some of them. Most spoke of the horror of the place and their desperation. But there were others who, we know, were using abortion as an extreme form of contraception. The jurors knew it, too.

McMahon's argument was impressive if you were not aware of the facts of Gosnell's long career. Rather than being the unjust victim of a supposedly publicity-hungry DA's rush to judgment, Gosnell had escaped justice for decades. Neither McMahon nor the prosecution would tell the jury, but the reality was that Gosnell had been involved in illegal abortions from at least the "Mother's Day Massacre" in 1972. In that notorious incident, Gosnell and another illegal abortionist named Harvey Karman had used an experimental device called "the super coil"—a ball with razor blades attached to it—to perform abortions on fifteen women who had been bussed to Philadelphia from Chicago. The device didn't work as planned, and several of the women had to be hospitalized with internal bleeding and other complications. Nothing happened to Gosnell then. Nothing happened when the National Abortion Federation denied his clinic accreditation. Nothing happened when the state Department of Health found numerous violations of Pennsylvania's Abortion Control Act. Nothing happened when fellow doctors reported Gosnell for running a shoddy operation that endangered women's lives. Nothing happened when Semika Shaw died. Rush to judgment? Gosnell had been getting away with murder for so long, his prosecution was about as far away from a rush to judgment as could be.

But the jury would not hear about the Mother's Day Massacre or many of the other injuries that Gosnell inflicted on his patients over the years that led to lawsuits and out-of-court settlements. So McMahon could present his client as a hardworking, selfless man—a pillar of the community with a virtually unblemished record who ran afoul of an overzealous prosecutor.

McMahon painted a portrait of a great man who had devoted his life to the service of the poor. "Dr. Gosnell is a lifelong Philadelphian, graduated Central High School in 1959, went to Penn undergrad for a short time and transferred over to Dickinson college, graduated from Dickinson College. Went to Thomas Jefferson Medical College and he had a rotating internship at Jefferson Hospital and worked as a resident in OB/GYN at that place and got his medical license—his M.D.—during that period of time."

In McMahon's telling, Gosnell could have taken advantage of enormous opportunities when he graduated in 1969. The racial violence and student protests that had rocked Philadelphia in the mid-sixties had begun to subside and racial barriers were beginning to fall.

But Gosnell had rejected the "easy money and lifestyle" that would come with those opportunities, McMahon explained. "He was committed to the community that he came from. He was dedicated to the poor. He was dedicated to the urban male and female population of west Philadelphia and all over the city," the defense lawyer said. Gosnell felt "privileged" to serve his community. He rejected the salary he would have earned "in some fancy OB/GYN place" and chose to work in a drug rehabilitation program helping people who couldn't help themselves.

Perhaps Gosnell did feel that he wanted to help people less fortunate than he. Maybe he did so out of a heartfelt desire to do good. But of course, helping people means you are in a position of power—and that the people you are helping are naturally grateful. Perhaps Gosnell needed the needy patients as much as they needed him. Because Gosnell isn't as intelligent as he would like to think he is, working among Philadelphia's poor and uneducated was a convenient and self-aggrandizing way to build a thriving practice while avoiding exposure in the hyper-competitive medical climates of New York and Washington. And, running a drug rehab clinic, Gosnell discovered just how lucrative addicts could be for someone willing to write prescriptions in exchange for cold cash.

But as far as McMahon was concerned—and as far as the jury needed to be concerned—Gosnell's motivations were pure.

McMahon briefly summarized Gosnell's resumé. He was board certified in family practice medicine, and he ran the rehab clinic from 1969 until 1979. During the same period, he opened a general family practice in West Philadelphia seeing "various people…a lot of elderly patients."

Gosnell had an opportunity to leave Philadelphia in 1979, but chose instead to "strengthen his roots and ties to the community by buying 3801 Lancaster and opening the Women's Medical Society." In 1993, Gosnell bought an art gallery next door and expanded the clinic, "bringing medical care to the whole community."

Allegations of racism are toxic in America, and they are almost impossible to disprove. Either you believe them or you don't—and most Americans tend to believe them. It was one thing for the prosecution to say that Gosnell treated his white patients differently from his black patients. But if a black person claims he's a victim of racial discrimination, the tendency is to take him at his word. And on the doctor's behalf, McMahon contended not only that the prosecution's attempt to paint Gosnell as a racist was absurd, but that Gosnell was himself the victim of racism. The charges against him were "a targeted, elitist, racist prosecution of a doctor that has done nothing but give to the poor people of West Philadelphia." Just in case the jury did not get the point he was trying to make, the defense attorney urged the jury to look at the case unemotionally and end the "prosecutorial lynching of Dr. Kermit Gosnell."

From the beginning, McMahon made it clear he would challenge each and every piece of evidence and every assertion the prosecution brought to bear against the man he would portray as a cross between Dr. Kildare and Mother Teresa.

But there was one very important person in the courtroom who was completely unimpressed with McMahon's presentation of Kermit Gosnell: Kermit Gosnell.

Although he sat with a half smile on his face, apparently listening to and approving of everything McMahon said, Gosnell was seething with anger at his lawyer.

Gosnell hadn't been certain until the very last minute that he wanted McMahon to represent him. The attorney, in fact, had had to use all of his persuasive powers to keep his client from representing himself. As Gosnell told us, "We were on rocky ground. He hadn't fulfilled promises he made." The doctor wanted to sack McMahon just before the trial got underway. "I filed to be allowed to represent myself, although I didn't want to. But I had to do it because I couldn't depend on him doing what he said he would do," Gosnell explained.

What was Gosnell so peeved about? McMahon hadn't retrieved an updated copy of the doctor's resumé from his papers to enter into evidence. Like all good narcissists, Gosnell was very proud of himself and needed others to know his accomplishments. The doctor felt certain that when the jury saw his education and his ongoing learning and achievements in black and white, they would find it difficult to believe he could be capable of such monstrous acts. "My last copy of my resumé was a very important document because it did speak to my professionality and continuing education, and McMahon had promised to get that from the records and have that as a document [so] that each jury member would have it," Gosnell explained to us. "It not only cited the excellent educational basis that I had, but in addition it showed all my continuing educational efforts and involvements, including prestigious places and things that I have done. McMahon promised to do it, and promised to do it, but he never did."

It was this alleged failure that prompted Gosnell to draft an application to the court to dismiss the best defense attorney in town. It took a tense and lengthy meeting with McMahon for Gosnell to change his mind. "It's still a bone of contention as far as I'm concerned. But eventually, he convinced me that he would be very worthy of my support," Gosnell told us. "I agreed to go ahead with him."[14]

This was typical Gosnell—people should be honored to work for him, even if he happened to be facing capital murder charges and needed McMahon's talents more than McMahon needed Gosnell's business.

Fortunately for Gosnell, the rest of the courtroom was oblivious to these tensions. McMahon defended his client zealously, and for the length of the trial the half-smile never left Gosnell's face.

Gosnell still thinks that a lengthy resumé is important. In legal submissions trying to appeal his conviction much space is given to listing his educational achievements, his service as a military doctor in Vietnam, his awards, and his media appearances. He also claims to be currently working on a number of self-help manuals and papers whose titles include "Addictive Diseases; Mental Health and General Well Being" and a perhaps self-serving study of "Better Outcomes For Prisoners."[15]

In an attempt to mollify Gosnell and further round out the doctor's good character for the jury, McMahon listed his children's achievements because, as he rather dubiously told the jury, "the measure of a man can sometimes be looked at in the conduct of his children." "All have done well," McMahon said, "and what they've done should speak legions and volumes to the character and nature of Dr. Kermit Gosnell." On the other hand, Gosnell's children never came to the trial and have never visited him in prison. And after the trial, in 2014, his son Barron was shot and wounded as he attempted to burglarize a house.

McMahon, knowing that many of the complaints, injuries, and lawsuits Gosnell faced since the Mother's Day Massacre could not be produced into evidence, accused the government of blowing the tragedy of Karnamaya Mongar's death out of proportion. He even claimed that Gosnell's patients had far fewer complications than average.

The lawyer warned the jury not to condemn his client as a murderer just because Gosnell couldn't bring Mayo Clinic standards to West Philadelphia. McMahon was making a populist case for his client's innocence. The prosecution would bring in experts to say how Gosnell should have run his clinic, but the defense was saying, in effect, pay no attention to those elitist doctors who don't care for or about the poor.

"They're going to come in, university people, higher-ups, educated people. You know what these experts don't do? They don't run an urban clinic. They don't run a low income, urban, poor, poverty stricken clinic."

The prosecution experts, McMahon said, live in an "ivory tower."

"Well, if you want the Mayo Clinic, go to the Mayo Clinic," he told the jury. "But if you're poor, you're female and you don't have the opportunity that maybe some of us have, you go to West Philadelphia to get it done because you can afford it and you can get it done."

Gosnell was performing about a thousand abortions a year. The doctor had a high rate of return customers. If it was a house of horrors and he was a monster, McMahon argued, then why did the women keep coming back?

And as for Mongar, McMahon claimed—inaccurately—that Gosnell had performed about sixteen thousand abortions in his career and only one person had ever died. That was correct only if one ignored the death of Semika Shaw.

Glossing over the fact that Gosnell's unlicensed staff had medicated Mongar, McMahon said she "was treated the way that everyone else had been treated over thirty-one years.... She just happened to have other complications that caused her to die. She wasn't anything out of the ordinary, Karnamaya Mongar. She wasn't anything different than any of the other sixteen thousand abortions." Perhaps a little too casually, he added, "She came up here to get a job done and she got the job done."

McMahon emphasized that until Detective Wood started poking around, Mongar's death had been ruled an accident by the medical examiner.

As for the seven babies Gosnell allegedly murdered, McMahon's defense was straightforward: they were never alive to begin with. "The first rule of homicide," he said, "the first rule is someone has to be alive to kill them. That's the first rule." He asked the jury to remember that the workers at the clinic were not professional and their testimony about seeing babies move was not scientific evidence because they were not scientifically qualified to make those kinds of judgments.

And the charges that Gosnell routinely aborted babies over the twenty-four-week limit? McMahon explained how difficult it was to accurately determine the gestational age of a child; it's a guesstimate at best. The forty-seven babies recovered from the clinic proved nothing, McMahon said, except that aborted fetuses are treated in a "gross" way by every abortion clinic.

"Dr. Gosnell was having a dispute with his hazmat people about the bill, so they weren't coming to pick up [babies' remains] and, therefore, there was a backup—like not picking up your trash for a period of time. I know it's gross, but that's how fetuses are taken care of. There's a hazmat service that comes.... There's nothing nefarious or ugly about it." The reality of abortion, he said, is that "those materials have to be discarded."

For McMahon to save his client's life and keep him out of prison for the rest of this life, he needed to show—or at least plant the seeds of reasonable doubt—that the seven babies weren't alive when they were born. And he had arguments for each of them.

According to McMahon, Baby Boy A was not born alive because his mother had been injected with Digoxin, a small amount of which kills the baby in the womb.

Baby Boy B, recovered from the clinic's freezer, was not born alive according to McMahon because his lungs never aerated. The medical examiner had put the baby's lungs in a container of water. They did not float; therefore, they had no air in them—the baby hadn't taken a breath.

For the remaining five babies, McMahon claimed all the prosecution had to go on was hearsay from the unqualified people who worked at the clinic.

FBI agent Jason Huff was the prosecution's first witness. He explained the warren-like layout of the clinic. Toward the end of his time on the stand, Huff gave the jury a sense of Gosnell that was quite different from McMahon's glowing portrait. He told them about the teriyaki salmon incident and Gosnell's torn, bloody gloves. That was the moment the jury knew they were most definitely not dealing with "Mayo Clinic standards."

The problem for the prosecution was that eating dinner with torn and bloody gloves, while disgusting, is not a crime. They had to prove Gosnell guilty of murder in the face of a defense strategy that played up the fact that abortion is a bloody and often disgusting business.

Pescatore and Cameron tried to show how far removed from normal abortion practice Gosnell actually was. They had difficulty with this line of argument, though, because the reality of abortion is rarely discussed publicly. Abortion is a physically dirty, bloody, and graphic procedure, and so it was sometimes difficult to differentiate between legal abortions and Gosnell's activities—which McMahon represented as being well within industry norms. Presenting the unvarnished truth about abortion seemed to work well for the prosecution, at least at first. But the advantage often withered under McMahon's probing questions.

Dr. Karen Feisullin was an important witness for the prosecution. Unlike Gosnell, she was a respected, board-certified obstetrician-gynecologist, at Abington Memorial Hospital. At first glance, her life and medical practice could not have been further removed from that of Gosnell.

Feisullin's primary experience was with delivering babies in a hospital to women who wanted them—"desired pregnancies" as she described them to the jury. She told the court that sometimes as a pregnancy advanced, she would detect "fetal development issues" and the woman would decide, in consultation with her doctors, to have an abortion. These abortions were unwanted and they were unusual. Dr. Feisullin said she would do two to four of these procedures a week. Gosnell, by contrast, would do more than a dozen abortions a night on women who desperately wanted them and who had often come back more than once. We have seen how Semika Shaw, the twenty-two-year-old woman who died in 2000 of infection and sepsis two days after having a botched abortion at Gosnell's clinic, had already terminated four pregnancies, and how another woman interviewed by the *3801 Lancaster* documentary project said she'd had eight abortions with Gosnell over fourteen years.

Dr. Feisullin outlined for the jury what an abortion is and the different ways the procedure may be done. Up to nine weeks, a woman may end her pregnancy with a pill—the infamous RU-486, which actually involves two drugs and requires several visits to a doctor over a two-week period. After that, any abortion has to be done surgically. Feisullin explained there are two types of surgical abortion: "dilation and evacuation, where the cervix is dilated and the pregnancy is removed from the uterus; or you can induce labor to end the pregnancy as well."

Feisullin explained that in the second trimester the cervix needed to be dilated because, "as the pregnancy gets larger and you need more room to safely remove the fetus and the pregnancy. It's safer for the patient to kind of pre-dilate the cervix before the surgery so you don't have to use as many instruments," she said. "There's less risk of tearing the cervix—called cervical laceration—because when the cervix tears you can bleed a lot." Feisullin confirmed an oft-cited but much disputed claim by the pro-life movement that having an abortion can make later pregnancies riskier. She explained that tearing the cervix during an abortion can "cause problems with pregnancies in the future."

Feisullin described how doctors use laminaria—those dried seaweed strips—to open the cervix so that it is easier to get at the fetus for the abortion. Larger strips of laminaria are for pregnancies that are more advanced. The strips absorb fluids naturally secreted by the vagina and swell, opening the cervix to "allow access to the fetus." Then after the laminaria has done its work, a speculum is inserted. A speculum is like a pair of flat scissors worked in reverse; they go in unopened "and then they are opened inside the vagina and separate the vagina walls" so the doctor can "visualize the cervix."

To prove that it was possible to accurately determine the age of a fetus, the prosecution decided to show a series of pictures of fetuses at different stages of development. This had the effect of showing just how arbitrary the twenty-four-week cutoff is. Commenting on a picture of a twenty-week-old fetus, Feisullin pointed out that ribs were clearly visible, and a little bit of muscle. The eyes were not yet open but, "the body was formed, the limbs are formed." Feisullin was asked to comment on a picture of what she described as a "premature infant born at twenty-three weeks." She explained that infants born at that stage have a 40 to 50 percent chance of survival, although "they may have development problems as they grow."

Feisullin then explained for the jury what a legal, purportedly normal abortion is—how it's done, how it looks. "The patient is anesthetized…and once the patient gets positioned, legs go up—with stirrups, the patient's legs go up. The patients gets prepped, meaning the area where the surgery is going to take place…gets cleansed with iodine solution." The woman is draped with a blue sheet, and the abortionist starts his work with a curette—a long, sharp pointed metal instrument. The point is used to "break the water"—that is, pierce the amniotic sac—which is then sucked out. Feisullin explained that it was important to do this first because if the sac is still intact during the actual abortion procedure, "there is a risk of pushing the fetus out of the other end of the uterus." That means the baby would be stuck in the uterine wall, heightening "a risk of perforating."

Medical science has made tremendous advances in caring for premature infants. If a woman were to go into labor and give birth, there would be an excellent chance that a baby at that gestational age would be born alive. In the case of an abortion, however, a baby born alive presents a conundrum.

The solution, to prevent this, Feisullin explained, is to inject the fetus with potassium chloride or Digoxin, which kills the baby in the womb. Feisullin explained to the jury how those injections are supposed to work. "One of the highly trained sonographers in our high risk prenatal department…does it. He has an assistant who scans the pregnancy, scans the uterus [with an ultrasound], and then injects the potassium chloride into the baby's heart. And they watch until the heart stops beating. It's almost immediately."

She explained that, although it had never happened to her, there is no law against a live birth during an abortion. "The potassium chloride and the Digoxin are really just used so that you don't have a live birth, not that you can't proceed with a procedure without it," the doctor continued. "The heart doesn't have to stop beating before you do it [the abortion]."

And if the baby was born alive, as it often was in Gosnell's clinic? Feisullin was clear about what would happen at her hospital, which strictly adhered to the law. "It depends on the gestational age," she said. "But just, you know, as a human being, you would want to comfort, at least comfort care." Comfort what? The doctor couldn't quite bring herself to use a pronoun. "You know, if it's in a hospital, you could offer—potentially offer, like over twenty-three weeks, to resuscitate it, but, you know, really just keep it warm you know. It will eventually pass."

It was clear that the jury was listening intently to understand exactly what the doctor was saying. And it was clear that Feisullin was getting increasingly uncomfortable saying it. If a baby were born alive during an abortion she performed, she would allow the baby to die. Even in a hospital, where resuscitation is possible, and premature babies live and often thrive in a nearby neonatal intensive care unit. Eventually, the doctor told the jury, the baby would die from neglect.

Listening to the evidence, journalists could be seen looking at each other checking if they had actually heard what they thought they had just heard. At a trial where a doctor was facing murder charges for deliberately killing seven babies, one of the prosecution's star witnesses testified that allowing live babies to slowly die through neglect was standard medical practice.

Feisullin was adamant that she had never heard of a doctor using scissors to sever a baby's spinal cord to kill it. But when McMahon rose to cross-examine, he made the case that Gosnell's actions merely ensured the baby "would pass" a little sooner.

But first, McMahon wanted to show that Feisullin's hospital clinic and Gosnell's were at the opposite ends of the social spectrum and therefore the patients had different standards and expectations. Several times throughout his questioning, McMahon made Feisullin affirm that she worked at a "large suburban community hospital." He wanted to emphasize that she was not running an urban clinic catering primarily to black women, and that she was treating a "particular type of patient," which is "not one where people just come in to electively have abortions just because it's their choice."

Having pointed out some of the differences between Feisullin and Gosnell, McMahon then began to highlight the similarities. He described in graphic terms what a legal abortion looked like, and had Feisullin agree—with some reluctance—that his description was correct. But in the course of McMahon's cross-examination, Feisullin became more uncomfortable and angry as his descriptions became more graphic.

Wasn't it true, McMahon asked, that not all procedures were done in the same way but that in all cases "there's a process where tools are actually gone up into the uterus and basically pulling parts out and you may pull out an arm or a leg or some portion of that"?

"Correct," Feisullin answered.

"Until you've successfully evacuated the entire pieces of the fetus, correct?"

"Correct," she replied.

McMahon picked up a pair of scissors and held a picture of a fetus to show the jury that a legal abortion is no less bloody or messy than what his client was accused of doing.

"The forceps are placed in, and then, step B, body parts are pulled from the fetal body out of the vaginal canal. Right?"

"Correct," the doctor answered.

McMahon then tried to argue that Gosnell's practice of snipping the baby's neck could simply be part of an ordinary abortion procedure.

McMahon got Feisullin to describe what would happen if during an abortion the fetus were to be delivered breach—that is, legs first. Feisullin said that often the head would get stuck in the vaginal canal. In that case, she explained, "a suction catheter is inserted at the base of the skull to remove the contents of the head.... and the brain is suctioned out [so that] the skull collapses and it comes out easily."

McMahon then produced a medical diagram of an insertion being made in a baby in order for the brains to be sucked out.

Through skillful questioning, McMahon got the jury to see that Gosnell's use of scissors could have had an innocent explanation.

"The procedure that we were just talking about…is portrayed here, and this is what you were talking about; right?" he asked Feisullin.

"Exactly what I was talking about," she answered.

"Exactly what you were talking about, where the person doing the abortion grabs the baby's leg—breach, as you said. The baby is pulled out into the birth canal, right?"

"Uh-huh."

"And the abortion delivers the baby except for the head?"

"Right."

"Puts a scissors—they would jam scissors in the baby's skull; the scissors are then open to enlarge the hole, the scissors are removed and a suction cap is inserted, the brains are sucked out, causing the skull to collapse, and the baby is then removed—correct?"

"Yes."

"That's the method that you just described?"

"Yes," Feisullin replied. "I wasn't aware of the scissors. I've never performed this procedure, so I wasn't aware of that step going before the suction."

"However," McMahon continued, "some sort of penetration has to be made in the back of the neck—"

"Correct, uh-huh."

"To open up the neck so that the suction can do that; is that correct?"

"Right, uh-huh."

It was an effective cross-examination. McMahon had gotten a prosecution expert witness to say that there could be a perfectly legal explanation for fetuses having puncture wounds in the back of their necks. McMahon could discredit witnesses about the where and when of snipping, but he could not argue with photos and bodies that had clearly visible puncture wounds in the back of their necks. With Feisullin's answers, though, McMahon could offer a credible, medically accepted reason for the wounds.

The trouble with McMahon's argument was that it tried to normalize an abnormal procedure. He asked Feisullin what would happen if the fetus were a breach delivery. But throughout the two-month trial, the prosecution called witness after witness to testify that Gosnell snipped the necks all the time. It was his standard procedure—not a technique he used during the odd breach birth.

Feisullin, who said she had never performed the procedure McMahon was describing and "wasn't aware of the scissors" involved, also failed to note the similarity of the procedure he was asking about with the "partial-birth abortion" method that had been outlawed by Congress in 2003, when it was made a federal crime to perform "An abortion in which the person performing the abortion, deliberately and intentionally vaginally delivers a living fetus until...in the case of breach presentation, any part of the fetal trunk past the navel is outside the body of the mother, for the purpose of performing an overt act that the person knows will kill the partially delivered living fetus; and performs the overt act, other than completion of delivery, that kills the partially delivered living fetus."

If anyone was "deliberately and intentionally vaginally deliver[ing] a living fetus...for the purpose of performing an overt act that the person knows will kill the partially delivered living fetus; and perform[ing] the overt act," it was Kermit Gosnell. Except the babies were more than just "partially" delivered when he killed them.

Gosnell's crime wasn't partial-birth abortion. It was homicide. Those babies were intact. They all had brains. None had been suctioned out—as Christine Wechsler had discovered when she put the scalpel to those babies' skulls so many months earlier.

McMahon's defense had problems, but he was well on his way to creating some reasonable doubt. The question was whether he could create just enough.

EIGHT

GOSNELL VERSUS GUMP

Jack McMahon's defense strategy was classic: go on the offensive. He needed to damage the prosecution's case so profoundly that the jury would have enough reasonable doubt for an acquittal. And the prosecution's case was far from invulnerable. McMahon could raise legitimate questions about whether the seven babies had lived outside the womb. That was crucial if he wanted to save Gosnell from a possible death sentence.[1]

And McMahon had surprising success with this line of attack—in fact, he even surprised himself. McMahon had a more difficult time, however, defending Gosnell against the charges that he hadn't abided by Pennsylvania's twenty-four-hour waiting period law and that he had performed abortions on women who were twenty-four weeks or further along. But those charges were relatively insignificant compared with first-degree murder.

To ensure that his client did not face the death penalty, McMahon needed to convince the jury that Gosnell could not have murdered the seven babies because they were never alive outside the womb. He claimed that all of them were stillborn because Gosnell had injected their mothers with Digoxin, the legal poison that doctors use in legal late-term abortions.

Abortionists adopted Digoxin after the U.S. Supreme Court ruled in 2007 that the federal law banning partial-birth abortion was constitutional. If administered correctly, the drug kills babies in utero, before they are born, preventing the possibility of their being born alive. Dr. Karen Feisullin had testified that Digoxin is an acceptable drug for this purpose, although she preferred to use potassium chloride.

McMahon took every opportunity to argue that Gosnell used Digoxin liberally and—more important—*legally*. Given the use of Digoxin, he urged, the babies would not and could not have been born alive. But McMahon's argument had problems. Militating against McMahon's claims was the often confusing, contradictory, and occasionally untruthful testimony from Gosnell's staff, which did little to help the defense's case.

In truth, it's difficult to know if Gosnell was using Digoxin at all by the time of the clinic raid in 2010. The evidence is clear that he began giving some of his patients some Digoxin injections in 2007. What is unclear is just how regularly the drug was administered and whether or not it was administered properly.

McMahon was keen to highlight how Gosnell's abortion methods changed in 2007, with the Digoxin injections starting after the 2007 Supreme Court's decision. The idea was to show the jury that Gosnell was a doctor who complied with the law and adjusted to changes in the law—not the monster that prosecutors were making him out to be. "If he's a stone cold-blooded killer, a house of horrors runner, why would he change his methods to comport with the law?" McMahon asked. "If you're a killer, you don't change your methodology to comport with the law. You're a lawbreaker, a killer according to them. Why would you go to the process of getting Digoxin, getting the needle, inserting it into them, trying to comply with the law?"

Several prosecution witnesses backed up what McMahon was saying, at least to a certain extent. Adrienne Moton confirmed that Gosnell started using Digoxin around the end of 2007. Even Kareema Cross, easily the most hostile to Gosnell of all the prosecution's witnesses, said he used the drug. Several of his patients also confirmed they had received an injection they were told was Digoxin and had signed consent forms acknowledging the drug would be administered.

McMahon also pointed to the stillborn Baby Girl Manning—whose cause of death the medical examiner couldn't determine—as further evidence that Digoxin was a regular part of Gosnell's practice. In fact that incident was not so clear-cut, as Shanice Manning would testify that Gosnell never told her what drug he was injecting into her belly. And of course even if Gosnell claimed he was injecting Digoxin, that was no proof that the liquid was actually the poison and not some ineffective and cheap saline solution.

In fact, the prosecution had plenty of evidence to rebut McMahon's claim that Gosnell was a law-abiding doctor. His use of Digoxin in abortions had been sloppy from the start. And, almost certainly, those very abortions very quickly became criminal.

Steve Masoff, one of Gosnell's most valuable assistants because he at least had had formal medical training, testified that Gosnell always had trouble using Digoxin. He would give the injection, but an ultrasound would show it hadn't worked. Increasing the dosage didn't help. Apparently Gosnell didn't have the skill to find the baby's heart.

So after a while Gosnell just went through the motions of administering the drug. Massof testified that Gosnell told him the law only required him to *try*: "You don't have to be successful, but if you try that's all you need to do." Gosnell was lying, of course. Pennsylvania law is clear: the baby cannot be killed outside the woman's body. If the baby is born alive, nobody—not the doctor, not a nurse, not a physician's assistant, *nobody*—can do anything to accelerate the infant's death. That would be murder.

As time progressed, Massof testified, though Gosnell was still injecting Digoxin, the heart "was always beating." But was Gosnell even injecting Digoxin, however inexpertly? The one thing everyone seemed to agree on was that Gosnell was injecting women in the abdomen with a substance *resembling* Digoxin. But whether the drug was genuine became a matter of dispute, even among his staff. Gosnell marked all the files of women who were over twenty weeks pregnant with a "D." According to Massof, that meant they had been given Digoxin. Several members of his staff testified that that notation was standard procedure—even if the woman never received any type of injection. And Lynda Williams said that Gosnell had virtually stopped injecting the women in recent years. Tosha Lewis also testified that the number of Digoxin injections had dropped "significantly."

Truth is, there is no proof that Gosnell used Digoxin in the final years of his practice. There are many reasons to doubt that he did.

If he was injecting Digoxin, then why was snipping a baby's neck so routine? The drug is all but guaranteed to kill a baby in the womb, so why was it assumed that late abortions would be born alive and that the scissors would be necessary to "ensure fetal demise"? Gosnell injected Shay Abrams, Baby Boy A's mother, with something the defense claimed was Digoxin. But Abrams said she still felt the baby moving the next day. A toxicology test on her baby's body found no Digoxin.

And if Gosnell was routinely using Digoxin, why didn't police find any of the drug at the clinic the night of the task force raid in February 2010? John Taggart seized ninety-eight different drugs from the clinic and meticulously catalogued them all. There was no Digoxin. If Gosnell was using Digoxin, even haphazardly, he should have had at least some of it on hand.

Assistant DA Ed Cameron raised the possibility that the women were receiving bogus injections. He pointed out that Gosnell routinely skimped on even the cheapest of medical supplies. Several of his employees testified that he would reuse medical instruments intended for single use. After dramatically putting on a pair of gloves, Cameron picked up and showed the jury a plastic curette—a cheaply made medical tool used to scrape remaining fetal tissue out of a woman's uterus. Gosnell's employees had testified that the doctor had used it over and over again on an untold number of patients. Cameron looked at the jurors and said, "What I want you to think about for a minute is, you've got a doctor here—and I don't even know if we are doing anybody justice by calling him a doctor—reusing something that costs one dollar, maybe $1.25." The prosecutor pointed out that if Gosnell was so cheap—so greedy—that he wouldn't pay for a medical tool that cost a little more than a dollar, then why would he pay for an expensive drug like Digoxin, when reusing a pair of scissors cost nothing? "What do you think a doctor who is not willing to waste a dollar on something that's a one [time] use would do when it comes to buying a drug?" Cameron asked. "Would he actually use it?"

So even though Masoff had seen a form in patients' files denoting the use of Digoxin, and even though Gosnell's staff had seen him injecting something, sometimes, into some women, Cameron said he believed the evidence showed the drug was no longer used in the clinic. He reminded the jury of Lynda Williams's testimony. "He didn't use it often," she said. "He stopped using Digoxin. That's why he snipped necks."

But after the prosecution rested, McMahon dashed any hope the prosecutors may have had of an open-and-shut case. The defense moved for Judge Minehart to dismiss all charges.

McMahon then methodically went through all the charges, belittling the prosecution case and the evidence and witnesses they had produced. His argument for setting aside the claims that Gosnell had broken the late-term abortion and waiting period laws was fairly pro forma, lacking in energy. That part of the motion was a long shot anyway. As we have seen, on the one occasion that Gosnell had spoken to the authorities—the night of the first raid on his clinic—he had admitted to Jim Wood that maybe 10 percent of the abortions were past the legal limit. Then there were the documents where Gosnell had written the baby's age as 24.5 weeks. There wasn't much McMahon could do for his client on those charges, and it showed in his demeanor as he asked for them to be dismissed.

But McMahon became animated when he turned to attack the murder charges.

He began with Baby Boy B. Even the prosecution knew this charge would be difficult to prove. McMahon told the judge there was simply no evidence that the baby was ever alive—an essential element for a murder conviction. The current and the former Delaware County chief medical examiners had both testified that they could not say "to a reasonable degree of certainty, or any certainty, in fact that the baby was born alive."

McMahon also thought he had a chance to persuade the judge to dismiss the charges surrounding Baby Boy A—or Baby Abrams, as he was sometimes called in court. The defense lawyer claimed that because the mother was given Digoxin and had signed a consent form to receive the injection, it was inevitable that the baby was born dead.

Adrienne Moton had testified she had seen the baby the evening it was born and it looked like it was sleeping—there was no movement. That was no proof, McMahon said, that the baby ever lived outside the mother's body.

But the case for dismissing the charges relating to Baby Boy A ran up against the testimony of Kareema Cross.

Cross is arguably the reason Gosnell is serving multiple life sentences today. Unlike Gosnell's other unqualified employees, she fully cooperated with the investigation. When other former workers at the clinic claimed they couldn't remember a particular incident or detail, she remembered specific times and dates. When others sounded confused on the stand, Cross was clear and emphatic. For McMahon, her evidence was a bit too clear, too exact. He claimed she was present at a suspiciously high number of key incidents and offered just the right amount of information to fill in the evidential gaps in the prosecution case.

McMahon made jurors smile when he likened Cross to Forrest Gump, the witless manchild played by Tom Hanks in the movie of the same name, who somehow managed to be present and take part in numerous pivotal moments in world history. It was one of the few moments of levity in a very dark trial.

"Remember the movie Forrest Gump? He was everywhere. He ended up everywhere," McMahon said in his summation. "He ended up at the Kennedy assassination; he ended up everywhere. And that's what Kareema Cross is in this case. She's everywhere. She's in every one of these situations."

It might be pedantic to point out that the Forrest Gump character was present at many important turning points in history, but not the Kennedy assassination. Still, McMahon's overall point was well made. Many of the charges against Gosnell hinged on Cross's testimony; she was a very convenient witness for the prosecution; and she was open in her hostility towards her former boss.

Cross told the court how Gosnell often yelled at her, treated her badly, and even prevented her from claiming unemployment assistance. She was angry with him. Could her anger have led her to lie? McMahon also suggested another reason Cross might not be telling the truth. She had gotten a special treatment, an unbelievable sweetheart deal from the prosecution—in return for false evidence, he claimed.

"This is a young lady that was never charged in the state—ever," he said. "All these other people are charged. She's never charged with any crimes, even though she worked there all these years." Cross received probation in the federal case against Gosnell for his pill mill operation.

Addressing the judge, McMahon tried to capitalize on Cross's murky motivations. He pointed out that apart from Cross's testimony that she had seen Baby A move, the prosecution had offered no other evidence that it was alive outside the womb, and that the signed consent form indicating the mother had received Digoxin could not be ignored.

McMahon moved on to Baby C. Apart from a single claim by Lynda Williams that the baby had moved its arm once, he said the prosecution could offer no other evidence that the baby ever lived. He argued that live babies move in a different way from the "spasm" Williams said she saw.

The case of Baby D—who became known, unfortunately, as the "toilet baby"—should also be dismissed, McMahon said. Once again, the only evidence the prosecution had was Cross's testimony that she "thought" she had witnessed a "voluntary movement." Gosnell should not be convicted of capital murder because of someone's thought, McMahon argued.

McMahon said that Baby E—also known as the "crying baby"— was another part of a pattern of dubious charges propped up by very dubious witnesses. Ashley Baldwin said she heard a cry—or a whine. When she went into the room where she heard the cry coming from, she saw the baby but testified that it didn't appear to be alive. And the only corroborating testimony the prosecution had was from "Forrest Gump"—Cross—who also said she heard the baby cry. But, McMahon noted, Cross never actually went into the room to check whether the infant was alive.

The murder charges for Baby F and Baby G both relied on Steve Massof's testimony. Massof had said he witnessed Baby G move once. And other than Massof's estimate, the prosecution had no evidence that Baby F was old enough to survive outside the womb. McMahon argued it would be wrong to let the jury decide if a baby lived when they could not even be certain of its age. "It's every one of these children," McMahon complained. The prosecution, he said, "put the homicide on one motion—one! I've never heard anything like that."

Of course, one motion or movement may not look like much, but it *is* evidence of life. It is evidence of a beating heart and a body with blood pulsating through it. That was the point Cameron emphasized over and over in his rebuttal to McMahon's motions to dismiss. McMahon was misreading the law, Cameron argued. When a child is born and makes a movement, that child is alive. He said McMahon had tried to claim the law required a voluntary movement to constitute life, but the actual language of the law reads, "the beating of the heart, pulsation of the umbilical cord, definite movement of the voluntary muscle or any brain wave activity." All seven babies more than met those criteria, Cameron said.

Cameron began with Baby G and worked backwards. The prosecutor said Massof had said clearly in his testimony that he saw Baby G breathe before it was murdered. "That baby had a respiratory excursion," Cameron told the judge. "It breathed. He said he saw it lying on its side. 'I saw it breathe.' Then its neck was snipped."

Baby F had made a significant movement—its leg went up to its chest. "That's voluntary movement. That's all the statute required. That baby had its neck snipped. It was killed," Cameron told the judge.

Regarding Baby E, Cameron said there was no more definitive sign of life than a noise, "and I think anybody that sat in [the court] and heard Ashley Baldwin and Kareema Cross, that sound is just chilling, it was a whine. What more sign is that of a baby crying out, I'm alive? And what did he do? He killed it. To make a noise you have to breathe. To make a noise, you have to move the vocal cords. That baby was alive and still should be alive," he added.

Cameron pointed out that two witnesses had said Baby D, the "toilet baby," was alive. Adrienne Moton, in fact, had already pleaded guilty to murdering that baby. There was a wealth of evidence that Baby D was alive outside the womb. "In that particular case," Cameron explained to the judge, "we have that baby not only moving in the toilet but we have testimony that the baby was ten to fifteen inches long." He added that one witness described Baby D's head as "big as a pancake" and that Cross testified she saw the baby breathe.

Cameron described Baby C as the "arm-pulling baby." He reminded the judge that Lynda Williams had testified how she played with the baby before its neck was snipped. "Lynda Williams called somebody into the room [and said], hey, look at this: she pulled the baby's arm and the baby pulled back, pulled the arm in. It's another voluntary movement, and that's all that the law requires."

Cameron devoted more time arguing for Baby B to remain in the charges than he spent arguing for any other baby—which probably was a sign of the weakness of his case. In fact the assistant DA admitted that Baby B was not the strongest part of the prosecution's case. All they had was the body of a baby with a gestational age of twenty-eight or twenty-nine weeks that had been stabbed in the back of the neck. He also admitted that Dr. Gulino, chief medical examiner, could not make the lungs float and therefore show that the baby had definitively taken a breath before it died. But, Cameron argued, because the baby had been discovered frozen and then thawed out, the ME was in uncharted forensic territory. Gulino had testified he had never examined a frozen and then thawed baby of that age. He didn't know, and no other scientist knew, what effect freezing and thawing would have on the lungs. "You have to go beyond the fact Dr. Gulino could not show the lungs floated to show that it breathed," Cameron argued. "He said, 'I can't really, because this is unprecedented. I reached out over all the country. We don't know the effects of freezing.'"

But, Cameron contended, all of Baby B's organs were properly formed and functioning. In effect, the DA was saying that the baby *must* have been alive. It was more of an inference than an argument, and Cameron knew it. But he did his best, pointing to expert testimony from Dr. Daniel Conway, a physician and neonatologist at St. Christopher's Hospital for Children. Conway had said that a baby as far along as Baby B had a 70 to 80 percent chance of being born alive and surviving. Cameron also reminded the judge of Adrienne Moton's testimony that Gosnell only snipped the necks of babies that were moving.

But, perhaps to deflect attention from the weakness of the case for Baby B, Cameron claimed that Baby A's was the weakest murder charge before the court. It appeared that the mother had received a Digoxin injection. At the very least, Cameron said, she was injected with something that Gosnell said was Digoxin. If it had been administered correctly, the drug would have killed the baby. But Cameron hastened to add that the woman said she could still feel the baby move inside her a day later. And two witnesses—Moton and Cross—said they saw the baby breathe and move after it was born.

McMahon had also asked Judge Minehart to dismiss the murder charge in the case of Karnamaya Mongar. All of the medical experts, he said, had testified that she died from an overdose of meperidine, which is the generic form of the narcotic Demerol. At worst, McMahon argued, this was medical malpractice. But in all likelihood, he said, this was just the sort of thing that can happen at an abortion clinic every so often. For murder to be proven, McMahon said, Gosnell had to start out with a reckless intent. But he insisted Gosnell never intended or wanted to harm Mongar.

Cameron agreed with McMahon—to a point. If it was just a drug overdose then, yes, the law would require administering the drug to be a reckless act from the start. If so, then Mongar's death could be judged an accident. That would be true in a well-run clinic, he argued, where the instruments were cleaned and sanitized and the floors and furniture weren't stained with blood. But there was so much more going on at the Women's Medical Society that moved Mongar's death from accidental to murder pure and simple. "It was all the other conditions at that clinic, it was the repeated course of conduct; it was the filth, not being there, the administration of all of those things," Cameron argued. In short, Gosnell had operated a filthy and unsanitary clinic that he staffed with untrained and uneducated staff instructed to administer dangerous drugs to patients. When somebody died under those circumstances, it was no accident. It was inevitable—and therefore it was murder.

Cameron also questioned McMahon's interpretation of the law. A drunken truck driver had recently been found guilty of murder not because he started out with reckless conduct or malice aforethought. He didn't even know the person he killed. No, it was the driver's reckless behavior and the reckless circumstances he created that resulted in an innocent person's death. And that was enough for a murder verdict. "His conduct, in acting recklessly and consciously disregarding, which is what a doctor of all people did in this case, to cause the death of another person—you could not get more recklessness in this case," he said.

Judge Minehart didn't deliberate very long before delivering a major blow to the prosecution. Despite Cameron's apparent concern about the strength of his case for Baby A, the judge let that charge stand. But the murder charges for Babies B and G were summarily dismissed. The judge also dismissed the abuse of corpse charges. Kermit Gosnell would not have to answer for cutting the feet of babies and storing them.

Ironically, both sides reacted in an unexpected way. Kermit Gosnell saw the dismissal of these charges as a setback. "It was a surprise and it was worrying. I was worried that by dismissing some but not others that the jury would think there must be evidence for the ones that were left."

And the prosecution? Despite the fact that they had already lost two out of seven homicide charges, they were quietly content. Gosnell was still facing capital murder charges, and pressing the other charges, even though they had been dismissed, had allowed the prosecution to introduce evidence that would stay with the jury.[2]

But then the prosecution got a surprise. They expected McMahon to call a bevy of experts to undermine the prosecution's claim that the remaining babies on the charge sheet were born alive. Cameron also had a lot of work prepared in case Gosnell took the stand—though he and Pescatore expected McMahon would do everything in his power to prevent his talkative client from undermining his own case. "I had boxes of evidence prepared in case he took the stand," Cameron told us wistfully in an interview after the trial.[3]

McMahon rose. All eyes in the courtroom were fixed on the lawyer. And he announced that the defense would rest.

Juror Joe Carroll said he was shocked by the move. "I thought McMahon was pretty good," he told us. "He did a good job, but I couldn't understand. After the prosecution got done, they didn't bring one witness. He just said, 'We rest.'...I couldn't understand why nobody was testifying for the doctor."[4]

All that was left for both sides was to give their closing arguments. Then Gosnell's fate would be left to the jury.

NINE

PROFILES IN COURAGE?

The prosecution was determined to deliver a memorable and bulletproof closing argument. They had to.[1]

"We weren't extremely confident we were going to win the case," at that point in the trial, Pescatore recalls.[2]

As is the custom, the defense went first. McMahon reprised many of the same arguments he had made the day before in his motion to dismiss. But now that he had to persuade the jury rather than the judge, it was important for him to appeal to the jurors' honesty, fairness, and courage. Don't let the politics surrounding the trial deter you from looking at the facts, McMahon told them.

"Do you know, and many of you may not, that there is no verdict in the United States of America of innocent? No one in the history of our jurisprudence has been found innocent of any crime, because that's not your function to find any defendant, and particularly in this case, innocent." McMahon wanted the jury to understand that returning with a not guilty verdict wouldn't mean declaring Gosnell innocent, "because none of us, none of us have the knowledge to know what actually happened in any of these particular cases. We weren't there, the DA wasn't there, nobody was there. You can only go by what we talk about here, what the evidence says and what our analysis is."

The beauty—or the audacity—of McMahon's closing statement was the way he deftly appealed to the jury's emotions while urging the jurors to keep their emotions in check. The gruesome reality of abortion would be foremost in jurors' minds. So McMahon made a point of saying the case "is obviously not about abortion." He acknowledged the pro-life and pro-choice activists who had, eventually, been drawn to the case, and he assured the jury that he respected all sides "to the nth degree." Because abortion isn't pretty. "It's bloody, it's real, but you have to transcend that concept that it's bloody and it's real and decide what the issue is in this case, and that issue isn't [whether] abortion [is] bloody and ugly, because if that was the truth, you'd have an easy verdict in this case."

McMahon needed to plant the seeds of doubt in the jurors' heads. "There has been the most incredible rush to judgment without evidence, without facts, without reality that I have ever seen in the history of criminal jurisprudence," he said, repeating what he had said at the beginning of the trial. "These knee-jerk assumptions without evidence that everybody has made, it's not right, it's not fair, and it can happen to us all."

So if the case wasn't about abortion, then what was it about? "This was an elitist, racist prosecution," the defense attorney reiterated. "Dr. Gosnell is not the only one in Pennsylvania doing abortions, but he was an African American that was singled out for prosecution. He's a provider in an urban clinic." Just look at all the "elitist" expert witnesses the prosecution brought in, McMahon said.

The defense lawyer proceeded to work through the remaining charges against Gosnell. Again and again he pointed to the use of

Digoxin. If his client were really a cold-blooded killer, why would he change his protocol in 2007 to use this approved drug? How could those babies be born alive when Digoxin would have killed them in the womb? And didn't those mothers sign consent forms attesting they knew they would receive Digoxin as part of the procedure that they sought out as his clients to perform?

And if Gosnell was running such a "house of horrors," why did he have so many repeat customers? If those poor, uninsured women didn't have a problem with Gosnell, why should the jury? "You know, you can commit murder in the cleanest place in the world," McMahon told them. "You can go to the Mayo Clinic and kill people. You can go to the dirtiest place in the world and not kill people. It has no relation one to the other."

All Gosnell wanted to do, his lawyer assured the jury, was give "those desperate, troubled girls relief. He gave them a solution to their problem, and that's what he was doing."

At the end of a presentation that ran nearly two hours and fifteen minutes, McMahon told jurors about how, as a Catholic school kid in the early 1960s, the nuns made him and all of the students read John F. Kennedy's *A Profile in Courage*. He read the book over and over again, he said, because it is really about people who "defy public opinion out of honesty and integrity, people who faced public pressure, but did not buckle."

"And that's what I'm asking to you to do today," McMahon said. "If you do this, you will forever know and carry with you the personal knowledge, pride, and satisfaction that you, that you yourself, are a profile in courage."

Stirring stuff. But enough to acquit? Perhaps. The prosecution team was worried.[3]

Cameron gave the prosecution's closing argument. He was not in the best of shape when he stood up to speak. McMahon had become violently ill earlier in the week and had to go to the hospital for what turned out to be a severe respiratory infection. That delayed the conclusion of the trial for a couple of days. Unfortunately for Cameron, he had caught McMahon's bug.

But Cameron opted to carry on because the prosecution was anxious about further delay. As Cameron's planned two-hour summation entered its third hour, his fatigue was apparent as he struggled with certain names and events without the benefit of referring to his notes.

Cameron began by warning the jurors that he was about to put them to sleep; he really could see no way around it if he was to "go through all of the facts of the case." His closing argument was a methodical, scientific recounting of the charges. Cameron outlined all of the prosecution's evidence pointing toward a conviction. He became emotional at times. And he took a few potshots at McMahon along the way. None of the jurors fell asleep.

The first thing Cameron had to do was demolish McMahon's Digoxin defense. That was crucial. If he could show the jurors that McMahon's argument was built on flimsy assumptions, then the jury would have a much easier time returning a conviction. So the prosecutor reminded the jury that Officer Taggart had found no Digoxin on the premises. He reminded them that Gosnell was greedy and unlikely to buy a drug if he didn't have to. He pointed out that staff member after staff member had testified that the doctor rarely used Digoxin and, when he did, he was so incompetent that it would not have been effective.

Cameron also couldn't let McMahon's cheap assertion about the "racist" and "elitist" nature of the prosecution go unanswered. "Last time I checked, my boss was African American," he told the jury. "Last time I checked, when I listened to all those women who testified, every one of these babies, they covered the spectra—they're black, they're white, they're Asian." Cameron also pointed out that the decision to prosecute Gosnell was made by a racially mixed grand jury.

In truth, Joanne Pescatore and Christine Wechsler guided the grand jury significantly. On the other hand, when we spoke with trial jurors after the trial ended, they said the prosecutors' allegations of racism never really moved them. They said they felt Gosnell's actions had little to do with race. They believed it was about Gosnell looking after wealthier clients.

"It was because people had more money. You have more money, you wanted special treatment," said juror Joe Carroll.[4]

Then Cameron resurrected the dramatic words of McMahon's opening statement and turned them on their author. McMahon had said that just because something was said in court didn't make it true; there had to be evidence to back it up. Now Cameron used that same logic to take apart McMahon's opening statements. This line of attack had the useful side effect of increasing tensions between the lawyer and his client, who was still smarting from McMahon's failure to present his full resumé to the jury.

Cameron pointed out that McMahon had presented no evidence to back up his assertion that Gosnell was a successful doctor. He had offered no evidence to support his contention that Gosnell had the lowest rate of complications in the entire country. And he hadn't produced a single piece of evidence to prove that Gosnell had, in fact, ever run any successful drug rehabilitation programs.

Cameron even took some time to rebut the defense's claims about Gosnell's children. After all, McMahon had claimed that the success of a man's children was often the measure of the man. But Cameron pointed out that McMahon had produced no evidence to show that Gosnell's children were as successful as he had claimed. For that matter, McMahon had produced no evidence that Gosnell actually had any children at all.

Cameron quoted one of the expert witnesses, Dr. Andrew Herlich, who had testified that being a doctor is "not a right, but a responsibility." Gosnell, the prosecutor said, had abused his responsibility.

Cameron gave the jurors a lesson about the Hippocratic Oath. "Being a doctor," he said, "is not just about going to medical school and getting a degree. It's about going out there and honoring the tenets of this oath." And Gosnell had violated each and every part of it.

Had he applied, "for the benefit of the sick, all measures which are required, avoiding those twin traps of over treatment and therapeutic nihilism"? Had he remembered that "'there is an art to medicine as well as science, and that warmth, sympathy, and understanding may outweigh the surgeon's knife or the chemist's drug'? Right there we know what he did was a violation of that oath," Cameron said. "He wasn't there. These women were given extreme levels of medication to cause birth, to cause delivery. Right there he violated." Cameron also reminded the jury how Gosnell had violated his patients' privacy by leaving their files unsecured throughout the clinic.

Then he quoted the final words of the Hippocratic Oath. "'Most especially must I tread with care in matters of life and death. If it is given to me to save a life, all thanks. But it may also be within my power to take a life. This awesome responsibility must be faced with great humbleness and awareness of my own frailty. Above all, I must not play God.' Above all, you must not play God," Cameron said. "You must not take a life." What had Gosnell done if not play God over and over with the lives of his patients and their babies?

Then the prosecutor recounted the testimony of Gosnell's employees. Yes, some of them had made deals with the prosecution. But their evidence was consistent and strikingly similar, and a number of them had admitted to taking part in the murders themselves.

Cameron became emotional when he brought up Shay Abrams's baby—Baby A—who was 29.5 weeks old when Gosnell killed him. "That baby would be four and a half years old right now," he said. "I wish in God's name there was something that we could do so that baby could walk in that door and do what a four and a half year old could do. But instead, what happened to that baby? It had scissors jabbed into its neck and it slowly suffocated to death."

Gosnell was a greedy and acquisitive man, Cameron said. He put his vacation home above the safety of his patients—especially Karnamaya Mongar. Gosnell wouldn't even use proper anesthetics. Cameron reminded them of Steve Massof's testimony; Massof had said Gosnell preferred older—and more dangerous—anesthetic drugs because they were cheaper. "I remember Masoff saying [they] did use Nalbuphine, which is a safer drug but [they] switched away from it because it was too expensive. I guess [they] had to take the money that would have been used for Demerol to put it into the shore house—to put it into the quarter million dollars that was in...his daughter's bedroom." Dangerous drugs, an untrained staff, and, of course, an absent doctor—all of that added up to homicide, Cameron argued. What was Gosnell's response when his assistant told him over the phone that Mongar was reacting badly to her anesthetic? Give her more drugs.

Cameron talked about how Elinor Barsony, one of the state health inspectors who had seen Gosnell's clinic years earlier, found a disgusting house of horrors when she accompanied the police and federal agents on the night of the February 2010 raid. Cameron was harsh in his characterization of Barsony—he called her the "uninspector." But he relied heavily on her description of what she had found during the raid to prove that Gosnell was running a clinic that was so unsafe and unsanitary that it made Mongar's death a murder, not just an accident. "She talked about how the equipment was outdated...dirty...the staff confused and unqualified, and there were women who were medicated before the doctor arrived."

And then Cameron reminded them about the paramedics who had responded to the clinic's 911 call. They arrived to find Mrs.

Mongar lying unattended—getting no help from anyone in the clinic. They saw a confused doctor and a dying woman without any intubation or any other sign of the treatment that would have been appropriate for someone in her condition. Cameron also mentioned, almost in passing, that the ambulance personnel noticed no one giving Mongar CPR.

When he decided to call no witnesses in Gosnell's defense, McMahon had made a mistake—and Cameron took full advantage of it. The failure of the defense to present their own evidence meant that everything McMahon had said in his opening argument—every premise, every assertion, every claim—was wide open to attack and ridicule.

The local press had reported, and McMahon repeated, that the reason Gosnell kept so many fetuses in the freezer at 3801 Lancaster was a contract dispute with his waste disposal service. McMahon admitted that it was unfortunate and "gross" even to think about the bodies as trash, but asserted that that is what they are considered under the law. Cameron pointed out to the jury that McMahon had never produced a single shred of evidence—not one witness, email, or letter—to prove that there was any such dispute, or that the fetuses were collected regularly by a legitimate waste disposal company. "I think it's more like those dollar curettes he was reusing," Cameron quipped. The doctor was simply too cheap and too greedy to properly dispose of the bodies. Hadn't Jimmy Johnson testified to finding an arm plugging the drain of a sink? Cameron also reminded the jury that John Taggart had found the remains of fetuses in the waste disposal of a sink at the clinic. "I'm thinking about the fact that it's a lot easier just to put stuff down the garbage disposal," he said.

And because Gosnell never took the stand, Cameron could focus on the one time he spoke freely with the authorities—the night of the raid. He was more than happy to answer Jim Wood's questions then, as he noshed on salmon teriyaki in his torn and bloody gloves. Even though it was a short interview, Cameron was able to show that Gosnell had lied in some of his answers and admitted to serious crimes in others.

"He lied about what happened with Mrs. Mongar. What did he say? 'I was there the whole time.' He said there were nurses there. There were no nurses there. [He said] I didn't know it was improper to administer medication with no doctor present." Cameron was scathing. "Come on! That's doctor 101," he told the jury.

Cameron reminded jurors that Gosnell had admitted to Wood that 10 to 20 percent of the fetuses in the building were over twenty-four weeks in gestational age—beyond the legal limit under the state's Abortion Control Act. "He's admitting…10 to 20 percent of the time he was violating the law in doing those abortions," Cameron said.

Cameron said that he and Jack McMahon had worked together in the past, and despite their frequent professional clashes they were quite friendly outside the courtroom. But that didn't prevent the prosecutor from ridiculing the defense lawyer's claim that Gosnell's employees were qualified to give injections, medications, and ultra-sounds because the doctor had shown them how during a twenty-minute "training." "I guess that's the Jack McMahon School of Medicine," he sneered.

Getting really personal, Cameron also noted that McMahon's daughter had been in the courtroom earlier.

"Jack's daughter was here," he said. "I don't know if she's still in the courtroom now. Do you think that for one second Jack would let his daughter lay on that table, would let those women who testified in this case give her medication without a doctor being present? I don't think so."

Cameron knew he needed to overcome the "Forrest Gump" problem in the prosecution case. Many of the more serious charges really did hinge on Kareema Cross being in the right place at the right time. Cameron detailed what Cross had witnessed and how she had tried to make Gosnell aware of potential problems, as when she had warned Gosnell that Sherry West and Lynda Williams didn't seem to care about the patients and were often over-medicating them. "His only reply was, 'You're not their boss,'" Cameron reminded the jury. Kareema Cross was so worried about conditions at the clinic that when she wanted an abortion herself, she went elsewhere.

Was Cross angry with Gosnell? Yes, Cameron said. But her anger was irrelevant to her evidence. "I mean, she was a little mad because he opposed her unemployment compensation. Well, let me tell you— if people were to accuse people of murder just because their boss opposed their unemployment and their unemployment compensation was denied, there would be a lot more murder cases in this city," he said. Cameron wanted to make sure that the jury knew Kareema Cross was no Forrest Gump being used to railroad an innocent Gosnell. "I would suggest to you that she was credible, she was believable," he argued to the jury.

The prosecutor ended his closing argument by sharing a recent personal experience with the jury. "It's really, really difficult, I would suggest, to keep the emotion out of this case—especially as I get older and I see what life is all about and what death is all about. And it kind of came home to me a couple of weeks ago," he told them. "I had a dog that got sick, and you know what they did with the dog that got sick? I took it to the vet and they took it into a room and they gave it a shot to go to sleep," he explained. "Then when it was asleep, they gave it a shot to cause it to die. These babies didn't even get that. My dog was treated better than he treated babies and women, and that's because he didn't care." The babies born at Gosnell's clinic were literally treated worse than a dog.

Gosnell had created an assembly line—Cameron called it "the Henry Ford model of doing business"—with no regard for any of the women in the community he supposedly served. "That's why he's got a quarter of [a] million dollars hidden in his daughter's bedroom; why he's got a shore house, which I wish I could afford."

When he mentioned the shore house, Cameron threw a glance at McMahon. The defense lawyer sat stoney-faced. It was well known in Philadelphia legal circles that Gosnell had found an unusual way to pay his large legal bill. McMahon is now the proud owner of a luxury vacation home, courtesy of America's biggest serial killer.

Like McMahon, Cameron wrapped up his argument with an appeal to the jurors to show courage. He invoked the courage of the police in Boston, who one week earlier had been involved in a massive manhunt for Tamerlan and Dzhokhar Tsarnaev, the Chechen brothers who bombed the Boston Marathon. A Boston police officer had been killed trying to apprehend them. "That's what courage is about," he told them. "For years we've been trying to find out what courage is and when we see it we honor it. What courage basically comes down to as human beings is to protect the lives of others, to go out of your way to save others."

"When a baby comes out of its mother and it moves and breathes and it's alive, you have to do the courageous...you have to do the right thing," Cameron said. "You have to protect it."

The prosecutor reminded the jury that when McMahon had cross-examined some of Gosnell's employees, hoping to undermine their horrific evidence, he had asked them angrily, "'Are you human?' Well, I tell you, the person we should be asking that question of is sitting right there," he said, jabbing his finger at Gosnell. "Are you human?" he shouted at the doctor. "To med these women up, to stick knives or scissors into the backs of babies to kill them? He is the one in this case that doesn't deserve to be called human."

Cameron told the jury that almost everyone honors the dead and treats them with respect. Even his own dog was cremated and put in an appropriate container. But what did Gosnell do? "He put them in

Limeade containers. He put them through the garbage disposal. He put them in the freezer. He didn't even have the basic humanity to treat them appropriately after he killed them."

Karnamaya Mongar couldn't speak English—"couldn't say a word," Cameron said—as she lay dying on Gosnell's table. Likewise, the dead babies had no way to speak—no way to beg for their lives. The prosecutor urged the jury to show courage—"be the voice of Mrs. Mongar and the babies," and find Gosnell guilty on five counts of murder.

In the end, Ed Cameron's emotional exhortations probably weren't necessary. The prosecution may have been nervous, and Gosnell may have been confident of an acquittal, but most jurors had made up their minds to convict him long before the closing arguments.

Nevertheless, it took nine days for the jury to return a verdict. It wasn't that anyone believed Gosnell was innocent. It was rather that they took their role seriously and followed the judge's instructions.

"Pretty much everyone thought he was guilty straight off," Joe Carroll told us. "There was a couple of people that wanted to just hang him, break him from the start," he said. "He's guilty and that's that.... We just couldn't do that. You *can* do that, but that's not what the judge charged us with. He gave us a sheet with every charge. We knew he was guilty. But we had to go through every charge. He had cases and cases of files we had to go through."

Where there were disputes and tension in the jury room, they centered on individual charges, with some jurors believing there was not enough evidence to justify a guilty verdict in some instances. But it became clear very quickly that they would all vote to find Gosnell guilty of enough to send him to prison for life, if not to death row.

Karnamaya Mongar was the sticking point. Eleven jurors agreed with the prosecution that Gosnell was at least guilty of third-degree murder, a serious charge. Joe Carroll disagreed, for a reason that surprised the prosecution when they learned about it. He believed Sherry West, who had testified that Gosnell had attempted to revive her through CPR. For Carroll, that meant Gosnell hadn't been reckless. He hadn't committed a murder. At best, it was involuntary manslaughter, a much lesser charge. The other jurors flatly disagreed, and all of a sudden the arguments became long and tense. Carroll was firm. He believed that the long car journey, Mongar's pregnancy, and the procedure itself had contributed to her death. That meant Gosnell could not be guilty of murder.

"You can't say the man's guilty of murder when he gave her CPR," Carroll said. "I understand that he had the defibrillator there. It might not have worked, but other people [had] seen him giving CPR and called the ambulance, tried to resuscitate the woman."[5]

No one in the investigative or prosecution team would comment publicly, but privately one source told us they were incredulous that Carroll put so much significance on a piece of evidence that was completely uncorroborated. "When we heard after that he believed Sherry West on this, we couldn't believe it," the source told us. "There was no way in hell he gave her [CPR]. Absolutely no way."[6]

Eventually, the jurors reached a compromise of sorts. Carroll was unsure whether Baby E, the "crying baby," had been alive when Gosnell "snipped" its neck, or if the cry could have been just a last gasp for breath. So he wasn't certain if the baby had already expired when Gosnell arrived to stab it in the neck. Carroll agreed to change his vote on that baby if the others would agree to involuntary manslaughter on Mongar. They agreed, and the jury was ready to announce a verdict.[7]

The end of deliberations took everyone by surprise. At 11:00 a.m. the foreman had informed Judge Minehart the jury was deadlocked on two counts. Three hours later, they had a verdict. The courtroom was mostly empty when the jury filed in at 2:00 p.m. There were only a few journalists present, and none of the pro-life activists who had previously attended. Wechsler, Woody, and Taggart were all there. For the first time in their careers, all three of them wept when they heard a verdict announced.[8]

Gosnell could not believe he had been found guilty. He was determined to appeal.

But Gosnell's defense team had a much more serious and immediate problem to contend with. He had been found guilty on capital murder charges. There would be a separate hearing to determine whether Gosnell would get the death penalty, and the jury was not in a forgiving mood. A few jurors had wanted to find him guilty of the death penalty charges without so much as a discussion. Even Carroll, who had been so scrupulous about the circumstances of Mongar's death, was ready to sentence Gosnell to be executed. "I would have been willing to vote for the death penalty after all the facts came out," he told us.[9]

But then the prosecution came forward with a proposition. They knew that even if Gosnell were sentenced to death, he could string out the appeals process for so long that he would probably die of natural causes before he could be executed. Pennsylvania hadn't executed anyone since 1999, and had carried out only three executions since 1976. The prosecution offered that if Gosnell waived all rights to an appeal, they would ask for only a life sentence without parole.[10]

Gosnell hated the idea. In his mind, he was innocent. To this day, he claims he is innocent. He is certain history will vindicate him. So giving up his right to appeal seemed absurd. But the possibility of the death sentence was daunting, and Jack McMahon claimed Gosnell was worried about the sentencing phase—how his children would have to appeal for clemency and the effect the publicity would have on them. "He's a proud man. To bring his young family into court was something he did not want to do," McMahon told the judge.[11]

"A big factor for Dr. Gosnell was his family. They've been con-spicuously absent, and that's been intentional because of the media focus and whatnot. He has some younger children in high school...and bringing them all forward for a penalty phase is some-thing that troubled him," McMahon told CNN reporter Sarah Hoye.[12]

TEN

MEDIA
MALPRACTICE

*"The power is to set the agenda. What we print and
what we don't print matter a lot."*

—KATHARINE GRAHAM, former publisher of the *Washington Post*

If it hadn't been for a committed group of bloggers, new media jour-nalists, pro-life activists, and Twitter users, the Kermit Gosnell trial very likely would not have made national news. When the trial of America's biggest serial killer began in March 2013, it was treated almost entirely as a local story. And it would have remained that way if it had not been for thousands upon thousands of Twitter and Face-book users and some savvy journalists in the new media world who embarrassed the old-line media into giving the trial the attention it deserved.

A few local news outlets and pro-life organizations had noted the raid on Gosnell's clinic in 2010. Major newspapers and broadcasters including National Public Radio, ABC News, and the BBC had pub-lished stories about the grand jury's report and Gosnell's indictment in 2011, but the coverage quickly died down. None of those stories made the front pages, and none of them prompted follow-ups. When media organizations want to cover a topic, very often they use an initial report of an arrest or incident as a jumping-off point. Journalists at their best ask questions and explore many different angles. They explore the history of the story, the cultural relevance of the story—they often look at minor characters that the public might want to know more about. In short, they look at all the angles. But not on the Gosnell story. The rare story that did appear included some sort of apologia from pro-abortion activists about how Gosnell's indictment shouldn't be taken as an indictment of abortion itself. Typically, newspapers went with wire copy. The January 20, 2011, Associated Press dispatch by David Crary was headlined, "Philly Abortion Murder Case Fuels National Debate."[1] But as journalist Mollie Hemingway pointed out, the supposedly objective AP story "begins and ends with quotes from abortion rights activists and pro-choice framing overwhelms the piece." And, Hemingway noted, Crary didn't write another word about Gosnell until May 4, 2013. That story was headlined,"Philly Abortion Murder Trial Has National Impact." It read a lot like his story from two years earlier. AP did carry some trial news culled from local stringers, but its national reporter wasn't assigned to cover the case.[2]

Conservative new media and pro-life activists reported the Gosnell case from the very beginning, starting with the first police raid on the Women's Medical Society clinic in 2010. On Facebook, Twitter, and in multiple blogs, the story of the notorious abortion doctor from Philly was reported regularly until January 2011, when the grand jury's report exploded on the scene and Gosnell and his wife were arrested for murder. Along with Hemingway, J. D. Mullane, radio host and blogger Dana Loesch, satirist Iowahawk, writer Mark Steyn, Breitbart.com's John Nolte, the *National Catholic Register*, the Catholic news site LifeNews.com, and blogger and conservative syndicated columnist Michelle Malkin were all over the story. They covered the grand jury report, the arrests, and the trial. They explored the story from multiple angles, noting how the Pennsylvania Department of Health had failed to inspect Gosnell's clinic for years. They called attention to other states' abortion laws and pointed out how Gosnell could have gotten away with murder elsewhere, too. In short, they did the work that reporters in the national press should have been doing.

"I would love to critique the coverage of the trial of Kermit Gosnell, the abortion doctor whose mass murder trial is going on right now in Philadelphia," wrote Mollie Hemingway at the Get Religion blog on April 8, 2013. "The only problem is that there is a curious lack of media coverage." Apart from a short story the *New York Times* buried on page A17 on the trial's first day, she didn't have much to work with.[3]

Until Hemingway and other conservative and Christian bloggers began pointing out the dearth of coverage in early April 2013, the trial had received no attention on any of the network newscasts and, as the *Washington Examiner*'s David Freddoso pointed out, just seven mentions on cable news from the time it had begun on March 13—and six of those were on Fox News. (The other single mention was on CNN.)[4]

Hemingway is a smart, tenacious reporter who made her name writing about the myriad ways mainstream U.S. journalists make a hash of religion. Now a senior editor at the *Federalist*, Hemingway was one of the new media up-and-comers who pushed the Gosnell trial into the national spotlight where it belonged. "The fact that we were all talking about this shows that this was something that the mainstream media was not in touch with," Hemingway told us. "We were waiting for this to be massive news, as we know from all other media coverage of serial murderers and abortion topics.... Unlike stories about women who kill their boyfriends or whatever, where you get hourly updates on CNN, we were getting *nothing*."[5]

After the trial got underway in 2013, Twitter users by the thousands seized the opportunity to tag #Gosnell when they pointed out media hypocrisy in the coverage of mass shootings in Aurora, Colorado, and Newtown, Connecticut, or any periodic media frenzy over some politician's gaffe.

Some celebrities got involved, too. Actress Patricia Heaton, famous for her role as Ray Romano's wife on the CBS sitcom *Everybody Loves Raymond*, was a prominent voice calling attention to the trial. On April 5 Heaton tweeted, "The news coming out of the Gosnell abortion clinic trial is absolutely horrifying, yet not one network has done any coverage of it. Not one." Her complaint was retweeted 1,744 times.

Heaton tweeted regularly during the trial, and her tweets got noticed. "Media treats footballer's imaginary girlfriend as real," she wrote, referring to a bizarre story about San Diego Chargers linebacker Manti Te'o's fictional dead girlfriend, but "treats murdered babies in Philly abortion clinic as imaginary." That tweet was retweeted 5,694 times and favorited 987 times. Iowahawk tweeted, "What Romney did with a scissors in 1965: 20 acres of front page. What #Gosnell did with a scissors: crickets. #AirbrushingMassMurder." Mitt Romney, for anyone who cares to remember, reportedly cut off a fellow student's hair when he was a rambunctious lad at boarding school five decades ago. This earth shattering news dominated an entire news cycle during the 2012 election campaign.

A look at Twitter between March 18, 2013—the day the trial began—and March 31 tells an interesting tale of how old media was dragged into covering the story by a tidal wave of social media.

Only local media and a few pro-life activists tweeted on day one of the trial. One Twitter user with the memorable handle @ExPoleDancer wrote, "FYI—today was the first day of the trial of Philly abortionist/baby & woman killer Dr. Kermit #Gosnell. #philly #prolife." On March 20 Erica Voll tweeted, "This #Gosnell case is astounding. Watching the stream is like getting punched in the gut over and over again." On the opening day of testimony blogger

Pundette tweeted a link to a post in which she had urged her readers to "get over whatever prejudices are keeping them from getting on the right side of this issue, for the good of the victims of this ghastly culture, and for their own good as well."[6] Nationally syndicated columnist Mark Steyn picked up that post and commented on it at National Review Online. Steyn, a conservative writer, had taken an early interest in the case and commented often. He compared the mainstream media's tepid response to Gosnell with their coverage of the mass shooting at Sandy Hook Elementary School in Newtown, Connecticut, a few months earlier. "One solitary act of mass infanticide by a mentally-ill loner calls into question the constitutional right to guns, but a sustained conveyor belt of infanticide by an entire cadre of cold-blooded killers apparently has no implications for the constitutional right to abortion," Steyn wrote.[7]

Other Twitter users picked up on the same theme during the first week of the trial. "Hey@piersmorgan," Ben Crystal wrote to now-former CNN chat-show host Piers Morgan. "So @TheDemocrats slandering the @NRA for #Newtown is news; but #gosnell the abortionist/butcher is not? #Journalism!" "He kept severed feet in jars yet escaped mainstream media coverage #Gosnell trial continues," tweeted a user called @IdaFlo. Linden deCarmo, a self-described Christian, software architect, and "small government enthusiast," tweeted on March 21, "What ever happened 2 #ItBleedsItLeads? Do normal rules not apply when the accused supports 1 of the sacred cows of the left? #gosnell." Twitter user @tricky223, a "poleclimbing Redneck who clings to his religion and guns while entertaining a fetish for the Constitution," tweeted to ABC, CBS, and NBC News, "If the @NRA is responsible 4 Sandy Hook then isn't #PlannedParenthood responsible 4 #Gosnell the Butcher of Philly?" Pro-life activist Mary Mack replied to a snarky post-Newtown tweet by British comedian Ricky Gervais, who wondered, "Why don't pro-life groups picket gun shops instead of hospitals?" "Because guns dont kill people, #abortion docs kill people. Thats why. #Gosnell," she wrote. (Gervais offered no response.)

On March 27 the Associated Press published a story about the trial in which reporter Maryclaire Dale described Gosnell as "an elegant man who appears serene in court" and who "smiled softly as he listened to testimony."[8] The Media Research Center's Newsbusters. org website noted the AP dispatch was one of the few national news items to appear since the trial began—and it seemed to present Gosnell in an almost sympathetic light.[9]

The pressure ratcheted up a little more on March 31, two weeks after the trial opened, when *Wall Street Journal* columnist Peggy Noonan tried to force the Gosnell trial into the national conversation on NBC's *Meet the Press*. "The real story this week is the haunting and disturbing story of this doctor in Philadelphia, Gosnell, who is being tried this week," Noonan said. "And if you wanted to watch the testimony, it was hard to find. But if you wanted to have a sense what was happening, you could find it on the Internet or in the local papers." The three major broadcast news networks had barely uttered a word about the case up to that point. And Noonan's observation seemed to have no effect. There were no immediate follow-up stories, not even on NBC.[10]

But alternative media was covering the trial closely. LifeNews, for example, was posting several stories a day throughout late March and early April, including several pieces calling out the national media's blackout—not to mention politicians' silence—on the story. Twitter users escalated their naming and shaming. Jeffrey D. Dickson, a conservative activist with more than sixty thousand followers, tweeted on April 1, "Obama 'weeps' for the children of Newtown but is completely unmoved by the deaths of the abortion survivor babies of Kermit Gosnell." "Dear @abc @nbc @cbs @cnn we shouldn't have to rely on @PatriciaHeaton or the UK press to give us details on the

Gosnell trial," tweeted @KevininABQ on April 6. "Do your jobs." Hundreds of similar tweets appeared over the same period, all echoing that message.

A group of pro-life activists including Bryan Kemper of Priests for Life, Jill Stanek, and Steven Ertelt of LifeNews organized a tweetfest on April 12 from noon till midnight. Kemper, who was the motivator in chief for the tweetfest, wrote "On your mark get set GO! Who is #Gosnell-Tweet till your fingers bleed!"

And finally, someone in the mainstream media noticed.

Kirsten Powers is probably best known as a Fox News analyst and a columnist for the *Daily Beast* and *USA Today*, but she started out as a political operative for the Clinton-Gore presidential transition team in 1992 and spent five years in the administration as deputy assistant U.S. trade representative for public affairs. Although she was raised as an Episcopalian, she spent much of her adult life as an atheist. She became an evangelical Christian in her thirties, and she has called her conversion "a bit of a mindbender," given her generally liberal politics and her longtime aversion to religion. But she may be the only liberal newspaper columnist in America who is staunchly and outspokenly pro-life. It was Powers who gave the Gosnell trial the final push it needed into the national spotlight with her April 11, 2013, column in *USA Today*.

At the time *USA Today* had the largest weekday circulation among all national newspapers with 2.88 million readers, besting the *Wall Street Journal* (2.27 million readers) and the *New York Times* (1.89 million readers). The column by Powers was a scathing attack on her liberal colleagues in the mainstream media, and the subheadline on the piece was a seven-word indictment: "We've Forgotten What Belongs on Page One."[11]

In an interview with RealClearPolitics' editor Carl Cannon, Powers explained how the Gosnell story had come to her attention. Her best friend from college, who coincidentally also had found religion later in life and was strongly pro-life, "kept bugging me about this Gosnell thing." After her now-famous column appeared, Powers had to apologize to her friend because, she said, "even I had been on the phone with her, and she had been talking about it, and [I] had sort of been rolling my eyes, like, '*I'm sure*.'"

"If something like this was going on, I would know about it," she thought.

Powers was cleaning out her email box and came across all of the stories her friend had sent from pro-life websites and the local Philadelphia press. "I started reading them and just thought, 'This can't be true.' ... And I was so horrified by it. I just couldn't believe it wasn't being covered." But it wasn't. She pitched the idea for a column to her editor at *USA Today*. "I emailed the editor and said, 'We gotta do something on this,' thinking he would say no. You know, because it's just a little hot, this issue." To her surprise, he said yes—she should write it for later in the week. Then about an hour later she heard back from her editor, who said they'd want the article for the next day's paper. "So I had to write it in two hours and I knew, obviously, not too much about it because...I hadn't really been following it. It was a real scramble and a real high-wire act, getting it done." The most influential column of her career, knocked out over a couple of hours.[12]

The article began, "Infant beheadings. Severed baby feet in jars. A child screaming after it was delivered alive during an abortion procedure. Haven't heard about these sickening accusations? It's not your fault. Since the murder trial of Pennsylvania abortion doctor Kermit Gosnell began March 18, there has been precious little coverage of the case that should be on every news show and front page."

Powers recounted Steven Massof's testimony about snipping babies' spinal cords, "calling it, 'literally a beheading. It is separating the brain from the body.' ... Massof, who, like other witnesses, has himself pleaded guilty to serious crimes, testified, 'It would rain fetuses. Fetuses and blood all over the place.' Here is the headline the Associated Press put on a story about his testimony that he saw 100 babies born and then snipped: 'Staffer Describes Chaos at PA Abortion Clinic.'"

"'Chaos' isn't really the story here," Powers pointed out. "Butchering babies that were already born and were older than the state's 24-week limit for abortions is the story."

Powers did a Lexis-Nexis search and learned that none of the major network news shows had mentioned the Gosnell trial in the previous three months. The exception was Noonan's appearance on "Meet the Press," where she "hijacked a segment...meant to foment outrage over an anti-abortion rights law in some backward red state."

"You don't have to oppose abortion rights to find late-term abortion abhorrent or to find the Gosnell trial eminently newsworthy," Powers wrote. "This is not about being 'pro-choice' or 'pro-life.' It's about basic human rights. The deafening silence of too much of the media, once a force for justice in America, is a disgrace."[13]

With this column in a major newspaper, the story of the media's blackout of the Kermit Gosnell trial became a story too big to be ignored.

Powers's column went viral. Twitter lit up and, for the first time, Gosnell's name trended worldwide. There was no ignoring the trial and its grisly truths any longer.

Mollie Hemingway used the publication of Powers's column to go on Twitter and ask national reporters why they chose to ignore the trial. Many simply chose to ignore Hemingway's questions as well.

Hemingway recalled for us how frustrated she was with the coverage up to that point. "I remember being totally fed up," she said. Powers's column was the perfect way to challenge mainstream media journalists about their failure to pay attention to the story. But first Hemingway had a hurdle to overcome with her editor at Get Religion. He didn't like his writers to personally name reporters because, in his view, news production is a team effort. "You never know if it's the reporter who's to blame, an editor, an assignment editor, a managing editor, a copy editor—don't name people because it might be unfair to them." She agrees with that approach, generally. But, as she told us, "at some point that allows people to escape personal responsibility for their own role in the blackout of a major media event. Which is why I started personalizing it." Her editor agreed.[14]

Hemingway noticed that Sarah Kliff of the *Washington Post* had written at great length about the Susan G. Komen Foundation's decision in 2012 to stop funding Planned Parenthood—a decision the foundation rescinded after a huge media firestorm fueled by Kliff's reporting. Kliff had also written numerous stories about Sandra Fluke, the Georgetown Law School student who gained national fame when Rush Limbaugh called her a "slut" on the air for her demands for free birth control. Kliff had also written about Todd Akin, the former U.S. congressman and U.S. Senate candidate from Missouri whose campaign self-destructed when he said abortions were usually unnecessary for rape victims because "if it's legitimate rape, the female body has ways to try to shut the whole thing down." Yet Kliff hadn't written a word about Gosnell. Why not? Hemingway asked.

Kliff replied on Twitter, "Hi Molly—I cover policy for the *Washington Post*, not local crime, hence why I wrote about all the policy issues you mention."

That's funny. When Akin made his "legitimate rape" comment, Kliff asked every pro-life politician she could find to comment and managed to milk more than *three dozen* stories out of it. When a national talk radio personality said something nasty about an activist almost no one had ever heard of, Kliff managed to extract several stories out of that, too.[15] But an abortionist who killed hundreds or possibly thousands of babies that were born alive? A local crime and not worth a story about its wider significance.

Kliff's tone-deaf tweet to Hemingway garnered *hundreds* of snarky and angry replies. One of the wittiest was from RealClear-Politics editor Robert VerBruggen, who quipped, "Makes sense. Similarly, national gun-policy people do not cover local crime in places like Aurora or Newtown."[16] Surely Trayvon Martin's shooting death in Florida was a local crime story? And the Arizona murder trial of Jodi Arias that received wall-to-wall cable news coverage mere months before Gosnell's trial began? Or how about the case of Casey Anthony, the Orlando, Florida, woman whose exoneration in the murder of her two-year-old daughter received coverage comparable to that of O. J. Simpson's trial?

The idea that the trial of a serial murderer of newborn babies was not worthy of national attention is utter nonsense. The news is dominated by murder—the more grisly the better. That the perpetrator in this case was a doctor was better yet for potential viewer interest. A nice middle class doctor as serial killer would be fascinating to consumers of news. And the government corruption angle—the fact that *all* the government agencies charged with protecting the people of the Commonwealth of Pennsylvania failed to do anything to stop him—is the very *raison d'etre* of the Fourth Estate.

Journalists aren't always the most imaginative lot, but the policy implications of Gosnell's crimes weren't hard to see. Hemingway offered Kliff an easy one: "President Obama worked against the Born-Alive Infants Protection Act back in the Illinois Senate. He said he thought it was unnecessary and that he was worried it would undermine [*Roe v. Wade*]. How has the Gosnell case affected his thinking on protections for children such as the ones Gosnell is accused of killing?"[17]

Less than twenty-four hours after Kliff's idiotic "local crime" tweet went viral, the *Post*'s executive editor, Martin Baron, issued a *mea culpa*. "We believe the story is deserving of coverage by our own staff, and we intend to send a reporter for the resumption of the trial next week," he wrote. "In retrospect, we should have sent a reporter sooner."[18] The following Monday, Kliff herself backtracked. "When I described the case of abortion provider Kermit Gosnell on Twitter last week as a local crime story, I was clearly wrong," she wrote.[19]

Clearly.

By the way, the *Post*'s readers never read President Obama's thoughts about Gosnell or the Born Alive Act because Kliff never got around to asking him.

Suddenly, serious journalists were trying to explain where they'd been during the early weeks of the most shocking trial of the century. The fact is, the members of the media are just ordinary people with all their weaknesses, ideologies, and preferences. These ideologies and preferences tend to be liberal, and until the new media emerged on the Internet, the public had no real way of bypassing these ordinary people who acted as gatekeepers for the public's right to know. Their explanations were revelatory. Taken together, they offer a sobering reminder of the power of the media to control what is and is not news.

The *Atlantic*'s Conor Friedersdorf confessed that until April 11, "I wasn't aware of this story.... had I been asked at a trivia night about the identity of Kermit Gosnell, I would've been stumped and helplessly guessed a green Muppet. Then I saw Kirsten Powers' *USA Today* column. She makes a powerful, persuasive case that the Gosnell trial ought to be getting a lot more attention in the national press than it is getting.... The news value is undeniable."[20]

Slate's David Weigel wrote on April 12 that he couldn't explain why the media had fumbled the story so badly. "Somebody else can try," he wrote. "It's never made sense to me, how a local crime story becomes a national story.... If you're pro-choice, say, and you worry that the Gosnell story is being promoted only to weaken your cause, you really should read the grand jury report. 'DOH could and should have closed down Gosnell's clinic years before,' write the investigators. Why wasn't it? Were state regulators nervous about igniting a political fight about abortion? Is the regulatory system incompetent or under-funded? And are there other states where the same could be said? Social conservatives are largely right about the Gosnell story. Maybe it's not a raw political story. It's just the story of a potential mass murderer who operated for decades as government regulators did nothing."[21]

The same day, *Bloomberg* columnist Jeffrey Goldberg acknowledged the media blackout of the case. "It's too late now, though, to suppress coverage," he wrote. "Powers and others have shamed the media into paying attention, and the press is now on the case. It's remarkable that it took this long."[22]

By Monday, April 15, the *New York Times* deigned to analyze the media's scandalous lack of coverage. "[A]fter an online furor that the case was being ignored by the national news media because of troubling accounts of late-term abortions," wrote Trip Gabriel, "reporters from major newspapers and television networks descended Monday on the Court of Common Pleas. It was the latest example of the power of social media to drive a wide debate." Gabriel asked various media experts to explain what went wrong. Kelly McBride, a specialist in media ethics at the Poynter Institute, said the absence of coverage was likely nothing more than a big misunderstanding. But, she added, thank goodness for social media. "One of the ways the news media knows how to cover a story these days is because of the attention in social media," McBride told Gabriel. "That's how people judge whether there's an appetite for a story."

The *Times* also noted that some conservative news outlets hadn't paid much attention to the trial, either.[23] And it was a fair criticism. As Paul Fahri had pointed out in the previous day's *Washington Post*, a Lexis-Nexis search showed that the *Weekly Standard* and *National Review* hadn't published anything about the trial, and the *New York Post* had run exactly one commentary criticizing the lack of news coverage—a criticism that should have included the *Post*'s own treatment of the story. Fox News was the one national cable channel to cover the story from the beginning of the trial.[24]

Local Philadelphia-area reporter J. D. Mullane of the Bucks County *Courier Times* took a picture of the empty section reserved for journalists the day Powers's column appeared. He was risking contempt of court—Judge Minehart had banned all cameras from the courtroom—but the picture sent a powerful message. Mullane tweeted it, and it very quickly traveled.

———

Court was out of session the Friday after Powers's column appeared. When the court reconvened the following Monday, Judge Minehart addressed the jury first thing. "Ladies and gentlemen, it's come to my attention the media coverage of this case has increased.... " At the end of the day, Minehart admonished jurors again: "Ladies and gentlemen, I advise you that there has been enhanced media coverage apparently and you have to be vigilant not to listen to anything or read anything or watch anything on TV. We just want to keep your minds clear so you take the evidence from the witness stand."[25]

Margaret Sullivan, public editor for the *New York Times*, ridiculed the suggestion that her paper was ignoring the Gosnell case because of a "vast left-wing media conspiracy." "Until last week," she wrote, when the pro-life movement was successful in putting enough pressure on the media to cover the trial, most mainstream media outlets had virtually ignored it. I don't think that editors and reporters got together and decided not to give the Gosnell trial a lot of attention because it would highlight the evils of abortion. I *do* think that it wasn't on their radar screen—and that it should have been. The murders of seven newborn babies, done so horrifically, would be no ordinary crime. Any suggestion, including mine on Friday, that this is just another murder trial is a miscalculation. Judged on news value alone, the Gosnell trial deserves more coverage than it's had, in the *Times* and elsewhere. Those who have called for more attention to this grisly and disturbing trial are right. But some of them—because of their accusations of politics overcoming news judgment—are right for the wrong reasons.

Sullivan tried to assure readers that the newspaper's editors hadn't gone out of their way to shun the story. "The behavior of news organizations often owes more to chaos theory than conspiracy theory," she wrote.[26]

Sullivan's admission was welcome, even if she was still a little too defensive. Often the problem in newsrooms is the unexamined and unperceived bias that governs coverage. Fish don't notice they're in water until the fisherman's net hauls them out into the air. As *Slate*'s Weigel put it in his April 12 column, "Let's just state the obvious: National political reporters are, by and large, socially liberal. We are more likely to know a gay couple than to know someone who owns an 'assault weapon.' We are, generally, pro-choice. There is a bubble. Horror stories of abortionists are less likely to permeate that bubble than, say, a story about a right-wing pundit attacking an abortionist who then claims to have gotten death threats."[27]

Wall Street Journal columnist James Taranto described the journalistic dereliction in the Gosnell trial as the "banality of bias." He wrote shortly after Powers's *USA Today* column appeared, "Laziness, prejudice and pride are ordinary human failings. As we've seen from the press's treatment of the Gosnell story, they can lead those whose calling is to bear witness to avert their eyes from radical evil. Call it the banality of bias."[28]

Taranto's colleague Daniel Henninger echoed that theme in a column published the same week. "In these times of a media that need to fill a bottomless electronic news hole, a story as sensational as the Gosnell abortion trial should be everywhere. But as conservative bloggers and a few liberal writers such as Kirsten Powers have established in recent weeks, most major newspapers and TV networks have produced little or cursory coverage of this trial. The two exceptions are the Associated Press and Fox News."[29]

Henninger was right. Even his own newspaper didn't cover the case. A search of the *Journal's* archive for Kermit Gosnell produces one mention prior to April 11, 2013. That was a story about Pennsylvania's grand jury system, focused on the Jerry Sandusky child abuse case.

Marc Lamont Hill, host of HuffPost Live, readily acknowledged the bias at work. "For what it's worth, I do think that those of us on the left have made a decision not to cover this trial because we worry that it'll compromise abortion rights," he said. "Whether you agree with abortion or not, I do think there's a direct connection between the media's failure to cover this and our own political commitments on the left. I think it's a bad idea, I think it's dangerous, but I think that's the way it is."[30]

The best that most media outlets could say of their coverage of the trial was that at least they published *something*. A wire story here, a wire story there. But they weren't interested in the case. They didn't follow up. They didn't look at the case from different angles. They didn't ask good questions. They didn't think there were any good questions to ask.

Would daily coverage of the Gosnell trial have been excessive? Certainly no more excessive than the incessant coverage of Todd Akin or Sandra Fluke or any number of scandals, real and perceived, and political hijinks that are part and parcel of the twenty-four-hour news cycle.

Compare for a moment the Gosnell coverage with the coverage of the Trayvon Martin case. Martin was the seventeen-year-old African American in Sanford, Florida, who got into an altercation with a neighborhood watch volunteer named George Zimmerman and was shot to death. Martin's manner of death was controversial, and his encounter with Zimmerman was the subject of conflicting accounts. Kermit Gosnell was accused of killing multiple babies and their manner of death was similarly controversial. The victims in both cases were black. Unlike the Gosnell case, however, reporters asked President Obama about Trayvon Martin, and the president famously replied that Martin "could have been my son."

Martin's death was arguably a "local crime," too. But the disparity in coverage was massive. In the Trayvon Martin case, reporters were quick to seize on a public policy angle (Florida's "Stand Your Ground" self-defense law) as well as a racial angle (until the Martin case, nobody had ever heard the term "white Hispanic") and flog both within an inch of their lives. The *New York Times* published 858 articles about Martin, including news stories, features, analyses, editorials, and op-eds. By contrast, the *Times* published just thirty-eight articles about or referring to the Gosnell case—including Margaret Sullivan's piece admitting that the story deserved a great deal more coverage than it had received.

We saw similar results at CNN.com and FoxNews.com. At CNN, a search for "Trayvon Martin" yielded 816 hits; "Kermit Gosnell" resulted in just twenty-five hits.

The ostensibly right-wing Fox News published *30,800* articles about Trayvon Martin or at least mentioning his name. And Gosnell? Just *506* mentions of the abortionist online.

Sparse coverage of that sort is completely contrary to what typically happens when a horrific crime occurs. Mollie Hemingway noted the stark contrast between the media's blackout of Gosnell and the wall-to-wall coverage of the racially motivated mass shooting on June 17, 2015, at the Emanuel African Methodist Episcopal Church in Charleston, South Carolina. A white man named Dylann Roof walked into the church and participated in a Bible study before pulling a gun and killing nine people in cold blood. He said his goal was to start a race war. Later, pictures emerged of him holding the Confederate flag. "You had hundreds upon hundreds of stories dealing with really interesting issues related to how different people interpret Confederate symbols. It's not hard for reporters to figure out that would be an interesting angle here. But for some reason they were just completely unable to look into [Gosnell]." The coverage of the Charleston shooting was so exhaustive that the Confederate flag became a national political hot button. South Carolina Governor Nikki Haley eventually ordered the flag removed from the statehouse grounds, saying "it never should have been there." City councils and state legislatures across the country rushed to ban Confederate symbols and change the names of streets and parks named after Confederate leaders. Without question, the massive media coverage drove that decision making. It isn't difficult to imagine that more extensive coverage of the Gosnell case could have led to changes to state abortion laws, too.

But from the beginning of the Gosnell case, as details emerged about what the doctor was doing at his Women's Medical Society clinic, partisans of abortion rushed to downplay and dismiss the significance of the story. Gosnell was an outlier, a "rogue operator." That was how Katha Pollitt, a columnist for the hard-left *Nation* magazine, described the doctor. Pollitt set the tone in a January 2011 article, published the week of the grand jury report, which totally misrepresented key aspects of the case. The blood-spattered floors, cat feces, and broken equipment were examples of "what illegal abortion looks like." The real problem, Pollitt maintained, was that Pennsylvania's "antichoice" lawmakers had been so keen to restrict abortion that they didn't demand proper oversight. As Carol Tracy of the Women's Law Project told Pollitt, "The problem here was that Pennsylvania has always focused on eliminating abortion, not on abortion as healthcare."[31] But the fact is, illegal abortions were nowhere near the majority of procedures Gosnell and his co-conspirators performed—unless you count them all as illegal for his defiance of the twenty-four-hour-in-advance counseling requirement. But that counseling requirement is, ironically, the very kind of "antichoice" legislation that Pollitt was blaming for Gosnell's house of horrors. The vast majority of the abortions at his clinic were performed on fetuses that were below Pennsylvania's legal limit of twenty-three weeks and six days.

Pollitt contended, in all seriousness, that Pennsylvania's restrictions on abortion had made Gosnell possible. Never mind Tom Ridge's hands-off policy, which ended inspections at abortion clinics, but which Pollitt seemed to find difficult to believe of a Republican without some sort of nefarious ulterior motive. No, it was the laws mandating parental notification, twenty-four-hour waiting periods, and "biased" counseling (because informing women about adoption is "biased")—laws that Gosnell had regularly broken—and a lack of state subsidies for abortions for low-income women that laid the foundation for Gosnell to build and maintain his house of horrors.[32]

The lack of coverage of the Gosnell case puts the lie to the old cliché that the role of the journalist is to "afflict the comfortable and comfort the afflicted." The truth is, establishment media outlets have their preferred subjects that resonate with them. These subjects are what they like to write and talk about. And when they get interested in a story—they really get interested.

In June 2015, for example, *New York Times* public editor Margaret Sullivan had to defend her paper's obsession with a book called *Primates of Park Avenue: A Memoir*. The book describes Wednesday Martin's experience of moving to the Upper East Side of Manhattan. It's a silly, ephemeral book about the comfortable lives of upper class women—no different from much of what passes for memoir these days, but appealing to the class prejudices of a certain type of elite New Yorker. The *Times* featured the book on the cover of its Sunday Review; published not one but *two* reviews; two opinion columns; several blog posts; and a news story about the phenomenon. Finally, Sullivan had to write a column sheepishly explaining the newsroom's obsession with a book that was already piling up in the used stacks at The Strand bookstore in Lower Manhattan.[33]

Kermit Gosnell's victims weren't comfortable. Not at all. They were poor and mostly minorities. And they didn't fit an easy or comfortable media narrative. Trayvon Martin was supposed to be a victim of a racist gun culture. Michael Brown in Ferguson, Missouri, was the victim of an out-of-control police force that pitted armed white cops against unarmed black kids. Gosnell's victims didn't fit an easy or comfortable media narrative, but their stories raised disturbing questions that should have been pursued by any reporter worth his or her salt.

What was Semika Shaw? She was a poor black woman who had a botched abortion and died. Outside of a conscientious former clinic employee, nobody knew her name or thought it worth knowing until Gosnell's crimes were brought to light. Most of Gosnell's other victims were poor and black, too. Many of them hobbled away from the Women's Medical Society; some of them contracted sexually transmitted diseases from unsterilized, reused instruments; and more than a few wound up in Philadelphia hospitals with complications from Gosnell's botched procedures. Gosnell murdered black babies. Oh, and Gosnell himself was black. But strangely he provided better treatment to his white patients. Why did none of this appeal to liberal journalists with their highly attuned sense of social justice? There were at least half a dozen entry points where journalists could have used the Gosnell case to look at all sorts of different issues. "In addition to all that basic 'just the facts' type of stuff, there are angles to fuel literally hundreds of stories in every paper that is interested in topics of women's health and abortion and immigration issues, and all those kinds of things," Mollie Hemingway told us. "You did not see that. You did not see many stories about these underlying issues."[34]

A black serial killer's black victims simply didn't fit the standard media narrative about race. And Gosnell's crimes were even worse for the pro-choice narrative about abortion. Since the Gosnell case, the evidence continues to pile up—there seems to be a media blackout on anything that makes abortion providers look bad.

In the summer of 2015, a group called the Center for Medical Progress began releasing a series of videos that showed, among other things, top executives of Planned Parenthood casually discussing how to harvest organs from freshly aborted fetuses and what price a baby's intact lungs, liver, and brain might fetch from a biotech research firm. The first video, posted on the Center's website and on YouTube on July 14, showed a conversation between Planned Parenthood Senior Medical Director Deborah Nucatola and undercover CMP staffers who had presented themselves as buyers for a California biotechnology company. In between bites of salad and sips of red wine, Nucatola described with a certain clinical detachment how she uses an ultrasound to make sure she can extract the best baby parts in one piece.

"So then you're just kind of cognizant of where you put your graspers, you try to intentionally go above and below the thorax, so that, you know, we've been very good at getting heart, lung, liver, because we know that," Nucatola explains. "So I'm not gonna crush that part, I'm going to basically crush below, I'm gonna crush above, and I'm gonna see if I can get it all intact."[35]

The story practically wrote itself: Planned Parenthood sells aborted baby parts. The executives' ghoulishness made an appalling scenario even more horrific. Over the next several weeks, the Center for Medical Progress posted more videos. In one, another executive helpfully explains that pricing a baby's organs and limbs is "just [a] matter of line items." As for the cost, "We bake that into our contract."[36] The videos raised serious legal and policy questions. Planned Parenthood claims to be in the business of women's health, but the series of video exposés makes a compelling case that it's in the baby parts business. Was the $1.2 billion organization changing medical protocols to make more money? Federal law prohibits selling fetal tissue for profit. Was Planned Parenthood profiting from selling "donated" tissue? Did the women who procured abortions from their local Planned Parenthood clinic even realize they were "donating" their fetuses? And just what is Planned Parenthood doing with the more than five hundred million dollars a year in taxpayer subsidies it receives? Federal law bans tax dollars from paying for abortions. Wouldn't an audit be in order?

The *Washington Post* was first out with the story in July. The headline on the *Post*'s website was remarkably accurate: "Undercover Video Shows Planned Parenthood Exec Discussing Organ Harvesting." Yes, that is exactly what the video showed. The story itself offered a balanced account that presented Planned Parenthood's reaction and the perspective of the people who oppose using organs from aborted babies for scientific research.[37]

But by the time the story appeared in the newspaper the next day, it had undergone a radical series of changes. The new headline read,

"Undercover Video Shows Planned Parenthood Official Discussing Fetal Organs Used for Research." Oh, was that all? Never mind then, nothing to see. And the story itself wasn't as balanced. Nucatola was demoted from a Planned Parenthood executive to a mere "official," and the story gave more space to Planned Parenthood's prepared statements denouncing the video.[38]

Very quickly, a narrative took hold. Whatever Planned Parenthood was doing, it was perfectly legal. The videos were "heavily edited"—never mind that the Center for Medical Progress released the full videos along with transcripts of the conversations. And instead of probing whether or not Planned Parenthood was breaking the law or misusing taxpayer funds, the media and several government agencies, including the California Department of Justice, began looking into the Center for Medical Progress and its backers.

Then, through the summer of 2015, as the Center for Medical Progress continued to release more videos containing more astonishing footage of Planned Parenthood officials and their business partners exhibiting a chillingly callous attitude toward the bodies of babies whose demise they profit from—and also an evident willingness to break the law—the media simply did their best to ignore the story.

The media blackout seemed to hold pretty well until the night of September 16, 2015, when Republican presidential candidate Carly Fiorina gave a short, impassioned plea to defund Planned Parenthood in light of the Center for Medical Progress revelations.

"I dare Hillary Clinton, Barack Obama to watch these tapes," Fiorina said. "Watch a fully formed fetus on the table, its heart beating, its legs kicking, while someone says we have to keep it alive to harvest its brain. This is about the character of our nation, and if we will not stand up and force President Obama to veto this bill, shame on us."[39]

It was a powerful moment. And one that must have come as a surprise to the twenty-three million viewers tuning in to watch on CNN, many of whom must have been asking themselves what this woman was going on about.

The Planned Parenthood videos were a national scandal. But national news outlets once again did their best to bury the story and discredit and marginalize the whistleblowers. Within an hour of the debate, media "fact checkers" were trying to brand Fiorina a liar. Planned Parenthood and its PR firm, SKDKnickerbocker, inundated journalists with talking points claiming that Fiorina had made up the whole thing. And journalists were all too happy to oblige them.

Leading the pack was none other than Sarah Kliff, now writing at Vox.com. "Carly Fiorina is wrong about the Planned Parenthood tapes," she wrote. "I know because I watched them."

"The things Fiorina describes—the legs kicking, the intact 'fully formed fetus,' the heart beating, the remarks about having to 'harvest its brain'—are pure fiction," Kliff insisted.[40]

Well, no—not quite. Once again, Mollie Hemingway had to correct the record. She pointed out in an article at the *Federalist* that Fiorina was probably referring to the Center for Medical Progress video posted on August 19, which did in fact show "a fully formed fetus, heart beating and legs kicking. And it shows this while Holly O'Donnell, a former organ harvester who worked for StemExpress at a Planned Parenthood affiliate, graphically discuss[es] the harvesting of a brain from a baby whose heart was beating."[41] The press also seized on a supposedly independent "forensic analysis" of the videos that raised questions about whether the transcripts of the videos were accurate. Never mind that Planned Parenthood had commissioned the analysis.[42] Or that a separate analysis not paid for by Planned Parenthood arrived at an entirely different conclusion.[43] But the stories also failed to show any journalistic curiosity. A significant point in the audit was that professional transcribers could not state with authority that a technician—in one of the headline-grabbing scenes from the video—actually uttered the phrase "it's a boy." The audio may not have been very clear, but Center for Medical Progress executive director David Daleiden says that's what the technician in fact said. Of course, the obvious solution for any journalist interested in real reporting on the story would have been to track down the technician and hear the truth directly from the source. But not a single reporter pursued that course. Instead, they went with the easy narrative that one indistinct phrase might discredit hundreds of hours of undercover work.

Then the press used the occasion of a Harris County, Texas grand jury's recommendation in January of 2016 to indict Daleiden for his undercover activity as an excuse to dismiss the CMP findings and claim vindication for Planned Parenthood. The same media outlets virtually ignored the dismissal of all charges a short time later.

How quickly the press forgets its own promises to practice better, more balanced journalism. With the serial admissions of bias in the Gosnell case came solemn vows from media mavens to do a better job covering difficult abortion stories in the future. The Kermit Gosnell trial was a teachable moment for the media. They'd been duly chastened and learned their lesson.

But when the Planned Parenthood videos appeared two years later, all of those vows and lessons were quickly forgotten. And once a Houston grand jury decided to indict the whistleblowers, well, "To me it's almost like an abusive spouse saying, 'Oh, baby, I promise, I'm going to do better a job.' And then they don't," Hemingway told us. "It's really damaging to the relationship."

ELEVEN

AMERICA'S BIGGEST SERIAL KILLER?

"The majority of serial killers are not reclusive, social misfits who live alone. They are not monsters and may not appear strange. Many serial killers hide in plain sight within their communities. Serial murderers often have families and homes, are gainfully employed, and appear to be normal members of the community. Because many serial murderers can blend in so effortlessly, they are oftentimes overlooked by law enforcement and the public."
—**FEDERAL BUREAU OF INVESTIGATION**[1]

"Kermit Gosnell is probably the most successful serial killer in the history of the world."
—**TERRY MORAN**, ABC News[2]

Like many serial killers, Kermit Gosnell had a lovely upbringing.[3] He was raised an only child in a middle class Philadelphia family. Doted on by his mother from an early age, he attended Dimner Beeber Junior High and graduated in 1959 from the prestigious Central High School.

Founded in 1836, Philadelphia's Central High is ranked as one of the best schools in the United States because of the high academic achievement of its students. Bill Cosby, Jeremiah Wright, and Noam Chomsky are among its famous (or infamous) graduates. Seth Williams, the current Philadelphia district attorney who made sure Gosnell never killed again, is another Central High alumnus.

When we interviewed Gosnell, the one well-known student he remembered clearly from his years at Central High was Ira Einhorn, an environmental activist who helped organize the first Earth Day in Philadelphia. Einhorn became much better known as "the Unicorn Killer." In 1977, he murdered his ex-girlfriend, Holly Maddux, and stuffed her body into a trunk in his wardrobe. She wasn't found for a year and a half. Einhorn escaped to Europe after his arrest, where he remained for twenty-three years. When he was eventually extradited and stood trial in his own defense, Einhorn claimed the CIA had killed Maddux in a bizarre conspiracy.

Gosnell started his undergraduate studies at the University of Pennsylvania but graduated from Dickinson College, gaming the racial quota system; it would have been more difficult to get into medical school if he had stayed at Penn.[4] He went on to study medicine at Thomas Jefferson University in Philadelphia, and then worked in the city until he was arrested.

Gosnell became a community activist in Mantua, a blighted, crime-ridden neighborhood in West Philadelphia. He was well liked and respected. He established a halfway house for drug addicts, as well as a program to help at-risk teens. A 1972 *Philadelphia Inquirer* story mentioned Gosnell as one of the finalists for the Junior Chamber of Commerce's "Young Philadelphian of the Year" because of his work at the halfway house.

During Gosnell's trial, Jack McMahon pushed hard on this narrative of selfless benevolence. He argued that Gosnell chose a life of service to the poor over the life of ease he could have easily chosen instead.

McMahon may have exaggerated Gosnell's opportunities and his sacrifice—after all, the defense never produced any evidence to back up these claims. But the doctor does seem to have made some real contributions. Gosnell's neighbors told us he was very generous with his time and particularly kind to the local children, whom he would treat for free if they had a fall playing in the street. He loved music. Like many Americans, he was concerned about staying healthy. He was a runner and competed in triathlons. He regularly chided his staff members who smoked and told them to quit their dangerous habit. He was an avid horticulturalist who often won top prize for his orchids in citywide competitions.[5]

McMahon claimed that Gosnell was "educated, professional, dedicated to the community, and an excellent father." In addition to raising six children of his own (with three wives), Gosnell unofficially fostered a child named Sherida Kennedy, who came to live with him and Pearl when she was only a month old. Her mother had many of the same problems as the women Gosnell tended to employ.

How could such a man be a serial killer? It turns out that almost everything we think we know about serial killers is wrong. The FBI—through its Behavioral Analysis Unit, made famous by the CBS television series *Criminal Minds*—has produced reams of research on serial killers. In the course of that research, they have discovered that most of the characteristics traditionally assigned to serial killers are simply myths.

MYTH: SERIAL KILLERS ARE ONLY MOTIVATED BY SEX.

"All serial murders are not sexually-based. There are many other motivations for serial murders including anger, thrill, financial gain, and attention seeking."[6]

It became clear from our research that financial gain was a huge motivator for Gosnell. Among the many calls we received from his former patients was one from a man who remembers very clearly seeing Gosnell at the clinic on a day when the reception area was crowded with patients. As the man waited in the cramped seating area, he saw Gosnell emerge from a treatment room in the back. The doctor sat down next to one of his workers and, smiling broadly, said, "Finally, I am making money."[7]

Judge Renée Cardwell-Hughes told us it was clear from the grand jury testimony that money was Gosnell's prime motivation. "He was a greedy, greedy, greedy person," she said. "That's why he wouldn't pay to have the facility cleaned. That's why he let the contract for appropriate [waste] disposal lapse. He was greedy. But he had convinced himself because he still believed himself to be a pillar of the community."[8]

Juror Joe Carroll agrees. He told an ABC News reporter after the trial, "Most of us felt it came down to a greed factor. The services…it was like a machine. They came in, he gave them a service, and bam, the women were gone."[9]

Gosnell typically demanded cash payments from his patients. Women who were already well past the twenty-four-week limit for legal abortion would be sent away for weeks until they came up with sufficient cash to pay for an abortion. And then, no matter how pregnant they were, Gosnell would take their money and "ensure fetal demise."

Gosnell kept cash in safes throughout the clinic. And, of course, there was the cabinet in his daughter's bedroom where police discovered more than two hundred and forty thousand dollars in cash. Gosnell would do anything for money, it seems. He reused pieces of equipment that cost a dollar. In the midst of his baby-killing "factory," as Ed Cameron described it, the Good Doctor also ran a "fertility clinic" where for one hundred and fifty dollars women were told to drink baking soda and vinegar. Oh, and they were advised to vary the times they had sex. The success rate for the Dr. Gosnell fertility advice is not clear, but it was another nice little earner.

Gosnell also may have been motivated by his anger. Many people who knew him told us about his ferocious temper, which could flare up at any time. A lot of that anger he took out on his patients, yelling and screaming at them and punching them with his fist when they complained of pain or woke during their abortions.[10]

And attention-seeking may have motivated him, too. He liked being in the same club as George Tiller and the other late-term abortion doctors, he liked the spotlight, the feeling of power. And now he thinks of himself as a martyr.

MYTH: SERIAL KILLERS ARE ALL WHITE MALES.

Gosnell is African American, and there is a persistent myth that serial killers are all white men. But that's not true. There are serial killers from all ethnic groups: White, African American, Hispanic, and Asian.

- Lonnie David Franklin Jr., A.K.A. the Grim Sleeper (African American) was convicted on May 5, 2016, of killing nine women and one teenage girl in Los Angeles, California
- Charles Ng (Chinese) was born and raised by wealthy parents in Hong Kong. He was convicted of killing six men, three women, and two babies in Northern California with his partner, Leonard Lake. The pair is believed to have raped, tortured, and killed as many as twenty-five victims. Ng is currently on death row in San Quentin
- Derrick Todd Lee (African American), nicknamed the Baton Rouge Serial Killer, was responsible for the murders of at least seven women in and around Baton Rouge, Louisiana. His killings spanned eleven years—in

part because authorities believed they were looking for a white male

- Coral Eugene Watts (African American), called the Sunday Morning Slasher, claimed to have murdered forty women. He confessed to twelve killings in the state of Texas alone and was also implicated in at least ten murders in Michigan

- Rafael Resendez-Ramirez (Latino), also known as the Railroad Killer, was an illegal alien from Mexico. He murdered at least nine and as many as fifteen people in Kentucky, Texas, Florida, and Illinois

- Rory Conde (Latino), dubbed the Tamiami Trail Strangler, was a Colombian national who strangled and sodomized (in that order) six prostitutes in Miami

MYTH: SERIAL KILLERS ARE ALL DYSFUNCTIONAL LONERS.

Dr. Elizabeth Yardley, director of the Centre for Applied Criminology at Birmingham City University in the UK, explained in a July 2015 article in *Real Crime* magazine that "many serial killers look like a pillar of the community on first sight," something she described as "possibly the scariest trait of all" among the murderers she has studied.[11]

There was no shortage of people who reached out to tell us what a nice man Gosnell was. We received dozens of calls from his former patients who wanted us to know that they really liked the doctor. People with good things to say about the doctor have written to our Gosnell Movie Facebook page. One patient of Gosnell's, a man who had damaged his feet while golfing in wet shoes ten years ago, told us that Gosnell was very good to him and refused payment.[12]

Adrienne Moton gave us a glowing description of Gosnell. To hear her tell it, Gosnell could have been anybody's genial next-door neighbor. "Gosnell, to me, he was a fun guy, caring. When I look back and see all this stuff that came out, I'm shocked. I'm shocked because I looked up to him. A lot of people looked up to him," she said. "He helped a lot of people," Moton told us. "Outside of the office, he was a fun person, laughed, chilled. He was into playing music. He knew I liked to sing, so he always tried to play the piano, and I'd sing along, which didn't work out too great...He was a health junkie. He loved working out, doing the garden, planting. He was laid back and got along with anybody."[13]

And she's not the only one who found Gosnell charming. We spoke to a secretary at a church in the neighborhood of the clinic. This neighbor, who wishes to remain anonymous, is still in complete shock about what Gosnell was doing. She had been a neighbor for years, and she and Gosnell used to have lots of fun together. She remembers having snowball fights in Gosnell's front yard. When we interviewed her at the church, she said she couldn't believe the headlines that had appeared in the local newspapers. "It's not the guy I knew," she told us.[14]

These pleasant descriptions tally well with the profile of other serial killers who were charming and outgoing. Ted Bundy appeared to be a well-liked man and an upstanding citizen. According to a *New York Times* article at the time, "People familiar with his early years say he was a Boy Scout, a B-plus college student; he loved children, read poetry and was a rising figure in Republican politics in Seattle. The year the murders began there, he was the assistant director of the Seattle Crime Prevention Advisory Commission and wrote a pamphlet for women on rape prevention."[15]

John Wayne Gacy, who murdered thirty-three boys and young men in Chicago, was loved by his neighbors, who described him as outgoing and helpful. He was very active in Democratic Party politics and even met First Lady Rosalynn Carter. He performed as a "Pogo the Clown" for children in hospitals.

A *Philadelphia Daily News* story on Gosnell included glowing testimonials from former patients: "When I wasn't working, I didn't have money to pay him," said Deborah Gray, fifty-seven, of West Philadelphia, a patient of Gosnell's for thirty-seven years. "I had no health insurance, but he would put the money I owed him on the books. If you were ever sick and couldn't get to his office, he would call in to the pharmacy for you."

"Many times people have not been able to fully pay me for my services," Gosnell noted. "As a principle, I have not refused to provide them care."

Debra Reynolds compares Gosnell to "an old-fashioned doctor in a country town that you could call any time." Reynolds, fifty-two, of West Philly, said Gosnell treated her and provided her with medication even though she was once uninsured for ten years. "He's done so many things for the love of this community," she added.[16]

MYTH: ALL SERIAL KILLERS ARE EITHER INSANE OR EVIL GENIUSES.

There was never any question about the soundness of Gosnell's mind. But, then again, few serial killers have been judged legally insane. The vast majority have been fit to stand trial. By and large, though, they do suffer from a variety of serious personality disorders. Psychiatrists we have spoken to say that Gosnell appears to suffer from narcissism.

In all our dealings with Gosnell the narcissism is evident. He talks about his exceptional intelligence, his brilliance at music, his poetry. In an appeal document he has penned in prison he writes of himself in the third person: "poetry of Defendant has been published in a variety of venues—including Dickinson College Bulletin, Philadelphia magazine, Buddhist Newsletter and a recent Documentary 3801 Lancaster." The last reference is particularly ironic given that the documentary *3801 Lancaster* is a damning portrait of Dr. Gosnell and his monstrous business.[17]

And serial killers are not especially intelligent. In film and television, serial killers always seem to be one step ahead of the police. The FBI says this isn't true in reality. It is certainly not true in the case of Kermit Gosnell. He was no criminal mastermind. He got away with his decades-long killing spree largely because of the incompetence of multiple government agencies that neglected to do their jobs. In the end, it took just one smart detective to discover and end the massacre at 3801 Lancaster Avenue.

MYTH: SERIAL KILLERS WANT TO GET CAUGHT.

When they start out, serial killers are inexperienced; with experience they make fewer and fewer mistakes. According to the FBI, "As serial killers continue to offend without being captured, they can become empowered, feeling they will never be identified...they feel that they *can't* get caught." This description fits Gosnell to a tee. Nothing he did alerted the authorities. He was invincible until he came into the sights of Detective Jim Wood.

To qualify as a serial killer, you must be guilty of the unlawful killings of two or more victims in separate events. Gosnell easily qualifies. He was convicted of first-degree murder in the deaths of three babies, whom he murdered on three separate occasions. To earn the title of America's biggest serial killer, he'd have had to kill a lot more people than that. And he did.

But exactly how big a serial killer is Gosnell? We have plenty of evidence to support our claim that he is the biggest serial killer in American history.

First, there was never any suggestion that the three babies Gosnell was convicted of murdering were unusual. The prosecutors simply selected the cases in which they believed they had the strongest likelihood of winning a conviction. But those babies died in a way that was standard practice at the Women's Medical Society clinic. Gosnell's modus operandi was to kill babies born alive by cutting their spinal cords. "Over the years, there were hundreds of 'snippings,'" the grand jury concluded. Their report is filled with evidence from a multitude of witnesses saying that hundreds of babies were killed in this way. Tina Baldwin said she witnessed Gosnell snip babies' necks "hundreds of times."

And then of course there were the Sunday babies, whose remains and files Gosnell destroyed. The grand jury heard from several witnesses about those babies—babies whose mothers were so far along in their pregnancies that Gosnell wouldn't allow his staff to assist in their abortions. Only his wife Pearl was present for those killings. Over thirty years, the number of Sunday murders would be in the hundreds, at least. "We may never know the details of these cases," the grand jury reported. "We do know, however, that, during the rest of the week, Gosnell routinely aborted and killed babies in the sixth and seventh month of pregnancy. The Sunday babies must have been bigger still."

Like the clichéd serial killer, Gosnell kept souvenirs of his crimes. All of those little baby feet in formaldehyde-filled glass jars were trophies. Kareema Cross was so disturbed by them that she took photos of them as far back as 2008. If anyone from the Pennsylvania Department of Health had bothered to inspect the Women's Medical Society, they would have seen them at once. Gosnell didn't hide them.

But the feet were not his only trophies. Gosnell also collected pictures of women's genitals. He snapped pictures when his patients were unconscious during their abortions. Steve Massof testified that he often saw Gosnell take out his cell phone and take pictures, ostensibly for "research" or for "teaching." Gosnell was not in fact conducting any research that Massof was aware of, nor did he teach. The doctor told Massof that he had an academic interest in female genital mutilation, and that he was photographing women from African countries where the practice is widespread. He would show the photographs to Massof and say whether he thought a particular woman had been circumcised expertly or not. We have also been told Gosnell liked to show the pictures to Jimmy Johnson, the janitor. When Officer Taggart was searching Gosnell's house, he found a collection of these pictures in a drawer.

In any discussion of serial killers, a few notorious names—those of the most prolific killers—always get mentioned. Ted Bundy admitted to killing thirty women, but it could well have been more. Gary Ridgeway, also known as the Green River Killer, was convicted of murdering forty-eight, but later confessed to others. John Wayne Gacy was convicted of killing thirty-three people. Jeffrey Dahmer was convicted of murdering and partially ingesting fifteen people. David Berkowitz, New York City's "Son of Sam," shot and killed six people. Less well known but significant are Dennis Rader, who killed ten people in Wichita, Kansas, and Aileen Wuornos, portrayed by Charlize Theron in the film *Monster*, who killed six men. Wayne Williams was convicted of killing only two men, but he is believed to have killed anywhere from twenty-three to twenty-nine children in Atlanta. Robert Hansen confessed to four murders but is suspected of more than seventeen. Juan Corona was convicted of murdering twenty-five people.

Their crimes are all horrific, and the number of victims is heartbreaking. But all these most notorious serial killers stand in the shadow of Dr. Kermit Gosnell. Strangely, Gosnell appears in no list we have found of known U.S. serial killers, though he is the biggest of them all. In reality, Kermit Gosnell deserves the top spot on any list of serial murderers. He's earned it.

TWELVE

MEETING THE MONSTER

BY ANN McELHINNEY

---

*"It was as though in those last minutes he was sum-
ming up the lesson that this long course in human
wickedness had taught us—the lesson of the fearsome
word-and-thought-defying banality of evil."*

—HANNAH ARENDT[1]

---

*"The most striking aspect of the test results is the
patient's total denial of responsibility for everything
that has happened to him. He can produce an 'alibi'
for everything. He presents himself as a victim of circumstances and blames other people who are out to
get him...the patient attempts to assure a sympathetic
response by depicting himself as being at the mercy of a
hostile environment."*

—JOHN WAYNE GACY'S 1968 PSYCHIATRIC EVALUATION[2]

The last time I had visited a prison was in Chisinau, Moldova, a tiny,
screwed-up landlocked proto-communist country sandwiched
between Romania and the Ukraine. A mostly forgotten country, it
had a never-even-noticed civil war in 1991 when a pro-Russian population formed an even more miserable breakaway republic called

Transdniestria. Chisnau, Moldova's capital, has almost no electricity at night. Often the only light on the main street after dark was from the McDonald's—and that's because it has its own generator. I was there in 2002 on assignment for the Irish Times, looking at conditions in Children's Prison No. 3, which housed hundreds of children on remand for years. Some were there for simply stealing a bottle of wine. The conditions were horrendous, the atmosphere dreary and threatening. It was a nightmare scene.

The state Correctional Institute at Huntingdon, where Kermit Gosnell is now a prisoner, is a long way from Moldova. The town is bright and prosperous like the surrounding Pennsylvania countryside. But Huntingdon Prison still seems dreary and threatening, like the prison in Moldova. Despite the massive security precautions, I never felt completely safe there, especially sitting in the large open-plan room where prisoners and visitors chat.

That was one of the biggest shocks of our visit. Kermit Gosnell may be one of America's biggest serial killers, in a prison full of other killers, but during visiting time they all sit in comfortable chairs within touching distance of their visitors. I was to find that out the hard way; Kermit Gosnell was very much within touching distance of me for the whole of our visit.[3]

Huntingdon is Pennsylvania's oldest prison. It opened in 1889 as a facility for delinquent boys and young men. Now it's a maximum-security facility housing more than two thousand inmates. The prison became nationally known in August 1999 because of the Norman Johnston escape. Johnston was serving four consecutive life terms for the murders of four teenagers in the 1970s. He escaped by losing forty pounds, allowing him to squeeze through the window in his cell. After a massive manhunt, a lot of panic, and nineteen days on the run, he was recaptured and returned to Huntingdon, where he remains today.

Our visit with Kermit Gosnell came after we talked several times on the phone. When you talk to Gosnell, either by phone or in person, the first thing that strikes you is his calmness. The first time he called, he sounded like a man coming in from playing eighteen holes of golf and ready for the nineteenth-hole cocktail, not someone serving three consecutive life terms who knows he'll die in prison.

Phelim and I drove from Philadelphia and stayed at a charming B&B in Solvang the night before our visit. At the B&B, we got plenty of questions about why we were in the area, but we dodged them by just saying we had some business in the area. Explaining that we were there to meet America's biggest serial killer might have made for some awkward conversations.

Huntingdon retains much of its original nineteenth-century stone architecture. The grounds are surrounded by high double razor wire fences with watchtowers and armed guards.

In the visitor's reception building, a prison guard checked us in. In his visitor application, Gosnell had described us as "friends."

I wore a big hoodie because I didn't want to appear wearing tight clothes. But it turns out that hoodies are a big no-no in a maximum-security facility. And there is no discussion or compromise. The top I had underneath was tight and low cut. I pulled it up as much as I could.

The entrance to the prison itself is imposing and grey, cold and frightening. Getting past the metal detectors was not easy. Phelim had no trouble, but I set them off three times. The prison has posted warnings telling women not wear underwire bras because they can set off the alarms. Too late. The guards told me to go through once again and, mercifully, the alarm didn't sound. We were in.

We crossed the grey courtyard and entered the visiting room.

The visiting room is a long rectangular box. Guards supervise from a command booth at the entrance. Along the left hand wall stands a row of vending machines. Visitors may not bring in any-thing—no money, no food, no gifts. But they can bring credit cards, and, because only visitors may use the machines, they're expected to buy the inmates treats.

Gosnell recommended we come on a weekday, as weekends at the prison are very busy and we'd likely have more time if we visited during the week.

Unlike what you may have seen on television, at Huntingdon there are no barriers between the prisoners and their visitors. No thick glass screen. And just how secure was the room, really? What would happen if all the prisoners decided to attack and take hostages on cue? Would the guards respond in time? It's probably best not to dwell on such things.

The inmates wear brown pants and a matching brown tunic with yellow trim. The buzzing from the fluorescent lights is made more tolerable by the sound system's constant soundtrack of golden oldies—the Beach Boys, Diana Ross, Elvis Presley ("Hound Dog," not "Jailhouse Rock," alas).

The inmates and their visitors—children, girlfriends, wives, mothers, and grandmothers—sit on soft armchairs. When we were there, a group of Amish dressed in their distinctive nineteenth-century garb sat at the far end of the room. Every now and again, one of them would make a trip to the vending machines, which they used like pros. We found seats against the righthand wall, which gave us a view of the whole room—I didn't want my back to anyone. Phelim and I sat next to each other, so Gosnell could sit opposite us.

We both suffer from chronic punctuality, and even with the difficulty getting past the metal detector, we were seated in the visitors' room by 11:20 a.m., though Gosnell was to meet us at noon. We weren't even sure he would turn up. Prisoners are alerted when they have visitors, but they are not forced to meet them. It's entirely up to them.

Beside the prisoners' entrance is a big clock. We waited and watched.

Prisoners and their visitors talked, held hands, and snuggled. Some kissed, some played cards. We noticed shelves along the side of the guards' booth stacked with games like Scrabble and playing cards and children's toys and—*hallelujah!*—scrap paper and pencils! Not only had we been barred from bringing any food into the prison, we hadn't been allowed to bring recording devices, cameras, paper, or pens. So we had planned to interview Gosnell and then rush back to the car and record ourselves recounting everything we remembered. It wasn't ideal, but it was the best we thought we could do. So this discovery was brilliant. We could take notes of the interview. I grabbed a bunch of paper and two pencils.

While we waited for Gosnell to appear, I was getting attention from a large thick-necked inmate sitting in my line of sight who kept mouthing the words "I know you." I'd look away, and then when I looked back he'd catch my eye again and mouth again that he knew me. He was mistaken, and he was also straight out of central casting: the guy who had killed his own family with his bare hands. My imagination was in overdrive.

Gosnell walked into the room at noon precisely.

Tall and smiling, he put out his hand immediately to shake our hands. We sat down with him. He chose to sit in the seat directly opposite me. He opened his legs wide on each side of my legs, straddling me, and leaned forward to bring his whole body uncomfortably close to mine.

Gosnell was relaxed and chatty and started by telling us about his Irish heritage and showing off his freckles. He behaved like an American tourist in Ireland, all charm and chat. We asked how he got the name Kermit.

"I was called Kermit after Teddy Roosevelt's youngest son. My grandfather was a great admirer of Teddy Roosevelt and named my father Armfield Kermit Gosnell. There is a tradition going back four generations that the eldest son was named after the father's middle name, so I was called Kermit, his middle name."

For a man in his mid-seventies, Gosnell looks very healthy. His back is straight. Nothing in his demeanor suggested he's at all bothered about multiple life sentences without the possibility of parole. The only thing visibly off about Gosnell when we first met him was a long tear in the right leg of his prison uniform pants.

"I've been in this prison for a year and I prefer it. The food is better here," he told us, adding with a laugh, "The quantities are bigger." Gosnell was chatty and affable, with a very soft, mellifluous voice. He described being busy with reading and writing. After years reading medical literature for work, he says, it's "a wonderful relief" to be able to read fiction, especially crime and mystery novels by James Patterson, Michael Connelly, and P. D. James. Mysteries help him escape, he said. "I've especially liked ones where the heroes are convicts who work through their problems."

Gosnell's only problems in prison, he tells us, are "time and money." He's just so busy playing and listening to music, reading, attending religious services and classes, and exercising that the days seem to rush on by. He has a cell to himself, where he writes. "I'm hoping to have a typewriter soon, which will help make some of my writing legible." Money is an issue—he has none, and the lack of it restricts his activities.

One could be forgiven for thinking that Gosnell is treating his prison sentence as a welcome vacation from the hectic life he'd been leading before. But he doesn't see it that way. Gosnell says he's a workaholic, just like his father. "My father was very strict and never vacationed. He would say, 'Why would you vacation when you still have bills and expenses to pay?' Although when he was older, he said he regretted it."

Gosnell was not quite as strict with himself as his father was, but close. "We vacationed the last weekend of every month because the volume was down. Because people got paid on the first day of the month. In forty years," he says, "I was never away for more than four days."

Gosnell was anxious to talk about anything and everything, whether or not we asked. Without prompting, he told us his then-seventeen-year-old daughter, Jenna, had done "extremely well" on her SATs—scoring 2270 out of a possible 2400—and had already received her first acceptance to a college in Boston even though she was still a junior in high school. He's proud of his six children, who mostly seem to have done well in life and performed at or near the top of their classes. (His son Barron Alexander, who legally changed his name from Barron Alexander Gosnell after the doctor's arrest, has been found guilty of burglary and aggravated assault in 2014, after he broke into a house and cut someone with a bayonet.)[4] Jenna seems to be the academic star "even though she's had a great deal of trauma in the last five years," he said.

Gosnell described what happened the day his house was raided by the police, and how his daughter handled herself. "If you were awakened by two detectives at gunpoint at the age of twelve—[and] your mother, who would never even cross the street except at the corner with the light, is in jail for two months—and then you've lived in a neighbor's home for five months so as not to be [put] in the public housing authority—and then your dear father, with whom you bike regularly, run regularly, cycle regularly, [and] swim regularly, is in jail for five years—you wouldn't be surprised if academically she falters. But her last report card, her lowest grade in a major subject [was] a 96. Somehow she has maintained, and I'm very proud of her."

The answer seemed fairly obvious, but we asked Gosnell how he was coping, given the prospect of a long incarceration. He had a ready answer. "It helps that I very strongly believe myself to be innocent of the heinous crimes of which I am accused," he told us. "I sort of understand the circumstances and I continue to feel optimistic of the eventual outcome…the vindication of what I've done, why I've done it and how—[it] will all become accepted within my lifetime. It's out of sight and out of my control. But I feel strongly that that will occur."

If he felt so strongly about his innocence, why didn't he take the stand in his own defense? He blames his attorney, Jack McMahon. "It was his advice that I not testify," Gosnell explained. And he agreed at the time because his lawyer felt "my credibility had been so compromised and the openness to further attack seemed to be counterproductive." Besides, Gosnell felt he had already won the case, that McMahon had proven his innocence. "But we didn't get the verdict."

We spoke with Gosnell for two hours. We decided to talk very generally and allow him to lead the conversation at first, before we would ask him harder questions. He's a big talker and very fluent. Only a few times did he freeze up, searching his memory for a name, an address, or a date. When that happened, he lowered his head smiling (always smiling) and said, "No, no it's gone. I can't bring that name to mind right now. I will remember and let you know." But for most of the interview, Gosnell was exceptionally specific about names, places, and dates. In fact, when he claimed not to remember a significant detail from his case, we didn't find him very credible.

Gosnell's days at the prison are full. He talks about his time there with the tone of an executive juggling a complicated schedule. "I'm very busy," he said breezily. He takes classes, but can't always get what he wants. "I wanted to join the poetry class here, but it's completely full," he said with a sigh.

He's doing a lot of exercise. When he was first in custody after his arrest, prison staff told investigators that he put his mattress on the floor in his cell and jogged on it. He explained how he's keen to stay in shape, having been a triathlete all his life. "As a boy I always promised myself I would never look like the before pictures in the Atlas fitness ads. So I am working a lot on my upper body." But he has had some difficulties, because he doesn't have the right sneakers. "The prison doesn't stock my size in sneakers. A friend sent me money, but they have a new system here where they take a portion of our money to pay for court costs. So I don't have enough money for the sneakers. I'm a 16 4E."

Pescatore and Cameron had told us that Gosnell's phone calls were monitored during the trial and he spent a great deal of time talking about his feet.[5] Feet seem to be an obsession of his.

In one of the stranger moments of the interview, Gosnell slowly raised his hand, palm side out, to Phelim. It threw us both; it looked for all the world like he was giving Star Trek's Vulcan salute. But no, he wanted to show Phelim just how big his hands were so that we could understand just how big his feet were. "They gave me 15 medium, so I've opened up the sides so they can fit me and luckily my bunions have cleared up." As he rambled on and on about his big feet and showed us his long fingers, it was hard not to think of the babies who had died at those hands. If Gosnell made that connection, he was completely unconcerned.

Gosnell is convinced that he will be vindicated and that he is getting out of prison one day. Therefore, he needs to be in shape so he can do a triathlon the year he's released. It's a personal goal. "I believe I will get out. Unfortunately, once you are convicted, proving innocence is not enough in the process of filing an appeal."

He told us he is still very angry with McMahon. Yet discussing his lawyer, he maintained the same tone that he used to talk about his books, his daughter, and his bunions. "Jack McMahon didn't follow through with his commitments," he said. "I'm the kind of person, if I give a commitment I follow through. There are many things he promised that he didn't follow through. He was supposed to send me the notes of testimony"—the trial transcripts—"but he hasn't."

Gosnell repeated his lament from our first phone call: he wishes he had taken the stand in his own defense, but McMahon didn't think it wise. Listening to Gosnell speak, we could understand why. "He recommended I didn't testify, and I accepted his rationale. But he didn't present my resumé, with its four pages of accomplishments and ongoing education, all of which I did because I always wanted to make sure that I was at the cutting edge. I took two Harvard continuing education courses," he said. McMahon didn't have to be a legal genius to know that a jury would be appalled listening to Gosnell talk so arrogantly about his accomplishments when he was on trial for severing the spines of live babies.

The doctor wants to make clear that his medical work was almost missionary, it was a vocation, all about making the world a better place. And this vocation stemmed from a particularly life-altering event when he was a child. Everything he has done since came from that moment, he said. "April 1952 is an extremely important date in my life. I wanted to learn to swim and my uncle took me over to the Y. I wasn't allowed in because it was segregated." There was another Y for blacks. "I didn't feel bad for myself personally; I felt bad for my race. I was told by the gentleman to come back in September because they were thinking about changing the policy. I had to go to the YMCA on Christian Street, but it had no swimming pool." Because of this incident of racial discrimination, Gosnell said, he decided to dedicate himself to his community. "At the time in the fifties, the criticism was that educated black people left the community to do well outside their own community, but I committed not to do that."

But he also worked out how to use racial politics to his advantage. He realized that the medical school he wanted to apply to had a quota system that took a disproportionate number of black students from Dickinson college—a historical black university. "I chose not to continue my studies at the University of Pennsylvania because there was a better chance to get into Thomas Jefferson Medical College if you were at Dickinson College. Both colleges had eleven students that went on to Jefferson Medical School, but Dickinson was much smaller so, I had a much better chance."

"My teacher, Mr. Cotter, said I should apply to Princeton because my grades weren't excellent but I was great at doing exams. But I didn't want to go to Princeton, because it would take me away from the community." This elaborate explanation of why he didn't go to Princeton, like much of what Gosnell says, makes no sense. Attending an Ivy League school wouldn't have prevented him from returning to work in a poor black community. If anything, Ivy League–educated professionals are exactly what those poor neighborhoods need. The real reason he didn't go to Princeton was something a lot more pedestrian: Gosnell's just not that smart. He thinks he is, but he's not.

In conversation with Gosnell, music is never far away. The doctor is a pianist. And, of course, by his own reckoning he is a very talented one. "I'm a classical pianist," he said. "Without doubt I could have devoted myself to the music of Chopin. I've visited his ancestral home and been in the same room as his piano." Gosnell loves Chopin. He had played Chopin during the police raid on his home. At the prison the doctor is given lots of free time to devote to music. On Saturdays, he listens to the opera on the radio. The Metropolitan Opera has been broadcasting matinee concerts since 1931. It is the longest continuously running classical music program in radio history, and now in Dr. Kermit Gosnell, convicted serial killer, it has a devoted fan. "Of course, I have been fortunate enough to have been to the Met," he said with a smile. He always had to let us know he's sophisticated, a cut above the rest.

Being in prison, Gosnell says, has given him the time to pursue his interest in other types of music. He loves jazz and blues. He becomes animated describing the "wonderful musicians" with whom he plays in the prison. This is not what I had expected. The prison may look intimidating, but life there, for Gosnell at least, is pretty peachy. He's got pals and they jam together.

He says he loves the music of Jacques Brel, an enormously famous Belgian singer-songwriter who sang achingly romantic songs and famously died of lung cancer in 1978 at the young age of forty-nine. But Gosnell can't remember the name of Brel's most famous song. When I was younger, I was a huge fan of Brel's. I reminded him it's "Ne me quitte pas" ("Do not leave me"). Suddenly Gosnell looked into my eyes and started singing the first three lines of the song. His eyes were fixed on mine as he sang.

Ne me quitte pas

Il faut oublier

Tout peut s'oublier

Don't leave me

One must forget

Everything can be forgotten

America's biggest serial killer was serenading me, promising never to leave me. I haven't listened to Jacques Brel since.

As Gosnell spoke, he continually touched my leg. He also continually apologized for touching my leg, but he was never sorry enough to stop or even to move away. It was an accident, supposedly, that when he wanted to make a point his hand would rest on my leg—before he would realize what he was doing.

No one from his family had visited in the year he had been locked away in Huntingdon. His explanation for his lack of visitors was ridiculous. "My children live such busy lives," he told us. It's hard to imagine any loving family member being too busy to visit their father or husband in over a year in prison—not for his birthday or even Christmas. Huntingdon isn't easy to get to, but it's not impossible. It struck me that all the other inmates in the visitors' room had visitors. Gosnell just had us, and I didn't want to be there for any longer than I had to be. But if the lack of family visits upsets him, he certainly didn't show it.

I asked about friends. It's hard to imagine that the cultured man Gosnell portrays himself as could find anyone to make friends with in the prison. Not at all, he has lots of friends, he said. "Oh, of course, yes, I have wonderful friends here. In this room alone I have five brothers." He sounded like he was talking about a gentlemen's club, not a state prison housing murderers, rapists, and pedophiles. But Gosnell is street smart, and he's a survivor; he has adapted to his new surroundings, trying to dial back from the appalling arrogance that has characterized most of his adult dealings with people. "I don't have airs," he told us. "I'm not a higher being. I don't let people know how intelligent I am."

Talking about Chopin and Poland, Gosnell says that the Jewish people are very important to him. "I've always said my minor was in 'Jewish,'" he says, with a laugh. He attended Jewish junior high and middle school, he claims, and Jewish history became a fascination of his. "In 1978, I was invited to an alcohol and addictions conference in Warsaw. I was partly motivated to go because I wanted to visit Auschwitz and Birkenau. Those visits really helped me with my Jewish fraternity brothers." Gosnell claims that visiting the concentration camps helped him understand Jews much better. Because they never know when the next pogrom will come, they "like to keep their assets liquid," he explained. He is very impressed with that wisdom. It's not hard to imagine that he might well be thinking of himself, the martyr, the persecuted member of a minority, who had seventeen properties but who could have fled the United States during the grand jury process if he had kept more of his assets liquid. As we have seen, he had fled previously—after the Mother's Day Massacre. Gosnell says he never left Philadelphia.

"The paper I presented in Poland was about how community medical centers could be a focus for change in the community. I spent a year writing the abstract, learning Polish, going to Polish shops, eating in Polish restaurants. Drinking Polish vodka," he added with a twinkle in his eye. This was one of those times that showed how good Gosnell's memory is and how he can be extremely specific when he wants to be. He mentioned one of the Polish shops in Philadelphia he frequented at the time: "Krakus Market, on the corner of Richmond and Allegheny." When I looked it up later, sure enough, it's still there today. And the conference he referred to really happened; it was the Thirty-Second International Congress on Alcoholism and Drug Dependence, and it was indeed held in Warsaw, Poland, in September 1978.

When Gosnell describes visiting Auschwitz and Birkenau, he talks coldly of the experience before veering into an admiring tone that becomes very disturbing. "I have always emotionally wanted to know about oppression," he began. In Auschwitz, "what was most impressive were the bins where they kept the children's shoes, and children's hair, and the bins with specific parts of clothing. The bins were six by four, made of solid wood. Each of the bins kept exactly that item, but the sheer volume of it was very impressive." That was the only adjective he used: "impressive." Not heartbreaking or tragic or horrific. No, Gosnell thought the storage of the little shoes, clothing, and remains of small, innocent Jewish children who were massacred by the Nazis was "impressive."

Apart from the weird coldness of his demeanor, Gosnell was showing an enormous lack of self-awareness. This is a man who has been convicted of murdering children, and who kept trophies of their feet. And now he was waxing lyrical about how "impressive" the neat and orderly collection of murdered children's hair and personal effects by the Nazis was. Did the rows of baby feet he kept in the clinic's kitchen seem "impressive" to him, too?

Gosnell was so eager to impress us that he lied even when he didn't have to. He spoke about visiting a popular tourist attraction in Poland. "I wanted to visit Czestochowa where the Black Madonna is. I was very interested in it because of the racial element. You have to get on your back and scoot back to see it. I was in Czestochowa when Pope John Paul II had his outdoor Mass." John Paul II did indeed visit the Black Madonna of Czestochowa, but that was in June 1979. Gosnell was in Poland in '78. He lies easily.

Gosnell has found religion in prison—or perhaps it's more accurate to say that he has found *religions*. He attends multiple religious services, including Muslim prayers organized by the Nation of Islam. Add in his interest in Judaism, and what you get is a man who is essentially a religious tourist. "I'm studying the Koran, although I'm a Christian," he said. "I'm reading it in two translations.... My way of approach is to look at something I'm studying [in] more than one context. It's normal for me to be reading three different things if I'm exploring." He expresses an intellectual interest in all faiths, but not once in all of our conversations in person or by phone did he speak from the heart about his own faith.

By that stage in the interview, we had heard enough about Dr. Gosnell's delightful life in prison. We were there to ask some hard questions.

Gosnell has an answer for everything.

I started by asking him to talk about the night of the raid. Though he was describing what must have been one of the worst days of his life, he still managed to weave in some self-promotion—with a bit of fake humility thrown in.

"I was coming from Delaware from the other clinic. One of my friends always said my biggest problem was that I didn't let people know how intelligent I was—basically I've always had a problem with self-promotion, so I had to have two jobs. Snow had been predicted and we had had thirty inches of snow the previous week, so we were prepared for snow. But that day was pleasant. It was sunny. All of a sudden, I saw police vans, TV vans, and across the street there looked like firehoses."

After tooting his own horn, Gosnell managed to get in a dig at the Philadelphia police. Not long before the raid on his clinic, a police officer had been involved in a shooting at the bar across the street. "I immediately thought that there had been another murder at Scooter's, a bar often frequented by off-duty police. So there had been a couple of homicides," he said exaggerating what had really happened. "I came up 38th Street and got a parking place on the corner, and all the police ran over to me and all of a sudden I realized I was the object of interest. They informed me I was going to be raided and showed me the search warrant. It said they were looking for huge caches of drugs, particularly drugs that were used on Karnamaya Mongar."

At the time, he was relaxed about the search. Gosnell had done business for so long with no oversight—even as the literal bodies were piling up—that he was confident this new investigation would all blow over. There was one little detail on the search warrant that made him nervous, though. "Detective James Wood presented me with the search warrant. He was a short slender man with glasses. In the good cop-bad cop routine, he's the good cop. The only thing that alarmed me was the back of one of the state forms, which said twenty-four weeks—it was the first time I'd seen that and it rattled me," he said. This was the point at which Dr. Gosnell realized that he had made a crucial error in the extensive faking he had done to cover up his illegal late term abortions. He had manipulated the ultrasound machine to make the fetuses appear smaller than they really were, but he had aimed for the wrong gestational age. So his abortion files typically said the late term babies he aborted had been 24.5 weeks along. But the legal abortion limit in Pennsylvania is actually at twenty-four weeks exactly; it's illegal to perform an abortion if the fetus is older than twenty-three weeks and six days. (Incidentally, Gosnell's admission that he was "alarmed" when he learned about the twenty-four-week limit gives the lie to a preposterous claim he made later in the interview, when he told us that he believed the fetuses he estimated were 24.5 weeks along would count as legal—on the basis, as we have already discussed above, of his supposed expertise in statistics.)

Still, he tried to remain confident. "I knew I had provided care, and didn't feel I had done anything wrong, and [I thought] there was no chance of being charged or convicted," he said. In other words, Gosnell was a member of the protected community of abortionists shielded from the scrutiny of the law. By providing women with the "choice" to end their pregnancies, he was doing something noble, and there was no chance he would have to answer for it—even if the abortions he provided weren't legal.

Instead of seeing himself as a lawbreaker, Gosnell accused the investigators who uncovered his crimes of disregarding the law. "I got along pretty well with Dougherty, but in retrospect [law enforcement] were motivated by strong moral objectives rather than the law," he said. Gosnell made that claim repeatedly in our conversations with him. It's a recurring theme with Gosnell that he was targeted by Wood, DEA agent Steve Dougherty, and Jason Huff of the FBI because the three men were Catholic.

It's true all three men are Catholic and take their faith seriously. They are not, like Gosnell, religious gadflies professing to respect all faiths and therefore respecting none in particular. But it is nonsensical to suggest that the investigation was motivated by their religious beliefs. Wood, Huff, and Dougherty were part of a large multi-agency task force. There were checks and balances and plenty of oversight. People at the highest level of the investigation and in the district attorney's office were determined to ensure the case would be by the book and would "preserve abortion rights."

If anything, pro-abortion officials such as Judge Renée Cardwell-Hughes labored to keep the probe from shining any light on the ugliness of "abortion rights." She was quite open about where she would allow the grand jury investigation to go and where she would prevent it from going.

I had to ask Gosnell to explain why his medical clinic was so disgusting. His answer was a preposterous lie. It was just the weather and debris from a few overgrown houseplants, he said. "The reason why the place was a mess was that I had a variegated philodendron and an arcing dracaena that was over two floors, a gift from a patient. When the door was open, all the leaves came down. We also had newspapers in because we were expecting snow and they were wet and in shreds."

What about the cats? "There are several reasons for the cats," he explained. "I had cats because there was a Delaware patient who had paid one thousand dollars for a procedure and as she was in the waiting room, a mouse ran over her feet and that was just unacceptable. A woman who paid a thousand dollars for a procedure and to have a mouse run across her feet! After we got the cats, no more problems. I got two cats. When you have mice, it's always advised to get two cats because it increases the chances of one of them being a mouser."

I asked him how he could allow the cats into the procedure rooms. Gosnell denied that ever happened. "The cats were not able to go into the procedure rooms. I had installed hospital standard sliding doors. They couldn't get in."

And then Gosnell had one of his brain freezes and so, presumably to jog his memory, he touched my leg. He apologized fairly quickly, but a few minutes later touched me again. He continued apologizing—and touching me.

Gosnell sat far too close to me, in my personal space. I was backed up against the wall in my chair, so I had nowhere to go. I was trapped. It was a horrible place to be. He leaned forward even more.

"What's the word for someone who only does things for money?" he asked.

"Greedy," I answered.

"Ah, yes, I'm alleged to be greedy. But would a greedy person spend seventy-five hundred dollars on hospital standard sliding doors? The cats could not get in because they couldn't get through those doors." This was simply a lie. Patients and workers and detectives have all told us about the cats in the procedure rooms.

I asked him how it was that everyone who worked at his clinic described, under oath, the same murderous act on babies happening over and over and over again? First he evaded the question: "I'm not angry with any of the workers who gave evidence against me because they were in a position where they were concerned about their own freedom," he said. "I think the power of the court is appropriate for the protection of the rights of people, but the plea bargaining system causes problems in the balance of justice." Then he lied: "The workers didn't say the children breathed—they said the child moved. The neonatologist said one movement does not mean life."

This is wrong on two counts. The workers *did* see babies breathe, and testified to that fact under oath in court. As for the neonatologist Daniel Conway, he did not say, "One movement does not mean life." On the contrary, he testified that a baby could be alive and *not* be breathing.

I pressed on the issue of all his staff testifying under oath that the babies moved. His answer was typical Gosnell. "The cause in my mind was dreams," he said. "They imagined they saw movement because of the size. The specialist said movement did not mean life; it was a visualization by the staff because the size was so impressive. It was not objective. More like a nightmare."

There it was again, the word *impressive*. A normal human being seeing a dead baby with hands and feet and eyes and nails all perfectly formed would never use the word "impressive." "Tragic," "heartbreaking," "devastating," and "shocking," but never "impressive." But Kermit Gosnell is not like most people.

It's certainly true that working in the Gosnell clinic was a nightmare. But it was all very real, and everyone was awake, and everyone remembered.

Gosnell lies easily and selectively, and cleverly manipulates small pieces of information for his purposes. He complained that if what everyone accused him of was true, then why is it that he was not convicted of murdering the forty-seven babies recovered in the basement? "Jack McMahon used the expression 'a window in time.' If there had been a breath in any of the forty-seven fetuses found, then it would have shown in the tests and it didn't."

It is true that the medical examiner tried the aeration test on all of the babies found in the basement. That meant he took their lungs and put them in a container of water. If the lungs had air in them, indicating that the baby had taken a breath, they would float. None of them floated.

But Gosnell had nothing to say about medical examiner Sam Gulino's testimony about the aeration test. "The issue of the freezing and unfreezing concerns me, potentially masking my ability to identify lungs that normally would have been aerated," Gulino testified. "The reason being that we know that tissues when they're frozen and then unfrozen the cells in the tissues will actually break open, the liquid that's in the cells will then be inside the tissue. So it's possible—and again there's no literature that really speaks to this, so I can only go on what I know about the physiology of the body and what happens to tissues after death—that that process could potentially interfere with my ability to determine whether or not that fetus had breathed." Gulino simply couldn't make a yes-or-no determination of whether or not the babies in Gosnell's basement freezer had ever lived.

But Gulino did answer "No" to the most graphic question Ed Cameron put to him: "Can you think of any reason why a neck was severed if the baby was not born alive?"

In the end, the only reason Gosnell was not convicted in the deaths of any of the forty-seven babies was that their cause of death could not be determined.

I asked Gosnell why he marked so many files with 24.5 weeks if the legal cut-off for abortion in Pennsylvania is twenty-four weeks. Gosnell answered by explaining that the problem with most people is that they are not scientifically trained and don't understand that in science you always round down. This was the problem in the court, he said: the scientific illiteracy of the jury. "Arithmetically 24.5 is 24 weeks [and] 24.6 is 25. Because of my background, that is how I wrote it and that is compatible with the limits of legal terminations. It's common among fiscal people to round up." And Gosnell then gave a lengthy description of just how mathematically shrewd he is. He took general chemistry at Penn, every biology class at Dickinson, qualitative and quantitative analysis at Temple. He listed all these classes in detail and boasted of his intellectual superiority to the twelve jurors whose job it was in the end to stand in judgment over him. In his mind they simply weren't qualified. They were stupid and he was smart. But none of this specious reasoning brought the abortions in Gosnell's records within the gestational age limit on abortions in Pennsylvania—where for an abortion to be legal, the fetus has to be *less* than twenty-four weeks. And it didn't account for his manipulation of the ultrasounds, either.

I wanted to know why he had re-done so many ultrasounds—why would that be necessary?

"I'm old school. They don't understand. I took fundal height. I am rather good tactilely as a doctor. I'm good with my hands. Manually, I estimate the age. Of the forty-seven specimens found at the clinic, only two of the forty-seven were over twenty-four weeks. One was twenty-six to twenty-eight and one twenty-four to twenty-six. The error rate here is in the range of possibility."

Gosnell wasn't all that good with his hands. He used them to cut living babies' necks. He used them to grope the semi-literate women who worked for him because they wouldn't have been able to get work anywhere else. He used them to touch my leg frequently during our interview. And he used his hands to write hundreds of prescriptions for drug dealers that ruined an untold number of lives.

I asked Gosnell about Baby Boy A, the baby boy that moved and breathed and struggled to live—the baby too big to fit in the plastic Tupperware container that soon became his coffin. The baby whose picture had been shown repeatedly to the jury. Some of them had wept when they saw it.

"I don't remember him," Gosnell said.

And maybe he was telling the truth. With all the carnage at the clinic, it's possible that Gosnell couldn't distinguish one baby from another, or remember what happened to them. I reminded him that Baby Boy A was the baby he had infamously joked about, saying he was big enough to walk him to the bus stop. But Gosnell had an answer for this too. Apparently it was a teachable moment.

"It used to annoy me when my mother used to repeat stories," he said. "But then when I went to a family reunion I realized it was done to allow learning and refreshing and reflection. So the bus stop remark, I was just repeating what my great nurse, Mary Mosley, would always say. She was an O.R. nurse at Penn for thirty years. She always used to say"—and here Gosnell imitated a high-pitched woman's voice—"'Doctor, why, they waited so long—that one was so big he could have walked me to the bus stop.'" He laughed as he said it.

Gosnell often puts on accents and adopts the speech patterns of the people he's quoting. It's very creepy; it reminded me of the voice of Anthony Perkins speaking in his mother's voice in *Psycho*.

Gosnell explained that he thinks the law limiting abortions at twenty-four weeks is a good law, but he also said he would help late term patients get abortions elsewhere. "I think twenty-four weeks is a good limit, and when I thought the patient was beyond twenty-four weeks, I would refer the patient on to someone else at great cost. Because late abortions are very expensive."

He is such a liar. Kareema Cross told investigators that very late some evenings Gosnell would tell the last employee in the clinic not to lock up, because he had someone else coming in for a procedure. She was convinced that these were illegal third-trimester abortions. Otherwise why would the doctor not have asked one of the staff to stay?

As we have seen, one of the doctors Gosnell said he sent patients to was the famous late-term abortionist George Tiller, who was murdered by a pro-life fanatic at his church in Wichita, Kansas. "George Tiller and I were very good friends," Gosnell said. "He was a wonderful, warm, sensitive individual. I feel more comfortable in prison because if I had been let out, I could have faced the same fate."

I asked Gosnell about the "Sunday Babies"—the larger babies he is alleged to have killed on Sundays, when the clinic staff wasn't there. He denied any pattern of regularly doing very late term abortions on Sunday, but did acknowledge that he did sometimes do abortions on that day. "Sunday was my family day. Sunday procedures were the urgent problem cases—the Saturday cases that couldn't wait until Monday."

But I told him that his employees had said he was doing the really, really late cases on Sundays. He said this was easily explained. "Steven Massof made these claims because he got money for every case, and he was angry because he thought I was trying to short him out of twenty bucks for the Sunday patients."

Then I asked why no files of the Sunday cases had ever been located. "I may have taken the files home, but there was never any policy of keeping them separate," he replied.

Gosnell's crimes came to light in the course of Jim Wood's investigation into illegal prescription drug trafficking. Before Gosnell was suspected of murder, Wood and his colleagues at the FBI and DEA had amassed evidence showing Gosnell was running an illicit pill mill and writing thousands of prescriptions for OxyContin every month. When I asked about this, Gosnell came out with one of his most ludicrous lies. "Regarding OxyContin, I was in prison a year before I realized it could be abused the way it was abused. I've read a magazine in prison where the manufacturer has settled a case with damages for misrepresenting how addictive it was."

A regular doctor might possibly be able to get away with this profession of ignorance, but not a doctor whose resume touts his expertise on addiction issues. Gosnell ran a narcotics rehabilitation program. He claims to have lectured on the subject internationally. And he's the guy who was angry at his attorney for not giving his full resumé to the jury, "with its four pages of accomplishments and ongoing education." He said he had kept up with training and education because he wanted to remain "cutting edge." To claim he only became aware of the addictive properties of OxyContin in 2013 is a preposterous lie.

In fact, problems associated with the abuse of OxyContin first began to surface in the late 1990s. By the early 2000s, newspapers were printing stories—lots of them in both the national and the local media about pill mill doctors, robberies, and pharmacy break-ins, all because of the abuse of OxyContin by drug addicts. The FDA issued, warnings. It's impossible that any of this was news to Gosnell.

I wanted to see how Gosnell would react if I asked him about the 1972 Mother's Day Massacre. The mention of it made him break into a broad smile. "Oh you know about that? That was the same weekend I told my mom, 'I am going to do abortions.' And she said, 'Oh no, not abortions, Kermit!' She was concerned about my career. But she and I were extremely close. She became my best receptionist."

The National Organization for Women had contacted Gosnell and told him about a plan to bus fifteen women who had been denied second trimester abortions from Chicago to Philadelphia. The group wanted to use Gosnell's facility at 3801 Lancaster. Harvey Karman, psychologist and illegal abortionist, was in charge of this trip.

"I talked to Harvey Karman, and I said not a problem. And he said they were going to bring his super coil." The super coil was a plastic strip about forty centimeters long, wound into a tight spiral. As former Gosnell employee Randy Hutchins described it to the grand jury in 2010, the super coil was "basically plastic razors that were formed into a ball.... They were coated into a gel, so that they would remain closed. These would be inserted into the woman's uterus. And after several hours of body temperature...the gel would melt and these ninety-seven things would spring open, supposedly cutting up the fetus, and the fetus would be expelled."[6]

"The super coil was ineffective," Gosnell said blandly. "We put the coil in, it was supposed to do something but didn't."

"One second trimester woman had problems," he explained. "We were unable to get all the products from her, and she was bleeding heavily. But Harvey didn't want her to go to the hospital. I insisted. She had a hysterectomy. Her name was Carolyn. The rest of the people went back on the bus, and I don't think there were any other problems." In fact there were massive complications with the women whom Gosnell had used as guinea pigs for the super coil. According to the Centers for Disease Control, nine of the thirteen women examined afterwards had complications, three of those had major complications, two required surgery, and one underwent a hysterectomy.

But for Gosnell, it was a minor episode in his career. "I was grilled by the cops at the time. I think the fact that I was doing it not for profit but for altruistic reasons was why they didn't charge me. Harvey was charged because he was not registered to work in Pennsylvania." Karman was later convicted of a felony in an unrelated abortion in California. He killed a woman in a hotel room, trying to perform an abortion using a nutcracker.

Media reports of the Mother's Day Massacre say Gosnell left the country to avoid prosecution, and Randy Hutchins confirmed to investigators that Gosnell had told him so in several conversations. But now Gosnell denies he ever left. "I worked right through at my clinic," he said.

Only once was our conversation interrupted. A prison guard shouted, "All visitors remain seated. All prisoners stand up for a count." The guard walked the lines of the prisoners, counting. I sat in silence—relieved for a moment from the leery gaze and the lies of Kermit Gosnell.

He never really stopped talking for all the time we were there. And he never really stopped trying to make me feel uncomfortable. At one point, I lost concentration. We had been in the prison for more than two hours. He was rambling on about medicine and techniques. "Are you familiar with menstrual evacuation?" he suddenly asked me. "You'd understand menstrual evacuation." He looked at me and smiled. "Where you have something important to do when you were menstruating and we'd just syringe it out—it used to be very popular with feminists."

I had to get out at that point. I'd heard enough. I felt he was playing me, trying to shock or embarrass me. I said we had to head back to Philadelphia. He stood and shook our hands again. But then he asked us whether the next time we came could we bring some quarters for the vending machines? We didn't understand until the former millionaire explained that visiting time was an opportunity for visitors to get treats that were not part of the normal prison food. But prisoners were not allowed to use the vending machines. Could we please buy him some treats? We bought him a cheese plate wrapped in plastic and left.

Then something crazy happened. It's funny in retrospect, but it wasn't at the time.

As we hurried to the exit, a prison guard in the command post by the door shouted out for us to come back. We came up to the window. One prison guard was sitting, and the other was standing beside him.

The seated one screamed at us that we had not asked for permission to use the scrap paper. We had about twenty pages of notes each. He screamed again: "This a state prison!" He said he was going to put the papers with our notes in the trash. We tried to explain that we hadn't known we couldn't use the paper, and we tried to apologize. But he just screamed that we were not to interrupt him. The man standing beside him was expressionless.

The standoff continued for a few minutes, with us being screamed at and told to dump our notes and us standing there, trying to apologize but refusing to give up our notes.

He finally stopped screaming and relented. We were allowed to leave with the notes.

We walked away in silence, in shock, after interviewing a serial murderer of newborn babies for two hours and then having a prison guard relentlessly scream at us for using scrap paper without permission.

Phelim and I were silent as we drove away from the prison. A composer friend had sent some Chopin for us to listen to in the car. We listened to the second movement of the first piano concerto and didn't speak.

The countryside around the prison is lush and green, there was rain in the wind, and small drops were falling on the windshield.

I was numb. In all my life, I have never been in the presence of someone who so disturbed me. I'd been working on the Gosnell material for more than a year, reading horrific testimony and police reports, interviewing witnesses and co-accused baby killers. I knew what Gosnell had done, and the pictures of his victims would be with me always. But meeting him was different from reading about him.

We drove on in silence and let the bucolic landscape and the music soothe. How could anyone love Chopin—such beautiful music—and still be capable of committing such hideous acts? The music is so gentle and delicate; it's the music of the heart and the soul. How could Gosnell appreciate that music and be a monster? As soon as I had that thought, I remembered the imprisoned musicians at the Nazi concentration camps who were forced to play the most wonderful music.

The Nazis were capable of appreciating beautiful music. Their prisoners, half starved to death, played as their fellow inmates—men and women and children—were led off boxcars and walked their last steps toward the gas chambers.

THIRTEEN

AFTERMATH

"This doesn't even rise to the level of government run amok. It was government not running at all."
—**TOM CORBETT**, Pennsylvania governor (2011–15)[1]

In the aftermath of the Gosnell case, some people went to prison, some regulations in Pennsylvania were changed, and a bill to ban abortions after twenty weeks was introduced in Congress.

Tom Corbett was sworn in as the forty-sixth governor of Pennsylvania on January 18, 2011. Four days earlier, the grand jury had released its report detailing the horrors at 3801 Lancaster and the state's failure to do anything about it for years. "This doesn't even rise to the level of government run amok," Corbett said. "It was government not running at all." Corbett called the failures at the Department of Health and the Department of State "despicable." He flexed his executive muscle, sacked six managers, and started updating the state regulations that govern abortion clinics.

Among the highest-ranking officials to be shown the exit was Basil Merenda, who had served as secretary of state under Corbett's immediate predecessor, Ed Rendell. Before that, Merenda had been a deputy attorney general in New Jersey. According to a Fox News story, Merenda claimed that he had not been asked to appear before the grand jury and that Corbett's administration hadn't said a word to him about the case. Merenda insisted he never knew about Gosnell. "Do you think for one minute that if I had known what was going on with the Gosnell complaints that I would have tolerated that? Come on," Merenda told FoxNews.com. "You can't say I was involved in the Gosnell matter when I had absolutely no input."

Also sacked was Susan Mitchell, the deputy health secretary for quality assurance, who had rather obviously failed to live up to her job title. She had spent more than twenty years with the State Health Department. She had inspected Gosnell's clinic in 1989 and again in 1993 and found many serious deficiencies, which she dutifully noted in her file. But she took no effective action. And nothing happened. Gosnell went right on killing.

Corbett also fired Department of Health senior counsel Kenneth Brody, one of the officials who decided not to resume regular clinic inspections in 1999, and Christine Dutton, the lawyer who justified the State Health Department's indifference to Gosnell's carnage with those two callous words that so infuriated the grand jury: "People die."

Department of State counsel Mark Greenwald, who reviewed and decided not to act on Marcella Choung's allegations of malpractice and Gosnell's nine hundred thousand dollar settlement with Semika Shaw's family, resigned.[2]

On December 14, 2011, the Pennsylvania General Assembly passed Senate Bill 732, which treats abortion clinics the same as any other surgical facility in the state and mandates annual inspections. The bill was a direct consequence of the Gosnell case. Now any time the state Department of Health receives a complaint about an abortion clinic, officials must review it within forty-eight hours and visit the clinic within five working days.

Governor Corbett ordered the Departments of State and Health to collaborate more closely on investigations. "We boiled it down to this: People need to do their jobs," Corbett said. "It's not enough to prosecute the wrong-doing. We need to change the culture. That starts here. That starts now."[3]

We'll see.

Our research of the Gosnell case and its aftermath doesn't give us any confidence that much has changed at either department. Both seem incompetent at best, and willfully corrupt at worst. We received no cooperation from the very agencies that failed to act to stop Gosnell. Our queries were repeatedly rejected. They simply wouldn't answer our questions.

It was the same story with the Jefferson College of Nursing. Officials there refused to say whether any of their students had complained about the horrid state of Gosnell's clinic. We also wrote to the National Abortion Federation asking why they never reported Gosnell to the authorities even though one of their accreditors had been on the premises and deemed them "horrific." They never wrote back, either.

On December 17, 2013, nearly four years after the raid on the Women's Medical Society, Kermit Gosnell appeared in a federal court for sentencing arising from the federal drug charges associated with his pill mill operation. He had reluctantly agreed to plead guilty the previous summer. Jack McMahon represented him at the short hearing. No one else came to support the doctor—not his wife, not his kids, not any of his former employees or patients. And McMahon was only there because he was being paid.[4]

At one point in the hearing, McMahon said his client took exception to a reference prosecutors had made to his clinic being filthy and reeking of cat urine and feces. "He wasn't found guilty of cats," McMahon said.

The hearing only lasted two hours. Gosnell was wearing prison garb. Though short, the hearing was not without its own drama. U.S. District Judge Cynthia Rufe told the court that Gosnell had written her an eight-page single-spaced answer to the charges against him. He clearly hadn't told McMahon, who had to try to work out on the spot how to proceed.

Unlike at his murder trial, Gosnell choose to speak at his federal court hearing. He lectured Judge Rufe for forty-five minutes in a rambling mess of a speech. He did take full responsibility for the illegal drug business, but then attempted to justify his criminal enterprise as an act of kindness to the poor, disadvantaged, drug-addicted clients he wrote the scripts for. "It was almost like a concierge practice, in that I would take whatever time was necessary for an individual," Gosnell told the judge, in all sincerity.

And he told Judge Rufe that she was not the only person he had written to. He had addressed another letter to then–U.S. Attorney General Eric Holder, offering to help his fellow inmates with his "expertise" in medical sociology, "narcotic rehabilitation," and as a "transactional inter-relationalist"—whatever that meant. This was the same man who would tell us two years later that he didn't know that OxyContin was addictive until he read about it in prison.

Gosnell insisted that he was "well intentioned" and called his drug dealing business a "pain management clinic." McMahon argued that Gosnell sincerely believed in a "higher purpose for what he was doing."

None of this impressed the court. U.S. Attorney Jessica Natali argued that the undercover video and audio recordings made it quite clear that Gosnell was not altruistic—he was just greedy. He might be soft-spoken and articulate, but he was also a common drug dealer. The evidence collected in the drug investigation proved that. In one of the investigators' tapes, Gosnell could be heard complaining about how exhausting it was to sign two hundred phony scripts in one sitting.

Natali had no shortage of damning evidence against Gosnell. The criminal informants that the three amigos had cultivated nailed the doctor. All of his sweet-talking couldn't explain how one informant had picked up nineteen prescriptions under eight different names, or how another informant was getting prescriptions in the names of fifty-two different people, none of whom had a medical file at the clinic. "He was filling orders on demand, keeping costs low and volume high," Natali added.

The night Karnamaya Mongar died, Gosnell had taken the time to write eighteen scripts for the drug dealers he supplied. Nothing was going to interrupt his lucrative pill mill business.

This would be Gosnell's last court appearance on the matter, and it seemed right that what Jim Wood had started with his undercover narcotics investigation should end with the drug conviction. Without Woody's discovery of Gosnell's prescription drug business, the full horror of 3801 Lancaster Avenue might very well have continued to this day. Judge Rufe recognized that without the drug bust, "the additional crimes involving the [murder] charges, and the harm to individuals that occurred there, would not have been known for some time."

The judge was not impressed by Gosnell's rationalizations. He had "made a hypocrisy" of the Hippocratic Oath he had taken when he became a doctor, she said. The harm he caused could not be overstated.

Natali pointed out that Gosnell's drug dealing put the lie to his supposed concern for the community. "He didn't care about that community," she said. "He preyed on that community.... This was not a doctor treating people for pain. He was filling prescriptions on demand, with zero oversight."

Gosnell was given a thirty-year sentence for the drug dealing part of his practice, to run concurrently with the sentence to life in prison that he had already been given for his abortion-related crimes. He also had to pay a fine of fifty thousand dollars and forfeit two hundred thousand dollars linked to drug trafficking.

At the beginning of our research for the Gosnell movie and this book we asked Detective Jim Wood if he thought Gosnell would respond to our request for an interview. Jim said, "He will talk to you and as long as he is alive you'll be hearing from him." That has proved to be uncannily true.

From his prison cell Gosnell writes letters to us, many letters. In them, he offers elaborate exculpatory answers to the evidence against him.

He denies gruesome details of the 1972 Mother's Day Massacre, for example, saying the toll of injuries that was widely reported by authorities, was exaggerated and that the "description of the Supercoil [in the media] was totally erroneous—no razors, no temperature responsive gel, no springing out and not [sic] cutting." He admits that one woman did suffer a perforation and had to have a hysterectomy, but claims he was "unaware of any other complications." He denies fleeing to the Bahamas to avoid prosecution.[5]

Gosnell characterizes the grand jury report as a "ham sandwich indictment"[6]—referring to the lawyers' joke that grand juries are so easily manipulated that they will indict a ham sandwich. He denies that he ever used the term "snipping" at the clinic: "Snipping was a term apparently generated during the trial [I] don't have any prior recollection of its use."[7] He continues to try to explain away his callous joke that one of the fetuses he killed was so large it could have walked him to the bus stop. That was just an exasperated joke about women who waited so late to have abortions, and he never meant it to be taken literally: "Personally I biked or drove my truck and never took the bus!"[8]

In his letters, he also shares details from his childhood. Ballet, not Chopin, was his original artistic passion. "But at that time it was not a heterosexual vocation."[9]

He phones us, too. We'll be out for a walk or at a dinner and he'll phone. His tone is always the same—soft-spoken, jovial, and matter-of-fact, not at all what you'd expect from someone in prison for life. He is chatty, telling about the inconveniences of trying to get paper or typewriter, how he needs money to use the phone. He asks about us like we are old friends and ends phone calls with an excess of polite salutations. He has an answer for everything we ask him—simply put, everyone is wrong except for him and he's convinced he will be vindicated. He is a misunderstood, maligned philanthropist who only wished to serve the poor and whom, he writes, the authorities "investigated, castigated, persecuted, monsterized, prosecuted, convicted, and incarcerated." In prison he is writing poetry. One poem he sent us is called "Pruning." According to this poem, abortion is just another form of wise pruning: "Every seed has not its destiny to fulfill potential." Gosnell has written another poem entitled "Twenty Five Years of Being The Empty Chair" in which he expresses self-pity at the prospect of twenty-five years of "peeing without privacy," "repetitive mundane meals," and—strangely for a man whose mother is long dead—"without Mother's hug, Mother's laugh, Mother's cooking or cookies." He has sent us Bible passages with explanations of how he believes they justify abortion. For example:

> John 15: 2: Every branch in me that beareth not fruit he taketh away; and every branch that beareth fruit, he purgeth it, that it may bring forth more fruit.

Application: A woman "purged" brings forth more fruit.

In September 2015 Yashada Devi Gurung, Karnamaya Mongar's daughter, won a medical malpractice lawsuit against Gosnell. Judge Jacqueline Allen awarded $3.9 million, $650,000 in compensatory damages, and $3.25 million in punitive damages. While Gosnell didn't have insurance at the time Mrs. Mongar died, lawyers representing the family said the DA's office had identified property and other assets that they intend to pursue. "The DA's office did a thorough job and there are certain properties that may provide monetary relief to this family. They lost their matriarch," said Bernard Smalley, the lawyer representing the family.[10]

In June 2016 the Supreme Court overturned a Texas law that had mandated abortion clinics maintain hospital-like standards and that physicians have hospital admitting privileges. The Texas law had been passed because of the Gosnell case, and Gosnell was continually mentioned during the oral argument before the Supreme Court. The Gosnell grand jury had recommended that abortion clinics "should be explicitly regulated as ambulatory surgical facilities, so that they are inspected annually and held to the same standards as all other outpatient procedure centers." Lawmakers in Texas wanted to prevent another Gosnell by enacting these standards. The Supreme Court, however, did not agree. The decision was a massive victory for the pro-abortion side, which had argued that there must not be any "undue burden" on women's access to abortion. Pro-life advocates were appalled: "The abortion industry cannot be trusted to regulate itself and they know it. That's why they fought tooth and nail against commonsense health and safety standards and requirements for abortionists to have admitting privileges at nearby hospitals," said Marjorie Dannenfelser, president of the Susan B. Anthony List. "We have documented page after page of incidents of abuse, negligence, and brutality since

2008. This decision means the filth and exploitation will continue unchecked."[11]

We have been contacted by a lot of people during the course of research for the book and the movie. One woman's story deserves a mention here. She is a grandmother to a child that was aborted in Gosnell's clinic. Her son's girlfriend had said she had miscarried but eventually admitted to going to Gosnell's clinic. The grandmother contacted us because she said people too often forget about the fathers-to-be, and she wanted us to know, "I just thought you should know that some people really did want to step up to the plate and take responsibility for these young lives." She told us she prays for some good to come of the Gosnell story. "I pray for a wide awakening and repentance across the world for these precious lives, to God be the Glory."

On June 10, 2015, a small group of people gathered at Laurel Hill Cemetery overlooking the Schuylkill River to commemorate the forty-seven babies whose bodies were discovered frozen in Gosnell's clinic. The mourners consisted of clergy, pro-life activists, and others touched by the stories of how the children had died. Roman Catholic Archbishop Charles Chaput and pro-life activists had mounted a campaign to obtain custody of the babies' remains from the city so that they might be buried properly. They had learned, to their sadness, that the babies had already been buried by the city at Laurel Hill on September 12, 2013. The medical examiner's office explained that this was standard procedure for bodies not claimed by any next of kin. It's true. Near the burial site of the forty-seven Gosnell victims is a small tombstone marking where the city buried fifteen hundred unclaimed bodies in 2010.[12]

Alliance Defending Freedom attorney Catherine Glenn Foster acknowledged that, in the end, Philadelphia officials had fulfilled the wishes of all who wished to pay their respects to the babies. "Today, we can say that the City of Philadelphia has heard us, they gave these babies a place to be buried," she said. "These babies were like any other...precious little persons," Foster told the mourners gathered in the summer sun. "How a person dies doesn't make anyone less human.... Try as hard as he might, neither their killer nor his infamy could erase these babies' humanity. We will use this sacred place to cry, to remember and to say: 'This ends here.'"

During the memorial service, well-wishers placed a temporary marker and a small blue silk flower to indicate where the babies were buried. It read, "May God welcome the souls of these children killed by Kermit Gosnell, and the souls of all children killed by abortion into the joy of Heaven." The mourners also brought flowers and white wooden crosses.[13]

But the people who had petitioned for the babies' bodies felt that the city had let Gosnell's victims down. It was wrong, they said, that the children had been buried secretly. The Reverend Patrick Mahoney, director of the Washington, D.C.–based Christian Defense Coalition, said at the memorial, "I would simply say this to the medical examiner and the Philadelphia city government: These children were not unclaimed.... We came for months after months, seeking these children in love. They were not unclaimed. They were wanted, they were desired, they had meaning and purpose."[14]

It's a sentiment we share.

ACKNOWLEDGMENTS

Thanks to crowdfunding more than twenty-nine thousand people made it possible for us to produce the Gosnell movie. Very early on in our research we realized that much of what we were learning about Gosnell would never end up in the movie. There were just too many stories, too many details, there were scenes that were too gruesome and too unbelievable. If we had included them the audience might have thought we were exaggerating, but these incidents happened and as journalists we felt they should be known. There were the details about the many, many government bureaucrats and medical officials and abortion establishment who had totally failed to do their jobs and let Gosnell go on killing. There were so many missed opportunities. Their failure needed a full reckoning. We also felt the horrific stories of the brutal murders of the babies who died in the clinic, and the details of their short lives deserved to be recorded. A movie could never do all that.

We are so grateful to those contributors to the movie who believed in the importance of telling this story and trusted that we would do it justice; they made this book possible.

Among that group there are certain individuals who stand out for going the extra mile and then some. We are so thankful to Scott and Debbie McEachin, John and Lisa Harpole, Melanie Sturm, Sally and Paul Bender, David Houston, Robert Hamilton, M.D., Rebecca Hagelin, and Jessica Sena. We also want to thank our wonderful assistant Olivia Williams. She has helped us wade through complex and emotional transcripts, interviews and evidence and at all times she did it professionally and most importantly with a smile.

And there are many more people we would like to thank, but they have asked that we not include their names here. They are remaining anonymous for professional or personal reasons but they know that we could not have written this book without them. Thank you.

And we want to acknowledge all the people who were willing to talk to us—law enforcement officers, jurors, workers from the clinic, family members of some of the dead babies, and women who had gone to Gosnell for abortions.

We are especially grateful to Detective Jim Wood and former ADA Christine Wechsler for allowing us into their worlds. Their dedication to their jobs and their humanity and humor were a gift of light in the diabolical world Gosnell created.

Our publisher Regnery committed to this, our first book, before a word had been written and then gifted us with Elizabeth Kantor as our editor. We could not wish for a better editor than Elizabeth. She has been meticulous but kind; we are very thankful for her attention to the details.

But there is one name more than any other that needs to be acknowledged, celebrated, and thanked. Magdalena Segieda, our business partner, resident guru, always the grownup in the room, our dear friend. She's the one that makes every project we undertake, including this book, possible and we are eternally grateful. Marrying each other sixteen years ago was the best thing we ever did. The next best thing was hiring Magda ten years ago. It was a very lucky day for us, she is simply irreplaceable.

APPENDIX

FROM LETTERS SENT TO THE AUTHORS: A POEM BY GOSNELL AND BIBLE PASSAGES SELECTED BY HIM, WHICH HE CLAIMS JUSTIFY ABORTION.

TWENTY FIVE YEARS   OF BEING THE EMPTY CHAIR

TWENTY FIVE YEARS
behind bars   is more than a lifetime...

TWENTY FIVE YEARS
without Mother's hug, Mother's laugh, Mother's cooking or cookies
nor the tender touch   of one's love,   long lost...

TWENTY FIVE YEARS
of peeing without privacy,   of repetitive mundane meals...

TWENTY FIVE YEARS
of friendships forged   on shared sparsity   and poverty...

TWENTY FIVE YEARS
for those many   with recrimination, repentance   and regret...

TWENTY FIVE YEARS
without walking   or sheltering   one's own DNA...

TWENTY FIVE YEARS
of "CORRECTION"   thriving on punishment...

TWENTY FIVE YEARS
for those feeling forgotten,   that they lack forgiveness...

TWENTY FIVE YEARS
of watching   our Democracy   become the will of those most able...

TWENTY FIVE YEARS
when the glimmer   of an Officer's humanity is best hidden from his peers...

TWENTY FIVE YEARS
not understanding GOD'S WILL,   continually learning to accept...

TWENTY FIVE YEARS
Of waiting for change,   of watching our backs...

TWENTY FIVE YEARS behind bars   is more   than a lifetime....

PRUNING

Agricultural parables   abound in the Bible,
        generations of experiences,   explicit expressions,
             sustainance   of life   and survival...
    Every seed   has not its destiny   to fulfill potential...
    Some   fall in the path of birds,
        some   upon rocky ground,   or are scorched,,,
           some without roots wither,   others choked by thorns...
             Some   on good ground   yield plentifold...
    Fruit trees   only flourish over years
    when well pruned   in early spring...

A child,   taught to
                "love thy neighbor",
                     pursue service   more than material worth
                     and provide for the needy,
       was pleaded   when barely a clinician:
         by Sandy, "please save my children and my marriage..."
           by Mary, "this grandchild, barely nourished, is only fifteen..."
             by others,   and others,   and others...
                as safety and future fertility   were within his skills...
    Later,   much later,   allegation and misperceptions
       evoked condemnation, persecution,   and prosecution,
          not unlike   a Roman era...

INSPIRED PASSAGES* sought confirmation, justification   and comfort:

   Genesis 2.7; "And the Lord God formed man of the dust of the ground.
   and breathed into his nostrils the breath of life;
   and mans became a living soul."
        . Application: No life until breath.

INSPIRED PASSAGES* sought confirmation, justification   and comfort:

   Genesis 2.7; "And the Lord God formed man of the dust of the ground.
   and breathed into his nostrils the breath of life;
   and mans became a living soul."
          Application: No life until breath.
   Genesis 9.7; "And you, be ye fruitful, and multiply;
   bring forth abundantly in the earth, and multiply therein."
          Application: Provision and procreation are equally important.
   John 15.7; "If ye abide in me, and my words abide in you,
   ye shall ask what ye will, and it shall be done unto you."
          Application: Do for your neighbor, as you do for yourself.
   John 15.2; "Every branch in me that beareth not fruit he taketh away;
   and every branch that beareth fruit, he purgeth it,
   that it may bring forth more fruit."
          Application: A woman "purged" brings forth more fruit.
   John 7.23,24; "...are ye angry with me, because I have made a man
   every whit whole on the sabboth day? Judge not according to the
   appearance but judge righteous judgment."
          Application: Similarly, Law prefers to avoid the greater evil
   by bringing about the lesser of evils.
   James 2.14; "What doth it profit, my brethren, though a man say
   he hath faith, and have not works? can faith save him?
          Application: Faith is expressed, not by words, but by deeds.
   Respect, and judge not, those who act with strong belief   that life,
   that LIFE BEGINS   at that very moment
        when an ovum is pierced   and gametes entwine...
   Swiftly approaching
   in these most terrible times
                    is Final Judgment....

                                         kbgosnell/revised 2015

  * King James Version

NOTES

EPIGRAPH

1. Jonathan Sacks, "'Never Again—But Will We Ever Learn the Lessons of History?" April 17, 2004, http://www.rabbisacks.org/never-again-but-will-we-ever-learn-the-lessons-of-history/.
2. Hippocratic Oath (c. 400 B.C.) trans. from the Greek by Francis Adams, *Encyclopedia Britannica* (1849), https://www.britannica.com/topic/Hippocratic-oath.
3. "Planned Parenthood History and Successes," https://www.plannedparenthood.org/about-us/who-we-are/history-successes.
4. Margaret Sanger, *Woman and the New Race* (New York: Brentano, 1920), 63.

PREFACE

1. Kirsten Powers, "Philadelphia Abortion Clinic Horror: Column: We've Forgotten What Belongs on Page One," *USA Today*, April

11, 2013, http://www.usatoday.com/story/opinion/2013/04/10/
philadelphia-abortion-clinic-horror-column/2072577/.

ONE: FROM DRUG BUST TO HOUSE OF HORRORS

1. Interview of Christine Wechsler by the authors on September 9, 2014.
2. Interview of Kermit Gosnell by the authors on May 1, 2015.
3. Except as otherwise noted, material in this chapter is from numerous interviews of Jim Wood by the authors, both in person and on the phone; the interview of Kermit Gosnell by the authors on May 1, 2015 and on numerous occasions by phone; and from a confidential source whose identity we cannot reveal.
4. Interview of Christine Wechsler by the authors on September 9, 2014.
5. Interview of Joanne Pescatore by the authors on September 8, 2014.
6. Testimony of Jason Huff at Kermit Gosnell's trial, March 18, 2013.
7. R. Seth Williams, District Attorney, "Report of the Grand Jury in Re. County Investigating Grand Jury XXIII," January 14, 2011, http://www.phila.gov/districtattorney/pdfs/grandjurywomensmedical.pdf (hereafter "grand jury report"), 20.
8. Testimony of Elinor Barsony at Kermit Gosnell's trial, March 25, 2013.
9. Testimony of Elinor Barsony at Kermit Gosnell's trial.
10. Testimony of Elinor Barsony at the Kermit Gosnell trial, March 25, 2013.
11. Interview of Marcella Choung in the Pennsylvania Department of State report on Gosnell, July 7, 2010.
12. Grand jury report, 225.

13. Testimony of Dr. Sam Gulino at Kermit Gosnell's trial, April 15, 2013.

14. Testimony of Adrienne Moton at Kermit Gosnell's trial, March 19, 2013.

15. Testimony of Ashley Baldwin at Kermit Gosnell's trial, April 11, 2013.

16. The authors have seen the footage shot by Detective Jim Wood showing the discovery of the five jars of feet.

17. Testimony of James Johnson, janitor at 3801 Lancaster Ave testimony, at Kermit Gosnell's trial, April 16, 2013.

18. Elinor Barsony testified at Kermit Gosnell's trial on March 25, 2013, that when she returned to the clinic on February 22 there was a strong smell of disinfectant and it appeared Gosnell had cleaned the place.

19. Grand jury report, 22.

20. Interview of John Taggart by the authors on September 8, 2014.

21. Ibid.

TWO: "MURDER IN PLAIN SIGHT"

1. Simone Weil, *Simone Weil: An Anthology*, ed. Siân Miles (New York: Grove Press, 1986), 18.

2. W. H. Auden, "The Guilty Vicarage: Notes on the Detective Story, by an Addict," *The Complete Works of W. H. Auden: Prose*, vol.2, 1939–1948, ed. Edward Mendelson (Princeton: Princeton University Press, 2002), 263.

3. Grand jury report, 3.

4. Except as otherwise noted, material in this chapter is from the grand jury report and from the interview of Christine Wechsler by the authors on September 9, 2014.

5. Interview of Renée Cardwell-Hughes by the authors on September 11, 2014.

6. Gosnell submission to the appeals court, which the authors have seen.

7. "State Policies in Brief: An Overview of Abortion Law," Guttmacher Institute, October 1, 2015, http://www.guttmacher. org/statecenter/spibs/spib_OAL.pdf.

8. Stephanie Simon and Miguel Bustillo, "Abortion Provider Is Shot Dead: George Tiller, Attacked at His Church, Had Long Been a Focal Point of Protests," *Wall Street Journal*, June 1, 2009, http:// www.wsj.com/articles/SB124379172024269869.

9. 012 Pennsylvania Consolidated Statutes, Title 18—CRIMES AND OFFENSES, Chapter 55—Riot, Disorderly Conduct and Related Offenses, Section 5510— Abuse of corpse.

10. David Altrogge, *3801 Lancaster: American Tragedy*, 2013.

11. Kirsten Powers, "Gosnell's Abortion Atrocities No 'Aberration': Column," *USA Today*, April 29, 2013, http://www.usatoday.com/ story/opinion/2013/04/29/gosnells-abortion-atrocities-no-aberration-column/2122235/.

12. Altrogge, *3801 Lancaster.*

13. Interview of John Taggart by the authors on September 8, 2014.

THREE: DERELICTION OF DUTY

1. Interview of Renée Cardwell-Hughes by the authors September 11, 2014. Except as otherwise noted, material in this chapter is from that interview, the interview of Christine Wechsler by the authors, September 9, 2014, the interview of Monique Carr by the authors, May 20, 2010, the grand jury report, and a confidential source whose identity we cannot reveal.

2. Conversation with a source who was involved in the investigation but whose name cannot be revealed.

3. Dana DiFilippo, "D.A. Weighs Insurance-Fraud Charges for Gosnell," *Philadelphia Daily News*, March 28, 2011, http://

articles.philly.com/2011-03-28/news/29354194_1_insurance-fraud-charges-insurance-fraud-kermit-gosnell.

4. Ibid.

5. Joint FBI-DEA interview with Kareema Cross, March 10, 2010.

6. Interview of Joanne Pescatore by the authors on September 8, 2014.

7. Interview of Jim Wood by the authors on May 1, 2015.

8. Interview of John Taggart by the authors on September 8, 2014.

9. Pennsylvania Department of State report on Gosnell, July 7, 2010.

10. Kathryn Jean Lopez, "The Brutal Gosnell Reality," *National Review*, May 14, 2014, http://www.nationalreview.com/corner/348232/brutal-gosnell-reality-kathryn-jean-lopez.

11. "Kermit Gosnell on Trial for Abortion 'House of Horrors'" Susan B. Anthony List, March 19, 2013.

12. Interview of "Jalil" by the authors on August 29, 2015.

13. November 16, 2015, letter from Kermit Gosnell to the authors.

14. Interview of Kermit Gosnell by the authors on May 1, 2015.

15. Interview of Jim Wood by the authors on September 10, 2014.

16. "Gosnell behind 'Mother's Day Massacre' over 40 Years Ago That Injured 9 Women," Life Site News, April 16, 2013, https://www.lifesitenews.com/news/40-years-ago-gosnell-experimented-with-abortion-supercoil-that-slashed-wome.

17. Interview of Kermit Gosnell by the authors on May 1, 2015.

18. Interview of Jim Wood by the authors on September 10, 2014.

FOUR: WILLING ACCOMPLICES

1. Except as otherwise noted, material in this chapter is from numerous interviews of Jim Wood by the authors, both in person and on the phone; from the authors' interviews with Christine Wechsler on September 9, 2014; the grand jury report; the

transcript of Kermit Gosnell's trial; and a confidential source whose identity we cannot reveal.

2. Interview of Joanne Pescatore by the authors on September 8, 2014.

3. Interview of Jack McDermot by the authors on July 14, 2016.

4. Trial of Sherry West before Judge Benjamin Lerner in the Philadelphia Common Pleas Court, March 2004.

5. Interview of Liz Hampton by the authors on September 10, 2014, and Liz Hampton's statement to the grand jury.

6. Interview of Adrienne Moton by the authors on October 2, 2014.

7. Vince Lattanzio and Emad Khalil, "Gosnell's Wife Sentenced, Apologizes for Husband's Actions," NBC Philadelphia, May 29, 2013, http://www.nbcphiladelphia.com/news/local/Gosnells-Wife-Gets-Up-to-2-Years-Sentence-209377491.html.

8. Interview of Joe Carroll by the authors on September 9, 2014.

9. *Denise Doe Vs. Eileen O'Neill, Delta Women's Clinic and others.* Lawsuit filed December 1998, 19th Judicial District Court Parish of East Baton Rouge, Louisiana.

FIVE: "THE INDIAN WOMAN"

1. Except as otherwise noted, material in this chapter is from the grand jury report and the transcript of Kermit Gosnell's trial.

2. Interview of juror Joe Carroll by the authors on September 9, 2014.

SIX: THE BABIES

1. Except as otherwise noted, material in this chapter is from the grand jury report and the transcript of Kermit Gosnell's trial.

2. September 28, 2007, letter from Kermit Gosnell to Irene Lafore.

SEVEN: GOSNELL ON TRIAL

1. Except where otherwise noted, material in this chapter is from the interview of Christine Wechsler by the authors on September 9, 2014, the grand jury repor.t, the transcript of Kermit Gosnell's trial, and a confidential source whose identity we cannot reveal.

2. Elizabeth Harrington, "9 of 12 Jurors in Gosnell Trial Are 'Pro-Choice,'" CNS News, May 13, 2013, http://www.cnsnews.com/news/article/9-12-jurors-gosnell-trial-are-pro-choice, quoting Jacqueline London of NBC 10.

3. Interviews with members of the investigative and prosecution teams.

4. Kevin Dolak and Russell Goldman, "Kermit Gosnell Jury Cites Greed in Conviction of Abortion Doctor," ABC News, May 15, 2013, http://abcnews.go.com/US/kermit-gosnell-jury-cites-greed-conviction-abortion-doctor/story?id=19184760.

5. Interview of Joe Carroll by the authors on September 9, 2014.

6. Altrogge, *3801 Lancaster: An American Tragedy.*

7. Dana DiFilippo, "Victims Say Abortion Doctor Scarred Them for Life," *Philadelphia Inquirer,* January 21, 2011, http://articles.philly.com/2011-01-21/news/27041098_1_abortion-doctor-abortion-clinic-one-treatment-room, quoting the *Daily News.*

8. Altrogge, *3801 Lancaster*: *An American Tragedy.*

9. Interview of Pamela [last name withheld] by the authors, summer 2014.

10. Interview of J. D. Mullane by the authors on July 17, 2014.

11. Interview of Jim Wood by the authors on July 14, 2016.

12. Interview of Kermit Gosnell by the authors on May 1, 2015.

13. Ibid.

14. Interview of Kermit Gosnell by the authors on May 1, 2015.

15. From an eighteen-page legal submission by Gosnell, a copy of which the authors have seen.

EIGHT: GOSNELL VERSUS GUMP

1. Except where otherwise noted, material in this chapter is from the transcript of Kermit Gosnell's trial.
2. Interview of Christine Wechsler on October 4, 2015.
3. Interview of Ed Cameron by the authors on September 8, 2014.
4. Interview of Joe Carroll by the authors on September 9, 2014.

NINE: PROFILES IN COURAGE?

1. Except where otherwise noted, material in this chapter is from the transcript of Kermit Gosnell's trial.
2. Interview of Joanne Pescatore by the authors on September 8, 2014.
3. Ibid.
4. Interview of Joe Carroll by the authors on September 9, 2014.
5. Ibid.
6. Interview with anonymous member of the prosecution team.
7. Interview of Joe Carroll by the authors on September 9, 2014.
8. Telephone interview with Jim Wood on June 22, 2016.
9. Interview with Joe Carroll by the authors on September 9, 2014.
10. Interview of Joanne Pescatore by the authors on September 8, 2014.
11. Associated Press, "Convicted Abortion Doctor Gets Third Life Sentence," *Los Angeles Times*, May 15, 2013, http://www.latimes.com/nation/nationnow/la-na-nn-abortion-doctor-kermit-gosnell-gets-third-life-sentence-20130515-story.html.
12. Sarah Hoye, "Abortion Doctor Convicted of Murder Waives Appeal, Avoids Death Sentence," CNN, May 15, 2013, http://www.cnn.com/2013/05/14/justice/pennsylvania-abortion-doctor-trial/.

TEN: MEDIA MALPRACTICE

1. David Crary, "Philly Abortion Murder Case Fuels National Debate," *Boston Globe*, January 20, 2011, http://archive.boston.com/news/nation/articles/2011/01/20/philly_abortion_murder_case_fuels_national_debate/.

2. Mollie Hemingway, "Can the AP Be Trusted to Cover the Abortion Issue Fairly?" *Federalist*, March 14, 2014, http://thefederalist.com/2014/03/14/can-the-ap-be-trusted-to-cover-the-abortion-issue-fairly/.

3. Mollie Hemingway, "Should Media Cover—or Cover Up—Abortion Trial?" *Patheos*, April 8, 2013, http://www.patheos.com/blogs/getreligion/2013/04/should-media-cover-or-cover-up-abortion-trial/.

4. David Freddoso, "Guns and Babies: A Tale of Two Massacres," *Washington Examiner*, April 4, 2013, http://www.washingtonexaminer.com/article/2526271.

5. Interview of Mollie Hemingway by the authors, January 28, 2016.

6. Pundette, "Must-Read: Steyn on Gosnell, Planned Parenthood, and the Moral Corruption of America," *Pundit & Pundette*, February 10, 2011, http://www.punditandpundette.com/2011/02/must-read-steyn-on-gosnell-planned.html.

7. Mark Steyn, "The Unmourned," National Review Online, March 20, 2013, http://www.nationalreview.com/corner/343460/unmourned-mark-steyn.

8. Maryclaire Dale, "'Desperate' Workers to Testify in Abortion Trial," *Daily Times News*, March 25, 2013, http://www.delcotimes.com/article/DC/20130325/NEWS/303259990.

9. Tom Blumer, "AP's Maryclaire Dale: Gosnell 'An Elegant Man' Who 'Smiled Softly in Court,'" News Busters, March 27, 2013, http://newsbusters.org/blogs/tom-blumer/2013/03/27/aps-maryclaire-dale-gosnell-elegant-man-who-smiled-softly-court.

10. Matthew Balan, "Peggy Noonan Interrupts Blackout As Networks Continue to Ignore Abortionist's Trial," News Busters, April 1, 2013, http://newsbusters.org/blogs/matthew-balan/2013/04/01/peggy-noonan-interrupts-blackout-networks-continue-ignore.
11. Kirsten Powers, "Philadelphia Abortion Clinic Horror."
12. Cassy Fiano, "Kirsten Powers Reflects on Her Blockbuster Gosnell Column and the Complicity of the Pro-Abortion Media," Live Action News, February 23, 2014, http://liveactionnews.org/kirsten-powers-reflects-on-her-blockbuster-gosnell-column-and-the-complicity-of-the-pro-abortion-media/.
13. Powers, "Philadelphia Abortion Clinic Horror."
14. Interview of Mollie Hemingway, January 28, 2016.
15. Sarah Kliff, "Meet Sandra Fluke: The Woman You Didn't Hear at Congress' Contraceptives Hearing," *Washington Post*, February 16, 2012, https://www.washingtonpost.com/blogs/ezra-klein/post/meet-sandra-fluke-the-woman-you-didnt-hear-at-congress-contraceptives-hearing/2012/02/16/gIQAJh57HR_blog.html; "Lawmakers Debate Mandated Coverage of Contraceptives in Health-Care Law," *Washington Post*, February 16, 2012, https://www.washingtonpost.com/politics/2012/02/16/gIQAgf3jIR_story.html; N.C. Alzenman (with Sarah Kliff), "Birth Control Rule Won't Apply to All Student Plans at Colleges, White House Says," *Washington Post*, March 16, 2012, https://www.washingtonpost.com/national/health-science/white-house-fleshes-out-exemptions-to-birth-control-rule/2012/03/16/gIQAoLB5GS_story.html; Kliff, "Rep. Todd Akin Is Wrong about Rape and Pregnancy, but He's Not Alone," *Washington Post*, August 20, 2012, https://www.washingtonpost.com/blogs/ezra-klein/wp/2012/08/20/rep-todd-akin-is-wrong-about-rape-and-pregnancy-but-hes-not-alone/; Kliff, "In Akin's Remarks, a Clash between Pro-Life Politics and Principles," *Washington Post*,

August 21, 2012, https://www.washingtonpost.com/blogs/ezra-klein/wp/2012/08/21/in-akins-remarks-a-clash-between-pro-life-politics-and-principles/; Kliff, "Missouri Set to Reprise a Familiar Role: America's Abortion Battleground," *Washington Post*, August 21, 2012, https://www.washingtonpost.com/blogs/ezra-klein/wp/2012/08/21/missouri-set-to-reprise-a-familiar-role-americas-abortion-battleground/; Kliff, "Cecile Richards: 'I've Never Seen a Presidential Election Where Women's Access to Birth Control Is Practically on the Ballot,'" *Washington Post*, August 25, 2012, https://www.washingtonpost.com/blogs/ezra-klein/wp/2012/08/25/cecile-richards-ive-never-seen-a-presidential-election-where-womens-access-to-birth-control-is-practically-on-the-ballot/; Kliff, "In 2012 Campaign, Women's Health Plays a Role like Never Before," *Washington Post*, September 5, 2012, https://www.washingtonpost.com/politics/2012/02/16/gIQAgf3jIR_story.html; Kliff, "An Interview with DNC Speaker Sandra Fluke," *Washington Post*, September 5, 2012, https://www.washingtonpost.com/blogs/ezra-klein/wp/2012/09/05/an-interview-with-dnc-speaker-sandra-fluke/.

16. Mollie Hemingway, "WPost Reporter Explains Her Personal Gosnell Blackout," *Patheos*, April 12, 2013, http://www.patheos.com/blogs/getreligion/2013/04/a-wapo-reporter-explains-her-personal-gosnell-blackout/.

17. Ibid.

18. Erik Wemple, "*Washington Post* Pledges Gosnell Coverage," *Washington Post*, April 12, 2013, https://www.washingtonpost.com/blogs/erik-wemple/wp/2013/04/12/washington-post-pledges-gosnell-coverage/.

19. Sarah Kliff, "The Gosnell Case: Here's What You Need to Know," *Washington Post*, April 15, 2013, https://www.washingtonpost.

com/news/wonk/wp/2013/04/15/the-gosnell-case-heres-what-you-need-to-know/.

20. Conor Friedersdorf, "Why Dr. Kermit Gosnell's Trial Should Be a Front-Page Story: The Dead Babies. The Exploited Women. The Racism. The Numerous Governmental Failures. It Is Thoroughly Newsworthy," *Atlantic*, April 12, 2013, http://www.theatlantic. com/national/archive/2013/04/why-dr-kermit-gosnells-trial-should-be-a-front-page-story/274944/.

21. David Weigel, "Kermit Gosnell: The Alleged Mass-Murderer and the Bored Media," *Slate*, April 12, 2013, http://www.slate.com/ blogs/weigel/2013/04/12/kermit_gosnell_the_alleged_mass_ murderer_and_the_bored_media.html.

22. Jeffrey Goldberg, "Why Is the Press Ignoring the Kermit Gosnell Story?" Bloomberg, April 12, 2013, http://www.bloombergview. com/articles/2013-04-12/why-is-the-press-ignoring-the-kermit-gosnell-story-.

23. Trip Gabriel, "Online Furor Draws Press to Abortion Doctor's Trial," *New York Times*, April 15, 2013, http://www.nytimes. com/2013/04/16/us/online-furor-draws-press-to-abortion-doctors-trial.html.

24. Paul Fahri, "Is Media Bias to Blame for Lack of Gosnell Coverage? Or Something Far More Banal?" *Washington Post*, April 14, 2013, https://www.washingtonpost.com/lifestyle/style/is-media-bias-to-blame-for-lack-of-gosnell-coverage-or-something-far-more-banal/2013/04/14/473e6668-a536-11e2-a8e2-5b98cb59187f_story.html.

25. Trial transcripts, Monday, April 15, 2013.

26. Margaret Sullivan, "Politics Aside, the Gosnell Trial Deserves—and Is Getting—More Coverage," *New York Times*, April 15, 2013, http://publiceditor.blogs.nytimes.com/2013/04/15/politics-aside-the-gosnell-trial-deserves-and-is-getting-more-coverage/.

27. Weigel, "Kermit Gosnell."

28. James Taranto, "Best of the Web Today: The Banality of Bias," *Wall Street Journal*, April 16, 2013, http://www.wsj.com/articles/ SB10001424127887324030704578426892205886784.

29. Daniel Henninger, "Henninger: Clinging to Guns—and Abortion," *Wall Street Journal*, April 17, 2013, http://www.wsj.com/articles/SB10001424127887323309604578428900867620 018.

30. Erik Wemple, "Gosnell Case: HuffPost Host Says Left 'Made a Decision' to Not Cover Trial," *Washington Post*, April 16, 2013, https://www.washingtonpost.com/blogs/erik-wemple/ wp/2013/04/16/gosnell-case-huffpost-host-says-left-made-a-decision-to-not-cover-trial/.

31. Katha Pollitt, "Dr. Kermit Gosnell's Horror Show: This Is What Illegal Abortion Looks Like," *Nation*, January 27, 2011, http:// www.thenation.com/article/dr-kermit-gosnells-horror-show/.

32. Ibid.

33. Margaret Sullivan, "Primates of Times Square: A Case Study," *New York Times*, June 13, 2015, http://www.nytimes.com/2015/06/14/public-editor/new-york-times-public-editor-margaret-sullivan-on-primates-of-park-avenue-coverage.html.

34. Interview of Mollie Hemingway by the authors, January 28, 2016.

35. Center for Medical Progress, "Planned Parenthood Uses Partial-Birth Abortions to Sell Baby Parts," YouTube, April 14, 2015, https://www.youtube.com/watch?v=jjxwVuozMnU.

36. Center for Medical Progress, "Intact Fetuses 'Just a Matter of Line Items' for Planned Parenthood TX," YouTube, August 4, 2015, https://www.youtube.com/watch?v=egGUEvY7CEg.

37. Nicole Haas, "Nothing to See here! Wash Post BUSTED for Watering Down Planned Parenthood Atrocity," *BizPacReview*, July 17, 2015, http://www.bizpacreview.com/2015/07/17/

nothing-to-see-here-wash-post-busted-for-watering-down-planned-parenthood-atrocity-225882. Although the original *Post* story is not cached, *BizPacReview* published a screen capture of the original headline. That image is cached here at http://www. bizpacreview.com/wp-content/uploads/2015/07/art-1.png.

38. Sandhya Somashekhar and Danielle Paquette, "Undercover Video Shows Planned Parenthood Official Discussing Fetal Organs Used for Research," *Washington Post*, July 14, 2015, https://www. washingtonpost.com/politics/undercover-video-shows-planned-parenthood-exec-discussing-organ-harvesting/2015/07/14/ae330e34-2a4d-11e5-bd33-395c05608059_story.html?tid=ptv_rellink.

39. CNN transcript of GOP Presidential Debate, September 16, 2015, http://transcripts.cnn.com/TRANSCRIPTS/1509/16/se.02.html.

40. Kliff, "Carly Fiorina Is Wrong about the Planned Parenthood Tapes: I Know Because I Watched Them," *Vox*, September 17, 2015, http://www.vox.com/2015/9/16/9342165/carly-fiorina-planned-parenthood.

41. Mollie Hemingway, "Watch the Video Planned Parenthood and Its Media Allies Deny Exists: Carly Fiorina Challenges Hillary Clinton, Barack Obama and Others to Watch the Planned Parenthood Videos Depicting Organ Harvesting," *Federalist*, September 17, 2015, http://thefederalist.com/2015/09/17/watch-the-video-planned-parenthood-and-its-media-allies-deny-exists/.

42. Laura Bassett, "'Sting' Videos Of Planned Parenthood Are Totally Manipulated, Forensic Analysis Finds," Huffington Post, August 28, 2015, http://www.huffingtonpost.com/entry/planned-parenthood-sting-videos-forensic_us_55df2334e4b029b3f1b1be9f.

43. Steven Ertelt, "Forensic Analysis of Videos Exposing Planned Parenthood Finds 'No Evidence of Manipulation,'" LifeNews, September 29, 2015, http://www.lifenews.com/2015/09/29/

forensic-analysis-of-videos-exposing-planned-parenthood-finds-no-evidence-of-manipulation/.

ELEVEN: AMERICA'S BIGGEST SERIAL KILLER?

1. "Multi-Disciplinary Perspectives for Investigators," Behavioral Analysis Unit-2 National Center for the Analysis of Violent Crime Critical Incident Response Group, Federal Bureau of Investigation, https://www.fbi.gov/stats-services/publications/serial-murder.

2. Tweet from ABC's Terry Moran on April 12, 2013.

3. Except where otherwise noted, material in this chapter is from the grand jury report, the transcript of Kermit Gosnell's trial, an interview of Kermit Gosnell by the authors on May 1, 2015, and a confidential source whose identity we cannot reveal.

4. Interview of Kermit Gosnell by the authors on May 1, 2015.

5. Interview with Gosnell clinic neighbor who wishes to remain anonymous by the authors on September 8, 2014.

6. This and the FBI myth-busting that follows can be found in the FBI's "Multi-Disciplinary Perspectives for Investigators."

7. Interview of anonymous Gosnell patient by the authors, summer 2014.

8. Interview of Renée Cardwell-Hughes by the authors on September 11, 2014.

9. Kevin Dolak and Russel Goldman, "Kermit Gosnell Jury Cites Greed in Conviction of Abortion Doctor," ABC News, May 15, 2013, http://abcnews.go.com/US/kermit-gosnell-jury-cites-greed-conviction-abortion-doctor/story?id=19184760.

10. DiFilippo, "Victims say Abortion Doctor Scarred Them for Life."

11. Victoria Woolaston, "How to Spot a Serial Killer: Criminologists Reveal Five Traits the Most Notorious Murderers Have in Common," *Daily Mail*, July 21, 2015, http://www.dailymail.

co.uk/sciencetech/article-3169359/How-spot-serial-killer-Criminologists-reveal-five-key-traits-common-notorious-murderers.html.

12. Interview of Gosnell patient who wishes to remain anonymous by the authors, summer 2014.

13. Interview of Adrienne Moton by the authors on October 2, 2014.

14. Interview of clinic neighbor who wishes to remain anonymous by the authors on September 8, 2014.

15. Jon Nordheimer, "Bundy Is Put to Death in Florida after Admitting Trail of Killings," *New York Times*, January 25, 1989, http://www.nytimes.com/1989/01/25/us/bundy-is-put-to-death-in-florida-after-admitting-trail-of-killings.html.

16. David Gambacorta, "Doctor from Hell...Or Godsend?" *Philadelphia Inquirer*, March 11, 2010, http://articles.philly.com/2010-03-11/news/24957137_1_medical-license-abortions-clinic.

17. From an eighteen-page legal submission by Gosnell, a copy of which the authors have seen.

TWELVE: MEETING THE MONSTER

1. Hannah Arendt, *Eichmann in Jerusalem: A Report on the Banality of Evil* (New York: Viking, 1965).

2. Terry Sullivan and Peter T. Maiken, *Killer Clown: The John Wayne Gacy Murders* (Pinnacle, 2000), 270.

3. Except where otherwise noted, material in this chapter is from the interview of Kermit Gosnell by the authors on May 1, 2015.

4. Julie Shaw, "Gosnell's Son Sentenced in Bizarre Burglary," *Philadelphia Daily News*, November 30, 2015, http://www.philly.com/philly/news/20151130_Gosnell_s_son_sentenced_in_bizarre_burglary.html.

5. Interviews of Joanne Pescatore and Ed Cameron by the authors on September 8, 2014.

6. Grand jury report.

THIRTEEN: AFTERMATH

1. "Pennsylvania Governor Fires State Health Workers over Abortion Doc Horror," Fox News, February 16, 2011.

2. Ibid.

3. "Pa. Firings, Policy Changes in Wake of Gosnell Case," NewsWorks, February 15, 2011.

4. Kermit Gosnell's sentencing hearing, December 17, 2013.

5. November 19, 2015, letter from Kermit Gosnell to the authors.

6. Ibid.

7. November 19, 2015, letter from Kermit Gosnell to the authors.

8. Ibid.

9. Ibid.

10. "Family of Abortion Doctor Victim Wins $3.9 Million Court Decision," *Philadelphia Tribune*, September 22, 2015.

11. "Repeal anti-Gosnell law after Supreme Court ruling: Pennsylvania Democrat," Lifesite News, June 28, 2016.

12. "Prayer Group Stage Vigil for 'Gosnell Babies' at Laurel Hill Burial Site." NewsWorks, June 10, 2015.

13. Ibid.

14. Dana DiFilippo, "Bugs Swarm Memorial Service for 'Gosnell Babies,'" Philly.com, June 11, 2015.

~

Judge Jeffrey P. Minehart presided over the Gosnell trial in a neutral and unbiased way, and there is no intention to suggest otherwise.

INDEX